KT-441-600

Staff Library
Singleton Hospital
Tel: 01792 205666 Ext. 5281

Reweaving the Autistic Tapestry

Autism, Asperger Syndrome and ADHD

Lisa Blakemore-Brown

Jessica Kingsley Publishers
London and Philadelphia

The author and publishers gratefully acknowledge permission to reprint extracts from the following:

'A Groovy Kind of Love' Words and music by Tony Wine and Carole Bayer-Sager© 1965, Screen Gems-EMI Music Inc, USA. Reproduced by permission of Screen Gems-EMI Music Ltd, London WC2H 0EA.

APA (1994) *Diagnostic and Statistical Manual of Mental Disorders, Fourth Edition.* Washington, DC: American Psychiatric Association.

Gillberg, C. and Gillberg, I.C. (1989) 'Asperger Syndrome: Some epidemiological considerations: A research note.' *Journal of Child Psychology and Psychiatry 30,* 631-8. Cambridge University Press.

Szatmari, P., Bremner, R., and Nagy, J. (1989) 'Asperger's Syndrome: A review of clinical features.' *Canadian Journal of Psychiatry 34,* 554-60.

WHO (1989) *The International Classification of Disease, Tenth Revision.* Geneva: World Health Organisation.

All rights reserved. No paragraph of this publication may be reproduced, copied or transmitted save with written permission of the Copyright Act 1956 (as amended), or under the terms of any licence permitting limited copying issued by the Copyright Licensing Agency, 33–34 Alfred Place, London WC1E 7DP. Any person who does any unauthorised act in relation to this publication may be liable to prosecution and civil claims for damages.

The right of Lisa Blakemore-Brown to be identified as author of this work has been asserted by her in accordance with the Copyright, Designs and Patents Act 1988.

First published in the United Kingdom in 2002 by
Jessica Kingsley Publishers Ltd,
116 Pentonville Road, London
N1 9JB, England
and
325 Chestnut Street,
Philadelphia PA 19106, USA.

www.jkp.com

© Copyright 2002 Lisa Blakemore-Brown

Library of Congress Cataloging in Publication Data
A CIP catalog record for this book is available from the Library of Congress

British Library Cataloguing in Publication Data
A CIP catalogue record for this book is available from the British Library

ISBN 1 85302 748 0

Printed and Bound in Great Britain by
Athenaeum Press, Gateshead, Tyne and Wear

To my inspirational daughter
Lorna-Charlotte Amelia

WS
745
BLA

Library
Singleton Hospital
This book is due for return on or before the last date shown
Tel: 01792 2056

Reweaving the Autistic Tapestry

Singleton Staff Library
S010545

of related interest

Caring for a Child with Autism
Martine Ives and Nell Munro
ISBN 1 85302 996 3

The ADHD Handbook
A Guide for Parents and Professionals
Alison Munden and Jon Arcelus
ISBN 1 85302 756 1

Raising a Child with Autism
A Guide to Applied Behavior Analysis for Parents
Shira Richman
ISBN 1 85302 910 6

Diet Intervention and Autism
**Implementing the Gluten Free and Casein Free Diet for Autistic Children and Adults
– A Practical Guide for Parents**
Marilyn Le Breton
ISBN 1 85302 935 1

Autism – The Search for Coherence
Edited by John Richer and Sheila Coates
ISBN 1 85302 888 6

Our Journey Through High Functioning Autism and Asperger Syndrome
A Roadmap
Edited by Linda Andron
ISBN 1 85302 947 5

Asperger's Syndrome
A Guide for Parents and Professionals
Tony Attwood
ISBN 1 85302 577 1

Hitchhiking Through Asperger Syndrome
Lise Pyles
ISBN 1 85302 937 8

Asperger Syndrome in the Family
Redefining Normal
Liane Holliday Willey
ISBN 1 85302 873 8

Asperger Syndrome, the Universe and Everything
Kenneth Hall
ISBN 1 85302 930 0

Contents

Abbreviations

ABA	Applied Behavioural Analysis
ADD	attention deficit disorder
ADHD	attention deficit and hyperactivity disorder
AoE	Action on Entitlement
APA	American Psychiatric Association
ASBAH	Association for Spina Bifida and Hydrocephalus
ASD	autistic spectrum disorder
BAS	British Ability Scales
BPS	British Psychological Society
CBCL	Child Behaviour Checklist
CD	conduct disorder
CHADD	Children and Adults with Attention Deficit Disorders
CHAT	Checklist for Autism in Toddlers
CHI	closed head injuries
DAMP	disorders of attention, motor and perception (syndrome)
DCD	developmental co-ordination disorder
DNA	deoxyribonucleic acid
DSM-IV	*Diagnostic and Statistical Manual of Mental Disorders* (4th edition)
ENT	ear, nose and throat
ICD	International Classification of Diseases
IDEA	Individuals with Disabilities Education Act
IEP	individual education plan
IPSEA	Independent Panel for Special Education Advice

IQ	intelligence quotient
LD	learning difficulties
LEA	local education authority
MBD	minimal brain dysfunction
MLD	moderate learning difficulties
MSBP	Munchausen syndrome by proxy
NAS	National Autistic Society (UK)
NVD	non-verbal difficulties
OCD	obsessive compulsive disorder
ODD	oppositional defiance disorder
OT	occupational therapy
PE	physical education
PECS	Picture Exchange Communication System
PET	positron emission tomography
PGARD	Professional Group for Attention and Related Disorders
PKU	phenylketonuria
SaLT	Speech and Language Therapist
SEC	Special Educational Consortium
SEN	special educational needs
SLD	severe learning difficulties
SSRI	selective serotonin re-uptake inhibitor
SULP	Social Use of Language Programme
TEACCH	Treatment and Education of Autistic and Related Communication-Handicapped Children
UCI-CDC	University of California Irvine Child Development Center
UCLA	University of California, Los Angeles
WHO	World Health Organisation
WISC	Wechsler Intelligence Scale for Children
WORD	Wechsler Objective Reading Dimensions
WPPSI-R	Wechsler Pre-school and Primary Scale of Intelligence (Revised)

Acknowledgements

To all the children and families who struggle so valiantly through their lives with these disorders: thank you to those I have had the privilege of meeting for assessments.

My daughter and soulmate Lorne – without you this book would not have been written.

My brother Jack, his wife Sue and my nephew Alexander, who supported me at a very difficult time, and my mother Edna, who, at the age of 80 years, has had to live in chaos while this was finished. Thank you.

Carole Sutton, Christine Rafaat, Peter Harper, Margaret Wysling, Sue Jenner and lovely Brenda Fletcher at Promoting Parent Skills: I owe you so much. Thank you for your incredible support during some very hard years. Most of all, thank you for having faith in me.

Julia West, Lorna Wing, Judy Gould, Gillian Baird, Helen Irlen, Carrie Haslett, Michele Pemberton, Andrea Bilbow, all the wonderful people at the Independent Panel for Special Education Advice (IPSEA), legal and medical colleagues. Friends, old and new in the UK and in various countries, whose own commitment and support for this work have kept me going.

My dear friends Tom and June Lovejoy who have supported me and provided a sanctuary during my dark years.

To Ann, Vicky, Nicky and Eileen for always being there.

Finally, for Richard. Thank you for trying and for believing in me. It is to help people early who suffer as you do that this book has been written.

Introduction

Some children, the 'eccentric', the hyperactive and both, who have been described since ancient times, cannot learn in the same way as the majority. They cannot access the rich opportunities in their families, schools and communities. Attempts to improve diagnoses and to intervene have provided considerable detail and brought us to the edge of some confusion. This book will share some perceptions with you, based on the tapestry I have woven for myself out of knowledge, observation and reflection, which may contribute to nudging us into the next stage of understanding.

A group of children with entrenched problems challenge us to clarify their problems and to provide more focused interventions. From my observations and experience over many years I know that these children have presented an enigma; outcome in their real lives has been very poor. Undoubted damage or 'warped' genes in biological systems and processes of such systems have changed their life story. However we intervened using our centuries of knowledge, we failed to reach these special children.

The Golden Children
(for Graham Albert Jones, 1938-2001)

...and when the intervening's over, the lights turned out
A group remain...

These are the golden children who dance in the rain
Damaged sails and chips off blocks
They straggle the rocks
Of life, and endure
The pain

On crashing waves
The moon falls
And moonbeams bathe the squalls

Passion ate
Music and fate
Knowledge of life comes too late.

The 'threads' which make up first impressions appeared to be the same as those of the normal individual – to those with no knowledge of such disorders. But without any doubt subtle biological initial differences resulted in increasingly very different people. The instinctive pawn's moves of normal individual processes, emerging in the form of the unique individual after multiple similar processes repeat themselves, seemed to have been replaced by multiple knight's moves, which resulted in the emergence of the highly unusual individual. If this was all, we would rejoice in difference and potential for creative, novel thinking, and there are many thousands of people who are fortunate to have such minds.

This book, however, is concerned with children whose lives are grossly compromised by differences which shift into disorder.

These children struggle with entrenched problems, which occur in conditions described as autism, Asperger syndrome, attention deficit and hyperactivity disorder (ADHD) and other developmental disorders. Whatever we do, there may always be the 'golden children', for whom very little works, but we have a duty to them to strive to prevent their problems through biological and technological advances and, until that is possible, to improve their life chances, however minimal that improvement may appear to be.

Increasing incidence

The incidence of autism, Asperger syndrome and ADHD has dramatically risen during the 1990s, shifting into the public consciousness and raising urgent issues to do with prevention and amelioration. The increased incidence relates to three separate issues:

- an increase of awareness and diagnosis, especially in the recognition of what we mean by Asperger syndrome and ADHD
- a widening of criteria into spectrum models

- a real increase in the underlying problems in the population which may be linked with unknown pathogens.

As a consequence there has been an increase in the wider public's awareness of how spectrum features can actually extend into the wider population and our focused understanding of these disorders can have much wider applications.

Confusion

The varying diagnostic criteria, alternative perspectives in different professional departments and in different countries, differences of professional opinion and individual differences which do not seem to fit the stereotypes have led to great confusion both in families and among professionals.

The metaphor

The metaphor of the tapestry has helped me to weave together complexity at various levels of explanation which I explore in this book; this thinking finds a resonance on many levels with Chaos Theory (Gleick 1987).

This book has been written primarily to provide a springboard from which families, professionals and other interested individuals can examine some of these issues and creatively explore how human development, and in particular the development of positive social engagement with others and successful planning and action through life, is an interweaving dynamic process.

Knowing this, and using the same process to reach this state of awareness, mimics how children develop and break through into social worlds.

In this book I aim to focus on various areas of importance. If you sense repetition – it is intended. This helps the learning process. This process of iterative shifting from varied perspectives is crucial, and is condensed in extreme autism to operate at the level of patterns, objects and sensations in the environment, avoiding the use of this activity to engage with people. With often aggressive retaliation when people try to intrude, as interactions occur less and less, there is increasing repetition on things and sensations. In turn fears and confusions increase.

Your task, as the reader, is to use the process of repetitive shifting from varied perspectives until awareness emerges. Create your own harmony to meet your needs.

Dynamic interweave of skills

Awareness of evidence from the strong research base of both autistic spectrum disorders (ASD) and ADHD spectrum disorders, and interwoven factors, leads to a greater understanding of the nature of early signs of difficulty for many children with developmental disorders. The dynamic interweave of the various factors includes what are known as executive skills such as attention, regulation, motor-planning, orienting, inhibiting, shifting, sustaining, retaining, consolidating, and sequencing, in interaction with essential processes including emotional arousal, pausing and rhythm in sensory modalities. Instinctive reciprocal behaviours weave into the communicative context, inspired by the novel and the humorous, and held constant by structure and timing. This natural interweave leads to the emergence of a social being primed to learn, to understand other perspectives and to anticipate the consequences of his or her own and others' actions.

Developing an understanding of time and space, of the self and that self in time and space in relation to the position of others, of consequences of action and actions of others, and judgement of social cues and clues to engage positively with others are just some of the fundamental developmental outcomes.

For the most entrenched problems, there is a fundamental failure to find relevance and/or salience in human interactions which makes child rearing and teaching very difficult!

Interweave of features in classification systems

Current classification systems do not recognise autism and ADHD as interwoven, but clinical practice has led me to consider that they are, and that knowing which processes interweave improves the chances of helping the child.

Certain cardinal features help us to create silhouettes for groups of children, but rigid adherence to checklists leaves out many and also fails to recognise the interweave of features and processes. Models which help us to understand the interweave not only use knowledge from linear models but also seek to incorporate complexity from varied perspectives to create the metaphorical leap which helps us understand what drives complex systems forward.

Interweave of threads of severity/ability/co-morbidity

The obvious variations in terms of severity, the pattern of ability early in life and the nature and extent of the other problems require us to look more closely at the unique child and also to recognise shared problems which span apparently different populations, set in classification systems.

Weaving the clinical picture

Exploring the various weaves of common threads within the tapestry – in particular the fixed criteria set in classification systems – allows us to see how the particular tapestry (in this formulation, the clinical picture) changes hue (in this formulation, the diagnosis). For instance, some obvious common threads are:

- hyperactivity, attention or executive skills
- reciprocity
- social use of language
- non-verbal skills
- motor-planning skills.

All these can be recognised within the autistic, the ADHD, and the language impaired child and in those with non-verbal difficulties (NVD) and dyspraxia or motor co-ordination populations at varying levels of severity within the tapestry. Other populations with recognised medical problems such as Tourette syndrome and hydrocephalus can also experience similar problems.

However, each group has been defined by what has been considered to be its particular cardinal feature and this can vary according to the professional, the politics and the type of classification used – if any. If other threads are not considered – the questions not asked – the full picture will not emerge. This applies to research and the problems with comparing apparently homogenous populations – should we be surprised we get surprised?

The autistic population is defined by the reciprocity problem; the ADHD group is defined by the hyperactivity, attentional or executive problems; the NVD group by its non-verbal problems and the dyspraxic group by its motor-planning or co-ordination problems; the Tourette group by the involuntary tics (both vocal and motor) and the hydrocephalus group by the medical condition affecting the cerebrospinal fluid, as opposed to behaviour. Herein lies an issue which confuses parents. Some conditions are more obviously linked with clearly defined medical problems, which give rise to neurodevelopmental problems that in turn affect presenting behaviour. Others are defined by the behavioural presentations, which are related to neurodevelopmental problems with possibly medical implications. Parents can speak about being given different diagnoses that are effectively the same thing.

Within this band of uncertainty lie conflicting views about causality and what to do.

Using a tapestry approach it becomes clear that these difficulties cluster together, implicating interweaving common neurodevelopmental pathways in the brain. It also becomes clear that the hue can change in different contexts and that the hue reflects the essential interweave which is greater than the sum of its parts and thus moves us away from a single focus on each thread. This method has been used to establish models of how learning commonly occurs and is sustained.

Drawing up simple tapestries of features and severity of features

In talks over the years I have drawn a simple table of, say, the essential difficulties relating to communication, attentional and motor skills on the vertical axis and then drawn a line along the horizontal axis to depict how severe is the problem in a particular child. This made sense to me. If you then consider ability level and how this interacts, the child's basic tapestry is sewn and the image emerges. The first impressions or snapshot approach used by the lay public leads to stereotypes such as 'little professor' (Asperger), 'off the wall' (ADHD) and 'off the planet' (autism). These impressions leave out much detail but can be added to the detail in the overall tapestry.

Interventions have proved to me that the overall hue can change for the better by a focus on each thread as it *interacts* with the others.

From a wider diagnostic level of explanation, considering each thread as a slide-rule, as we slide along the reciprocity thread we can move from the Kanner (1943) autistic population definitions through to the Asperger population and then the ADHD population. By looking at other threads, such as the severity of hyperactivity and by looking more closely at the reciprocity thread, we may find, for instance, that a child may have exceptional hyperactivity, no language, motor problems, repetitive behaviour but few obsessions and just a few prosody problems.

From our family tapestry we may find no overt signs of any autism at all but a history of ADHD-type difficulties. From our early developmental tapestry we may find no obvious medical problems or injuries.

At that stage the criteria would place the child on the autistic spectrum, and therefore be a recognition of the need for intensive support. It is quite likely that there will be communication and motor problems in some members of the wider family who were considered only to be hyperactive as children.

Through the tapestry we would see that our efforts would need to focus on the hyperactivity as well as the poor communication skills and on drawing out the good skills. This child then has a good chance of shifting further back towards normal on the reciprocity thread before he or she even starts school. It could be that the hyperactivity was causally linked with compromising underlying neurodevelopmental systems to establish reciprocity skills in the very early years of life. Dependent on age, severity and response to detailed work to improve attentional and communication skills, we would be better equipped to determine whether interventions such as medication, medical investigations and diets should also be brought into the intervention tapestry.

Another child may have considerable prosody problems, rigidity, repetitive behaviour and obsessions, no language but lots of echolalia and imitation of chunks of favourite films and may also be hyperactive. If there is autism and ADHD within the wider family tapestry and also problems in the developmental tapestry, we have a tough job on our hands, requiring everything we know to be put in place as early as possible. The children with such tapestries are our greatest challenge in the pre-school years if we are to reweave their tapestry before formal schooling begins. The families also need positive support and help so that they can begin to reweave the whole family tapestry, which may have suffocated their potential in life for generations.

Repetitive interweaving leads to emerging perceptual awareness

This book discusses autism and ADHD and other commonly coexisting disorders through the metaphor of the tapestry, to illustrate the complex way development works. The metaphor also addresses how repetitive action leads to the emergence of images or stories of engagement when the plan is appropriate. In autism, there is no problem with repetitive action, but the lack of relevance and salience of the wider human environment totally alters the plan. In some cases, no image emerges at all.

Interweave of knowledge to weave more efficacious interventions

Applying the knowledge to interventions tapestries, using the same repetitive approach and researched methods, can reweave warped tapestries and the developing life story to improve the life chances of 'different' children. Positive effective interventions focusing on defined threads of the tapestry enable us to meet needs and make changes to children's lives so that they have a chance to shift into other defined populations where the difficulties are milder. This is not a surprise. It has worked in the opposite way for decades and is still obvious for many children; children with significant problems whose needs remain unmet move into other defined populations over time. They develop very serious adolescent and adult disorders. The only caution is that when parents provide support for children and change their designation, systems can refuse help, even though the child may still be in need. This argues for the involvement of honest and open systems in change programmes from the outset of serious concerns.

I have reached a position from my own weaving of tapestries where I believe that putting in place processes interweaving planned specific iterative actions which incorporate patterns of interpersonal actions, and which are undertaken in various communicative contexts, provides the best chance of creating change. A child's unique tapestry will determine what else is needed, including diets, medications, other therapies and how intense the programme should be. Tapestries charting closely monitored change should determine the likely duration and the ongoing maintenance plans.

Chaos Theory

The reasoning that led to using the metaphor of the tapestry is how I have always thought, but I was overjoyed in 2000 to find another person applying this thinking in work with people. Through serendipity, and the online *British Medical Journal* at www.bmj.com, I exchanged emails with Dr Vivian S. Rambihar, based in Toronto. Dr Rambihar has written about and also applies Chaos Theory to help him in his work as a cardiologist. He writes:

> Medicine, nursing and health, human sciences dealing with the complex dynamic interactions of science and society, in the art and science of caring, can benefit from the ideas of chaos. This may seem at odds with the current passion for evidence based medicine (nursing and health). The evidence base is the traditional Newtonian, statistical and later probabilistic science, rooted in the objectivity of the scientific method. The world, however is not like that. It is subjective, contextual, irregular and uncertain, with diversity, variety and variability that follow more closely the science of chaos and complexity. (Rambihar, V.S. 2000a, p.21)

Models incorporating Chaos Theory and tapestry thinking should enable more of us to develop a rich and meaningful awareness of those we have a duty to support, and in turn may move us closer to finding elusive explanations to enigmatic problems.

Chapter summaries

Chapter 1: The warp and the weft

This chapter describes the reasoning behind the metaphor of the tapestry and explores the various ways in which it is used in this book to understand children's development, developmental disorders and interventions.

Chapter 2: Brief cross-Atlantic history of two spectrum disorders

The two spectrum disorders, which I attempt to interweave with early interaction issues, are those of autism and ADHD. There are important historical cross-Atlantic issues including the use of different classification systems which help us to understand how similar behavioural traits have been described and managed differently in various countries.

My education, training and experience over a period of 30 years have brought me to consider that these two well-researched behavioural presentations overlap considerably; knowing this helps us to understand the disorders and potential shared interventions more clearly, to help not only in these disorders but also in many others which present with similar clusters.

Chapter 3: Causes, triggers and the interweave

This chapter discusses recent and current thinking, suggesting that there may be common threads at the genetic and biochemical level, which should help us to understand the failing processes and the resilience factors over time.

It is becoming increasingly possible to detect problems of rhythmic function in various body systems even before the infant is born through looking at various reflexes and responses which may reflect nervous system variation.

Geneticists are fast discovering the genes that link with these disorders, when these become operational and whether we can reweave that fundamental tapestry.

Damage to the nervous system leading to forms of encephalitis, through certain environmental influences which include vaccines and their effect on certain vulnerable children, has been clinically recognised since the start of the vaccination programmes in the early twentieth century.

Neuro-imaging techniques such as positron emission tomography (PET), which are undertaken as people engage in various activities, allow us to see which parts of the brain are functioning under such conditions in different groups of people. Such tests are not intended for mass diagnostic purposes in children, given the radiation issues and the costs, but in research they can inform us clinically about the functioning and needs of the populations with ASD and ADHD and other conditions which have a genetic base affecting various rhythmic functions. There is some evidence through the use of PET to suggest that people with Asperger syndrome may interpret information differently and with more emotion as they are using different neurological pathways. While some will argue that what we are seeing is simply how that brain has developed through environmental influence, the nature–nurture dichotomies must step back now given indisputable evidence for the dynamic tapestry effect of biological systems interwoven with the environment. Due to medical and technological advances, information from before children are born can also reveal problems, which could lead to terrible and confusing behavioural problems as the child matures but which can be better understood given the new technologies.

British specialists within autism now increasingly recognise the presenting and underlying interweave of ADHD spectrum disorders and ASD; Barkley (1997) now believes that ADHD should be viewed as a bio-psychosocial disorder of executive dysfunctions and self-regulation, both of which are fundamental problem features – in various forms – within the autistic spectrum, whatever else might be interwoven.

Neuropsychological findings in the head- and brain-injured population also offer important insights into these shared frontal lobe problems found in all these groups in various clusters and at varying levels of severity. These problems relate to a variety of cognitive functions which have been termed executive functions (Pennington and Ozonoff 1996) and which are found to be malfunctioning at varying levels of severity in ADHD and ASD. Glitches in the frontal lobes can interfere with making plans, putting plans into action and sustaining that action; we are only just beginning to explore the range of these problems.

Chapter 4: Definitions, descriptions and disorders
This chapter sets out currently used definitions, wider descriptions of the disorders and the pivotal defining feature. The origin and reasoning behind each name is briefly highlighted. In some cases the same names are being used for very similar problems, causing confusion. A slightly different focus on the same set of problems can lead to different sets of criteria in various countries and the use of different levels of explanation leading to a definition for a diagnosis can

also cause confusion. If these variations merely reflected academic discussion about differences of perspective, specialism and opinion, there would be less urgency to weave a broader perspective. However, the applied nature of our work demands that we use what we know to make diagnoses and decisions about the lives of children. Professional caution resulted in an earlier reluctance to label children, which has led to no support and in some cases disastrous irreversible outcomes. The openness of our working practice and the increasing demand to support the obviously failing children have meant that we have had to show some of our professional confusions – this is not a failing. In genuine professional practice in changing times we cannot pretend to know everything. We never know everything but all the time we apply what we learn as we develop. Professionals should not remain static.

Parents' greater knowledge and rights, coupled with the demands on professionals to meet targets and avoid lawsuits for failure to diagnose, make it imperative that we apply our minds to ensure that there is a broad consensus of opinion and a common working model which recognises the interweave of these disorders. This leads on to working positively with families through a dynamic process of discovery about the best forms of support for the child and family.

Chapter 5: The threads of social engagement

A central theme of the tapestry concerns how people interact successfully with the world through perception, emotion, thought, plans and actions and particularly how they interact reciprocally with others. These factors are interwoven in a rhythmic manner just like the basic rhythms of the heartbeat. Such crucially important skills are compromised, particularly within autism, at a biological and chemical level.

Very early rhythmic behaviours occur instinctively in the normal infant and so the tradition of exploring normal infant interaction within research into autism, for comparison, will be continued here (see Hobson 1989).

Inherited or acquired conditions can interfere with the regulation of these early instinctive processes, which lead on to a normal development of the self. For the latter to occur I believe that the individual must first be able to incorporate an understanding of the other person and then the wider world into developing self-perceptions.

I feel that it is impossible for the human infant to develop a true sense of self without first incorporating others' reactions into his or her basic tapestry of instinctive reactions – this combined process thus creating our social individual selves. Self-esteem, meaning a sense of self-worth, comes later and for some children it is their fundamental lack of a cohesive sense of self, as in autism, which is often misinterpreted as a lack of self-esteem.

In discussion with another speaker who had a fascination with word roots, at a Lifeline conference in Trinidad in 1995, I mentioned this thought and he referred to the way the word 'individual' had 'dual' embedded within it, remarking that without the 'dual' you have no individual!

The grossly selfish 'me' mentality, which has arisen from thinking that we must look after ourselves first if we are to look after others second, has led us up a route of potential social destruction. It is one thing to look after yourself once your true self is established and quite another to look out of yourself towards others to establish your true self in the first place!

Autistic children have well-recognised problems with regulating synchronous behaviour in order to incorporate others into the tapestry of their selves, or to stand in others' shoes, and the literature is replete with such evidence, most notably for me in the work of Trevarthen (e.g. Trevarthen 1977, 1979, 1993, 1998).

This chapter touches on some ideas about very basic processes which need to be woven together in the early interactions of normally developing infants. From evidence in my own research in the 1970s and 1980s I discuss the relevance of touch–talk–gaze processes interwoven with pauses which creates a musical rhythmic quality. Musical structures in relation to timing and phrasing and to prosodic features have been well researched and considered to be strongly related to the process of developing connections with others in dynamic ways (Stern 1977; Trevarthen 1979, 1993).

To get my point across in order to connect with the reader, I have included music in this chapter – but as it is a book I have had to use the simple lyrics of a modern love song. Love song lyrics combined with music can engender the processes which help people make reciprocal emotional connections; this is a step on from the obvious emotions which can be engendered in the self by hearing various types of music.

I have been given permission to use the Tony Wine and Carole Bayer-Sager (1965) lyrics to 'Groovy Kind of Love' sung by Phil Collins, which simply states the basic touch–talk–gaze processes that forge human connections.

To illustrate *failure* to forge such connections, with touch–talk–gaze processes not operating properly, I refer to a wonderful poem which I found through serendipity.

The night before speaking as chairwoman of Promoting Parenting Skills at a conference in Birmingham, UK, in September 1998, in which I was referring to the processes of touch–talk–gaze and to 'Groovy Kind of Love', I read in a broadsheet about a paper being presented that same week on a 'savant poet' by the Oxford psychologists Dowker, Hermelin and Pring (1998). Remarkable poems written by Kate, an autistic person in her mid-forties, had been analysed. Compared with the poems of a non-autistic but physically disabled female poet, it was found that there was less use of alliteration and rhyme and greater emphasis on self-analysis in Kate's poetry.

I briefly explore certain essential instinctive processes, which seem to produce engagement and compare this to how these connections can fade and disappear rapidly given brain disorders such as autism.

Some quotes from people and about people with autism, ADHD and Asperger syndrome and their parents are also given to illustrate my thinking about the development of these crucial connections.

Processes of self and other awareness, developing trust and empathy and the regulation of thought and action within that context are crucial for the smooth running of community and society and indeed for the ultimate survival of the species. Understanding disorders that interfere with such processes can help us to understand these fundamentally important issues.

Chapter 6: Failing systems

Fascination about the world, concern for others and personal integrity weave into a rainbow of hope. However, politics, money and power, deceit and controversy lurk behind every wonder of the real world, ready to strike like lightning as we pause to gaze. This is the rain in the rainbow. For many parents with children whose development is disordered, life can be like a permanent darkening storm. As they lose touch with their child through their withdrawal or opposition and then seek support, they may find that their child is not the only one who fails to listen. Many problems can beset the family which sets out on the unmade road to recognition and support for its child with special needs. Here are some known examples:

- A failure to inform families of potential problems given significant prematurity, birth problems or medical complications, and to give advice about ways of interacting and managing their child from the outset.

- A lack of recognition in the early toddler years when behaviours can be extremely difficult, parents most anxious and appropriate interventions the most effective.

- Blaming families instead of respecting them and helping them to identify the difficulties.

- The refusal to accept the existence of disorders – 'We don't recognise ADHD', for instance, has replaced a refusal to accept dyslexia, which is now more widely accepted after at least a decade out in the cold.

- Sabotage of attempts to obtain reliable information about a child from school systems as part of a multi-professional assessment.

- School refusal to co-operate with independent interventions.

- Cynicism – 'Oh, the current fashion.'

- Honesty – 'We don't have enough money.'

- Dishonesty – 'No, we can't assess him, he has no problems, I've got dozens of children whose needs are greater than your child, he is a model pupil' – but the child is kicked out of school three weeks later.

- Arrogance – 'It is not our policy to send children for specialist assessments, nor do we send children to specialist schools. All that's stopped. You can't go higher than us.'

- More arrogance – 'We do not accept the findings of independent specialist assessments. We employ our own advisers.'

- The use of various lists of criteria, different models within the research on each disorder and an over-reliance on the notion that single causes can be found for complex and dynamic processes have all contributed to the confusion which leads to a child failing.

This chapter looks at the thread of system failure.

Chapter 7: Tangled tapestries

Chapter 7 discusses how tapestries can become tangled by the triggering of glitches in the biological tapestry at certain points in time. This finds a resonance with the notion of sensitive dependence within Chaos Theory, which recognises that a slight change can cause a dramatic alteration to the weave of the tapestry. The wrong colour thread or a single stitch in the wrong direction amidst thousands going right can ruin the whole emerging image.

Contenders for tangling tapestries include:

- system failure to intervene early
- ignoring the problems and blaming the family, usually the mother
- the severity of particular disorders
- the nature of the contexts within which the child lives, plays and learns
- the number of other disorders or features
- the nature of the co-morbidities
- inappropriate or poorly applied interventions
- compounding environmental effects over time including personal frustration at failure.

As a result of the above, a clustering of factors can emerge as 'new' behaviours at different points through a child's development; these can become very severe without appropriate support and in turn further tangle the tapestry.

Chapter 8: Creating the tapestry

Chapter 8 outlines some simple plans for how to weave together pragmatic tapestries of risk factors, and to place these along a continuum of severity; and tapestries of resilience factors. Time-lines can help to create a chronology of events – the age of the child when events occurred and behaviours emerged. The context within which certain behaviours are exhibited is also crucially important and includes the way others relate and communicate with the child with developmental problems as well as multiple environmental factors including iatrogenic effects (problems caused by medical interventions, e.g. reactions to drugs or vaccines) and currently unknown allergic effects of certain diets and drugs during pregnancy.

It is hoped that many will be helped by the interweaving process of setting down features to see them more clearly rather than just reacting to behaviour, and of using colour and plans to represent their child's difficulties visually. This process should lead to a greater awareness and, when standing back from it all, to more focused and finely tuned interventions.

The relevant factors that form the threads are drawn from research and also from knowing the unique child. However, the multiple features of individuals and their interactions are infinite – so don't think you have to think of every-thing! This is only an idea, a rule of thumb to use if it helps.

Some readers may gain further insight into these processes by looking at Chaos Theory websites. They will be able to observe or create *fractals*, or patterns of 'chaos' which are self-similar but even slight differences could totally alter the pattern. Different scales of measurement and focus also change the pattern. Patterns are created using basic mathematical principles of addition and multiplication in a complex and repetitive interweaving process across the two axes (see Resources). Slight changes can create unpredictable outcomes. These fractals reflect the unique 'images' which emerge from woven people tap-estries, themselves created through often unseen and instinctive repetitive pro-cesses and unexpected influences which can entirely change the images.

Some people are happier with various lists and these can obviously be compiled from information set out in Appendix 2. However, the human tapestry is more than the sum of its parts. Our failure to transfer findings easily from the scientific method relates to the beguiling uncertainty of the human condition in interaction. What emerges from a population study will not explain the obvious individual variation which we are faced with daily in clinical situations. It will also miss crucial interactions which may drive the problem.

What individuals do in a one-to-one laboratory or clinic session is unlikely to match their quite different behaviour in a social context. One simple example of why this happens relates to the removal of the essential structure, guidance and rehearsal encouraged by the clinician or researcher. Some indi-viduals can lose the thread entirely. This is not about seeking attention, it is about attentional systems needing such methods and often a modification of language, repetitive and consistent rewards in order to fire up the motivational system to process, make plans, put plans in action or inhibit certain actions in the context of the real world.

Skills learnt in the therapy room or the clinic, often in isolation from the communication environment, do not easily transfer and if they do, they are not sustained. Highly infrequent and piecemeal support is probably not worth the expense and the effort for our severe tapestry kids.

Problems can also arise from the results of standardised testing which uses standardised language misunderstood by the child. Obviously we cannot change such procedures and then rely on the scores. Conversely, if children are more able but simply confused by the language used and/or unable to sustain their attention for the test, then test outcomes are also unreliable. Nevertheless, thousands of children, particularly those with autism and subtle language impairments, have been wrongly placed and inappropriately supported following the outcome of such assessments.

Within the tapestry model all information is important, especially when the intervention stage is reached. If optimal functioning can occur within a certain situation we need to alter our perspective to work out how the person can then shift and transfer to function similarly with other people and in other settings which are usually highly fragmented and confusing for our children, such as the noisy and stimulus-overloaded supermarket, the big classroom, the crazy playground, the theatre where people suddenly start clapping and laughing for no obvious reason and so on. If the verbal and nonverbal linguistics are highly confusing, this challenge could remain hidden. The pressure increases as the child moves through the system and is expected to function independently and with little of the augmentative support that is often provided in the early years in school.

Traditional classifications can be entered into the tapestry leading to an emergence of general images, which we could call Asperger syndrome or autism or ADHD, and knowledge of functioning in a clinic or experimental setting as well as the profile of results from assessments.

The process of drawing up multiple tapestries addresses the functioning of the unique child in context, including the mode of communication, emotions, fears and passions, flexibility, and understanding of the novel and the humorous.

This process should facilitate the development of an intuitive awareness of how the unique child's tapestry has developed over time and, crucially, how she or he learns and interacts with the real world. From this base of truly knowing the child, we are better placed to understand what to do in order to improve learning and living.

In order for accurate images to emerge, the crucial challenge in this process is to be able to shift perspectives from the detailed parts to the whole picture and vice versa, and then incorporate the two. We need to assimilate and balance our increasing understanding from various findings established by evidence-based science as it relates to the particular unique child and to understand the synergy in operation. To be able to assimilate information from both the traditional and the creative, the art and the science, requires that we do not become stuck in one or the other. How we feel as we do this can also be added to the contextual tapestry as creating the balanced interweave should give rise to greater feelings of compassion and understanding for the children we live and work with.

The earlier a child's difficulties can be recognised the better, but for those readers with older children whose problems have become tangled, don't give up – it's never too late to reweave the tapestry.

Chapter 9: Interventions

Once tapestries have been drawn up to include details from focused and comprehensive assessments by professionals, dependent on the extent of the difficulties, tapestries of intervention can be applied. This chapter discusses a number of interventions and the rationale behind them. Given the overlap of conditions through intertwined underlying processes, it follows that there exist certain principles related to how children have failed to learn despite interventions; there are also certain principles which appear to be common to successful interventions in a number of children with overlapping disorders.

I discuss some interventions which have shown some success within autism and ADHD, and refer to the crucial principles and features which seem to interweave to create a successful outcome and how they have been applied following the creation of a tapestry. These common features can be mapped onto the failing processes discussed in earlier chapters, which are found to interweave frequently in developmental disorders.

Controversy will always rage about the best approaches for children and there is a much-needed drive to ensure that information about interventions is clear and honest about expected change, in order to avoid creating false hope. With greater awareness and a professional interweave of increasing knowledge, we are better poised to support.

The intelligent consumer – parents – can now access all this information and it is important for them to be able to take control of decisions about their children. The increasing body of information about ADHD interventions and ASD interventions should help parents to make their own decisions about their child and to work in harmony with professionals who are supportive. The aim is to improve the functioning of the child, which in turn will benefit the child, the family and the wider community and society as a whole.

There are now numerous resources which can be used by families and support groups and Appendix 2 lists books, software, devices which can be purchased, phone numbers and addresses of organisations and helplines.

Tapestry Kids

At the end of Chapters 1–5 I have provided stories of some of the children and young people I have assessed over the years through using parts of their psychological reports, which I hope will help families. Descriptions of the tests used in these assessments are in Appendix 1. New assessment instruments are increasingly used to improve our understanding and the introduction of new neuropsychological assessments is adding to the knowledge that can be currently gleaned about a child. My own development and understanding are also constantly incorporating new thinking and it needs to be recognised that these reports were written some time ago. I hope, however, that they will provide insight into tapestry thinking and also tapestry disorders.

Limitation of space prevented me from including everyone I have seen, whose life experiences have enriched my own. The children range in age from pre-school to late adolescence. These children present with tapestries of problems, which are outlined in the reports. Each family has given written permission for their children to be mentioned and all names and other identifying features have been changed.

Chapter One

The warp and the weft
Weaving the developmental threads

> A tapestry is made by passing coloured threads among fixed warp threads.
>
> Chambers Twentieth Century Dictionary

Tapestries have been woven to depict fascinating, complex and colourful stories about people for centuries. In this book, the tapestry is used as a metaphor at various levels of explanation to illustrate the complexity and inter-weave of genetic potential and environmental triggers, in a story of how people themselves develop.

The way in which the unique person tapestry is constructed and unified into the wider social tapestry is still a beguiling mystery. Behaviours and inter-actions which can weave together into interwoven developmental disorders include autism, Asperger syndrome, ADHD, language spectrum disorders, dyslexic spectrum disorders including the dystonias and dyspraxia, Tourette syndrome, Irlen syndrome and other behavioural presentations as well as some of the shared difficulties experienced by children with specific medical conditions including central nervous system disorders such as hydrocephalus. Clusters of behaviours can interweave together but if they are understood only as purely separate disorders without understanding the threads, the interweave and other factors which also impact, interventions may be of little use.

The threads of these interwoven disorders can interfere with processing of the world and prevent synchronous relationships and the meeting of personal potential, warping the natural weave of the fabric of development and changing our life story.

> Weave: To make by crossing threads; to interlace; to work into a fabric; to depict by weaving; to construct; to unite, work into a whole. Weaving:

the act or art of forming a web; the intersecting of two distinct sets of fibres, threads or yarns – those passing longitudinally from end to end of the web forming the warp, those crossing and intersecting the *warp* at right angles forming the *weft.*

Chambers Twentieth Century Dictionary

A robust international literature on the above disorders points to their clear multiple genetic nature and, increasingly, we are understanding how environmental triggers even before birth can interweave. Clinically evident overlaps between the behaviours seen within disorders reveal common gene clusters and shared pathways. Some genetic researchers have explored the polygenetic nature of these disorders. Comings (1996), for instance, found that certain disorders cluster or weave together and are linked with three shared dopamine genes. He found that those people who inherited all three scored highest for ADHD and this was reduced as the number of inherited genes reduced. Comings (1996) also found support at a molecular level that other disorders such as Tourette syndrome, obsessive compulsive behaviours, conduct disorders, mania, and others could also be interlinked.

We are just beginning to understand the effects of such neurogenetic clusters, which may include metabolic disturbances, which interfere with brain and body function and ongoing development.

Weaving normal developmental tapestries requires the careful execution of a plan and the weaving process involves repetitive, rhythmic and balanced actions as the story is developed.

Problems with rhythm of different functions and at various levels of severity are always found within the tapestries of children with the above disorders. It is common to find early breathing and sleeping problems, a range of muscle difficulties, which could include feeding, digesting and bowel problems and some to the balanced use of the voice. Problems settling into a rhythmic reciprocal relationship with a caregiver from birth, when speech develops or from the time of a viral infection or brain insult are pivotal to autistic continuum disorders, with problems of regulation and execution of planning and action seen as pivotal to attention deficits. As we move along this ADHD thread we can find empathy problems which imply shared faulty mechanisms at different levels of severity presenting as different disorders. The changing hue of the same weave of difficulty is confirmed if interventions can shift some children back along the thread.

A person who has inherited the genes for such disorders is more likely to experience difficulties accommodating to environmental expectations and rhythmic timetables even before birth. It is also likely that they are more at risk of dormant potentials being triggered given certain environmental experiences to which others may not react at all, such as particular drugs and allergens.

Research has been able to detect certain motor movements, patterns of breathing, underactivity or overactivity and a limited startle response in the unborn infant and make predictions about the likelihood of developmental problems later. Hepper (1995) stated: 'As the behaviour of the foetus directly reflects its neurological functioning, observation of behaviour can provide information on neural well-being.' He went on to say that foetal behaviour at 18–20 weeks could be monitored through developing a standard neurological test, to allow the early identification of neurological problems.

Furthermore, the propensity for difficulties will also unfold over time as part of a maturational timetable, further interweaving with environmental triggers to create the unique tapestry. Here are some of the environmental threads which can tangle such genetically vulnerable life-story tapestries:

- adverse pre-natal conditions including viral infections, side-effects of prescription drugs, smoking, excess alcohol consumption
- birth injury including possible oxygen loss
- prematurity before frontal lobes are laid down, and related developmental and health problems including neurological damage through brain haemorrhages and the knock-on effects of poor organ function
- trauma from intrusive essential operations possibly associated with above
- side-effects or allergic reactions to medications and pollutant-contaminated foodstuffs on vulnerable infants and young children
- infant viral infections.

In turn, the interwoven inherited and acquired problems can lead to:

- difficulties with important rhythmic and self-regulating behaviours including sleeping, eating, interacting, processing, retaining and consolidating information, and putting plans in action in early learning

- head injuries as a result of impulsive, risk-taking behaviour which in turn lead on to executive dysfunctions including impulsivity, volatility, attention and concentration problems, poor planning and organising ability
- convulsions associated with any of the aforementioned and the effects on brain development.

Over time problems with social communication, motor skills, attention and inhibition may emerge more clearly and in some cases interweave with speech, language and motor delays. In turn, these difficulties will be further exacerbated by:

- a lack of recognition and early treatment or support
- others' reactions to difficult behaviour and/or illness
- social failure
- academic failure.

These problems can then result in secondary clusters of problems or disorders. Various threads weave to make the tapestry more complex over time and the intervention components and weave will determine good and bad outcomes.

When artists plan to weave a tapestry they have essentially the same basic tools as every other artist. The most obvious variations develop through the colours used, the images created and the developing stories. More detailed variations relate to the nature of the canvas, the threads, the plan and the execution of the plan, the weave and the tension in the process of weaving. Errors leading to glitches in the tapestry can occur at every stage and any stage. One tiny glitch can lead to dramatically different outcomes as changes are progressively added and multiplied.

The metaphor of the tapestry recognises similarities and differences at various levels – biological, neuropsychological, environmental – and additionally allows us to explore how the unique person tapestry emerges from the natural weave of the science and the art of developing thought and action in interaction with other people within a social milieu, the nature of the interweave determining outcome.

For some years the notion of the spectrum has helped us to recognise variability along a number of overlapping dimensions within various disorders. Within autism, Lorna Wing introduced the term 'autistic spectrum' to highlight a greater complexity than that implied within the 'continuum' (Wing 1996). The tapestry relating to disorders can be seen as being made up of multiple overlapping spectra relating to currently designated different disorders, and can work at different levels of explanation. Context is also included as well as the potential for change and the potential for the emergence of the unexpected.

Practically, this metaphor also allows us to look at the particular weave of certain clusters of factors which accumulate or weave together to form presenting features which we group into what have been termed as syndromes or disorders.

Attempting to understand how these clusters form, how they are described and diagnosed and how they are maintained over time allows us to understand how treatment or intervention tapestries can be woven together to change the developing child's life story.

This metaphor is proposed as a way to represent visually, understand and manage complex issues to help parents and professionals who find the term useful. Human tapestries are living dynamic forms. At every level it seems to be the nature, the severity and the interweave of the threads or circuits within and between different parts of the brain in interaction with the environment which determine ultimate behaviour.

The tapestry is proposed for those who are tired of the simple story and seek the defining quality of a mental canvas, which safely allows them to explore complexity without losing the thread.

Emerging images

The emergence of the image and then the story within the tapestry, like the emergence of representational thought and imagination in play, language, planning and sequencing life stories with others as we develop, results from the complex, intensive and highly repetitive weaving process.

Step inside my shoes

Problems with the emergence of important skills or with the sustaining of them are rife within the ADHD and the ASD groups. A most crucial thread in a human tapestry, and often problematic in these groups, has to be the thread of synchrony or reciprocity (Wing 1981). Through such processes a child learns from infancy to stand in someone else's shoes and in doing so improve the fit of his or her own. Understanding the other's perspective through synchrony helps individuals form their own sense of who they are in the world in relation to others.

One adolescent Asperger male told me how he would buy shoes exactly the same as those of his friend. Not satisfied with the same shoes, he would mould them to look worn in the same way and even organise the lacing in exactly the same way. This struck me as a perfect symbolic representation of the difficulties experienced by people with Asperger syndrome and autism. It is also an example of how the natural skills of imitation can remain at a concrete level, the image failing to emerge and then becoming distorted, leading to exhausting and obsessional attempts to compensate for the failure to engage instinctively in reciprocal interaction.

From infancy, rhythmic sensory and perceptual self-regulatory processes interwoven with those of others allow our sense of the social self to develop as understanding of other people emerges. These processes affect the emergence of increasingly complex thought, action and language. Children with autism have particular problems in this area but many without obvious repetitive behaviours have similar difficulties, often hidden from view beneath a normal veneer.

It's the way you say it

Language emerges from the weave of the synchronous communication tapestry. Infants instinctively use sounds repetitively, which interweave with associated gestures, alternations and facial expression as communication develops. Emotions and thought also weave together with language to make communication salient and motivating.

For many children with autism, the sounds they make are odd and not modified by the linguistic swirl in their social milieu. For some, normal babble sounds never turn into words. For others, sounds turn into words but the words disappear in the second year and sentences are not formed at all. Odd repetitive behaviour can emerge at that point. Parents may notice that their children do not seem to be building on their skills – in other words not learning. Like hamsters, they can tread the wheel forever, but still stay in the same spot. Desperately haunted parents of young autistic children I have assessed have frequently spoken about when they 'lost' their child into a world of his or her own. They say: 'That was when we lost her' or 'I lost my son around that time'. This realisation in the family does not always occur immediately, unless a child has suffered some sort of injury or illness with immediate dramatic effect. There is usually a gradual awareness, or emergence of recognition that their child is standing still in his or her learning, then appears to lose the babbling of words and the social connectedness.

One autistic child reacted to a viral infection after which time his joyful and animated baby talk was replaced by a dull droning sound. His obvious state of confusion led to him falling off a chair and hitting his head badly on a concrete patio. A seriously tangled tapestry was sewn into place very early for this tragic little boy. The repetitive weaving has no colour and no plan, so nothing emerges.

For many children who do go on to use language, semantic-pragmatic problems emerge; the accent can be oddly different from the accent of those around and sometimes sounds foreign – such as one little boy with an obvious American accent with parents who spoke broad English Midlands. Some will intersperse their disjointed sentences with snatches from repetitively watched videos, uncertain how to apply their knowledge and unable to incorporate the metalinguistic hue of the other person, appreciate their perspective and understand their needs as a listener and active participant in a dialogue.

Instinctive looking

Infants developing normally will alternate actions in interaction with people and then between people and things in their world according to very interesting fixed timetabled patterns; gradually the threads of play in concrete activities will coexist with the emergence of the more complex weave of pretend play.

Many children with later diagnosed ASD and ADHD are ill with medical problems during the first year of life and can not engage in the important activities even if they have the capacity to do so. There is a high rate of prematurity and birth problems amongst these groups and associated illness and neurological difficulties pre-term. The medically vulnerable group with ADHD and ASD type difficulties later appears to be the group of children whose prevalence has dramatically grown during the 1990s.

Many infants diagnosed with difficulties at the severe end of the autistic spectrum show little interest in people in the first year of life, failing to share attention through eye-gaze monitoring and looking at a shared object of interest, then pointing to items of interest. In some cases obvious motor problems evident at the earliest stages may prevent learning and action, which help to form relationships.

In other cases, interest in the social environment may be minimal, the lack of eye-gaze monitoring more related to salience of the stimuli and motivation. For some, a lack of interest in the wider environment which is not salient for them coexists with an over-focus on certain aspects, for instance, little shiny things, spinning objects or detail instead of any interest in people. Angled or peripheral looking at objects and people, darting glances or long stares contribute to the odd presentation of these autistic children, which was described initially by Kanner (1943).

An abnormal fascination with the TV in the early months of life may indicate that the child has a propensity for obsessional behaviour and is drawn to the multiple wavelengths. Even with a TV in the room, normally developing infants show more interest in toys and people. One could hypothesise that an excessive over-focus on these wavelengths rather than people during the first few weeks of life may completely alter that child's perceptions in relation to interaction with the world - a world of people with whom engagement involves synchronous actions with human wavelengths.

Others develop early skills normally and can be seen to do so on family videos, but then lose these early skills by 18 months when more complex communication and play skills should emerge.

Without the synchronous plan for weaving leading to interactions and transactions in the human tapestry, the image in the tapestry may never emerge, replaced instead by a magnification of constant repetitive activity.

Art reflects life

Essential processes, which breathe life into artistic representations in the widest sense, can be mapped onto the emergence of life itself and linked with poor processing in developmental glitches. For instance, the use of tempo and rhythm in music, pauses in film narrative, colour and pattern in art, evoke imagery and emotion in the perceiver; these processes can also be seen as crucially important in human behaviour, and most specifically in relation to infant development.

Plans and actions, basic regular rhythms incorporating important pauses are fundamental to development and compromised in attentional deficits and autistic spectrum disorders at varying levels of severity. Achieving balance and harmony in all things and in relation to all body systems is important.

The infant's perception of the world seems to shift from perceiving hidden symmetry in sound and light, to an imaginative position which incorporates the understanding of people; after much repetitive to-ing and fro-ing aware-ness can suddenly appear out of the blue – like the image in the tapestry.

Early repetitive, rhythmic and quite specific multi-modal behaviour in normal infants gives way to rhythmic novel interaction with people and is nec-essary for learning to orient and relate emotionally to the social world, but in the child with autism, these early instinctive skills never develop appropriately. In certain cases, if such skills appear to be evident early in infancy, the skills fail to shift to form the appropriate image and they return to thread form as basic perceptions of sensory patterns.

Forms of imitation, for instance, if occurring at all, can emerge within the severe autistic group in snatches of delayed echoing of sounds or in copied actions, which are not assimilated into a reciprocal tapestry. Unusual connec-tions and novel associations prove salient but can lead to rigid repetition of certain behaviours or certain phrases used whenever that particular association is perceived. The child with severe autism seems forever controlled and trapped within a relationship with hidden natural symmetries of colour, sound and natural patterns like angles.

Our knowledge and observations of autistic children easily lead to these conclusions and the savant poet, Kate (see Dowker, Hermelin and Pring 1998), illustrates her engagement not with people but with patterns in the environ-ment.

Donna Williams (1998) has written of her own experience with autism in which she confirms this thinking. Most interestingly, Donna Williams is also helped in reducing complex perceptual information through her use of Irlen coloured lenses, suggesting that the undoubtedly neurological distorted per-ceptions of wavelengths within the environment can be rectified by the appli-cation of the correcting harmonic colour combination for the individual.

Autistic spectrum disorders at the severe end of the spectrum can result in individuals remaining stuck at the level of basic information processing, which seems to bind them to a repetitive and addictive loop and which does not allow for appropriate temporal shifts or incremental leaps into representations of memory, thought and language followed by appropriate planned action.

Repetitive behaviours increase as abstract language fails to consolidate; early skills, if seen at all, fade away as the child withdraws into autism and there is decreasing motivation, if any was ever in evidence, to engage with people. Indeed people, their actions and expressions can become noxious. Remarkable Kate in Chapter 5 speaks of how she is getting on just fine using her brain to manipulate her fascinations in increasingly complex ways - until she is 'whacked' by society.

The artistic and musical processes of colour, pattern and rhythm are intertwined in the living tapestry with the science of life development. Complex neural circuitry in the brain weaves together and regulates internal and external biological systems. Glitches in the weave of these tapestries at various levels of explanation prevent the chemical, electrical and biological processes from operating smoothly.

These glitches affect not only social communication but also the ability to focus appropriately on salient features of the environment generally, to plan, organise and regulate action in relation to various modalities and situations. Children's instinctive understanding of time and their body's relative position in space is usually compromised within the autistic and the ADHD group but, given the tapestry nature of the circuitry, we can see how children may fit into certain concepts or descriptions of disorders as we explore the nature of the various threads and the severity of the problem defined by such threads.

For instance, as we move along the autistic reciprocity, language and motor skills threads, we find that the weave which matches the stereotype of the Asperger group and the children who meet the criteria for poor reciprocity will meet the criteria for an autistic continuum disorder but other threads will vary.

The stereotyped ADHD group will overlap in a number of areas but will have less obvious social communication problems or they may be hidden from view by increasingly difficult behaviour which is misinterpreted. Many other threads such as regulation of emotion, sticking in procrastination or leaping impulsively into action without a plan (both ends of the same neurochemical thread), processing more than one thing at a time and so on are commonly shared problems amongst these groups. Establishing the evidence of such behaviours and appropriately assessing them helps us to plan more appropriate interventions early in order to reweave the tapestry.

Neuropsychology is concerned with the relationship between brain and behaviour and weaves into an exploratory tapestry with other related fields of work. Certain neuropsychological deficits are shared in the disorders of autism and ADHD, and are found in more severe form in people who have suffered head and brain injuries. They affect the frontal lobe processes, often referred to as executive functions (Pennington and Ozonoff 1996). The underlying skills relate to focusing, sustaining that focus, planning, shifting and organising. More broadly, the central executive has to manage all these tasks, then the working memory must retain them in order to create images, which converge to develop complex thought.

Specific areas of the brain are implicated in relation to different tasks, and new brain-imaging techniques such as PET reveal which parts of the brain activate when certain tasks are completed. The neurotransmission system is linked with the motivational system and is felt to be implicated in many learning difficulties. Nevertheless, circuitry at various levels interweaves. Regardless of which threads are included in the unique disorder tapestry, for instance, significant reciprocity problems in autism and significant self-regulation problems in ADHD, recognition of shared threads or interwoven circuitry must help us with our interventions.

Some children are highly active with aggressive rage reactions and they regularly miss salient but subtle social cues and clues. Without the overactivity and rages they may have picked up on these features, but as the overactivity interweaves with the effect of failing to pick up on them, leading to more obvious social communication problems, we are less able to establish if one problem preceded the other, and if so, which one. Increasingly it seems that we need to address the interweave, the tapestry and its threads rather than forever search for single 'simple' causal answers.

There is an interesting interweave between motor problems, ADHD and developing social awareness (see Chapter 5). The recognition of this particular tapestry of difficulties is well known, and seen within the later diagnosed Asperger, dyspraxic or motor co-ordination and nonverbal developmental problems group, the individual children's behaviours are often baffling to many professionals, the intelligent children being seen as enigmas.

Highly active infants who may go on to be diagnosed as ADHD or ASD with hyperactivity may have managed to hurt their heads badly through risky actions, the effects of which will interweave with their development, as shared problems shown after any head injury relate to executive dysfunctions such as impulsivity and risk taking, not considering the consequences of actions, poor planning, poor concentration and attention, and poor temporal judgement. Those with an inherited ADHD, for instance, could be doubly disadvantaged by a head injury after a risky action. The problems accumulate as the tangled tapestry is woven.

For many children with ADHD in their tapestry, language and normal play seem to develop but impulsive behaviour restricts the skill building that is designed to result in the emergence of more complex thought, language and action. As the years pass, the gap between the child and his or her peers can widen to Grand Canyon proportions.

Impulsive behaviour is recognised as an inherited and acquired trait, which restricts important activities designed to allow the child to make multiple perceptual shifts in these early months and years of life. For instance, the failure to pause may prevent a child from assimilating important information (Grossman 1987) and it is well recognised that impulsive children cannot tolerate delays and waiting (Sonuga-Barke *et al.* 1996). I knew of one impulsive ASD child who had a very short name but he made it even shorter with a nickname so that he was not held up when writing the whole name. The intense inner restlessness which this can create leaves many young children saying they are bored, when their systems have not been able to hold information long enough to process it in order to make causal connections and engender interest.

They rush to finish to go – nowhere. Putting on the brakes allows the child to take on board information at all levels. I entitled one talk I gave to British psychologists 'Braking the Mode', a play on words which related to three issues:

1. the process of helping children to learn to brake and pause

2. linked to different modes – the visual, the auditory, the kinaesthetic etc.

3. resulting in 'breaking the mould' – or reweaving the tapestry.

Once information can be processed in a balanced manner, in turn the formed memories can be consolidated into representative and rational thought. Essentially, this is learning and applies to the management of information in every connection between children and their world.

For some, even when they are clearly consciously motivated to do certain things, the brain's motivational centre requires constant novelty or risk taking, and the danger which accompanies it, to trigger action.

Many children with neurodevelopmental problems are described as unmotivated as if this is a problem they can easily overcome just by taking responsibility for their learning. I find this offensive to individuals who desperately want to feel motivated, but their motivational system will not let them! It is we, as professionals, who need to take responsibility to ensure that we fully understand the child following comprehensive assessment. If their motivational systems, essentially driven by the neurotransmission system, are compromised we must ensure that we can provide interventions which can trigger responses in those systems before the child truly gives up.

For children who constantly complain of being bored, while underachieving in school, the family needs to impress the same message on them.

The interwoven existence of semantic-pragmatic disorder, particularly within autism, is well recognised. While there are obvious expressive problems which demand the involvement of speech and language therapists, especially if other obvious language disorders coexist, there are many children with hidden difficulties which are disguised to those with little understanding of this pernicious disorder.

In children of normal intelligence, there can be surprise at a child's failure to follow instructions and tendency to misconstrue events and intentions of other people. Many children with such hidden difficulties have developed secondary behavioural problems, which have often been misinterpreted. There is a dearth of understanding about such difficulties and about the interventions that can dramatically change them.

Children with semantic-pragmatic language disorders may also show an impulsive language style which seems egocentric and which is presented in the Asperger group with obvious neurotransmission implications given the impulsivity.

A number of children struggle with non-verbal confusion, failing to pick up on the social cues and clues in their social world. These features are well recognised within the autistic spectrum. Some children have significant problems generating language and if this cannot be remediated during the early years of life, they may never speak.

Many develop some language but the process of generating it appropriately remains very difficult, even though they know what they want to say. Such problems can leave an impression of much less intelligence given the tradition of regarding language use as the sole indicator of intelligence.

Street language, which is easy and makes an impact on peers, can be highly motivating, the children developing a camaraderie through their use of such language, which had previously eluded them.

Others develop to a high level of intellectual ability but fail to balance their life plans through self-regulated processes and will constantly need novel stimuli to sustain and motivate in order to ensure the emergence of new types of awareness and skills. The life-long frustration is obvious and desperately sad. Many of these individuals watch as others climb past them on academic, social and vocational ladders when they have the intelligence to do the work but lack other features, which restricts life choices. Great bitterness can follow. This restricts life chances even more as people increasingly avoid them.

Many intelligent individuals with differences which restrict can be totally misunderstood and misrepresented throughout their lives, possibly victimised and at the least passed over for the dusting of opportunities and the glittering prizes.

Trust of others can be compromised given problems with the ability to represent through the weaving of the representations of others into our own perceptions, which can lead to fears and phobias as a child develops. One phobic Asperger child told me that she simply could not imagine, no matter how hard she tried. If we cannot imagine or represent in our minds, for instance, the likely consequences of our own and others' actions, our inability to trust and a consequent fear of others and their intentions will increase, alongside a fear of change as we cannot predict likely outcomes and incorporate them into our life plans. The motivational system can become further limited by suffocating fears, lives spent running on the spot instead of moving forward, all energies focused on reasons to justify doing nothing. In these cases the tapestry acts like a suffocating blanket.

Many children who fit the Asperger criteria are too trusting. As a result they are more likely to be manipulated and taken for a ride. This must be watched out for amongst carers and parents.

The tapestry metaphor is also used, as it seems a rich and respectful model, which I hope will contribute to a better understanding of the uniqueness of each individual. Despite shared threads, self-similarity in Chaos Theory parlance, the emerging picture is of a unique person. Tapestries of better focused and appropriate support can be woven which incorporate the recognition of the individual needs and the recognised needs of the cluster groups which the individual's behaviour most clearly matches. This is why off-the-peg solutions are not applicable to these children without careful fine-tuning.

There is also a flexibility, which reflects life and allows for reweaving through positive experiences and interventions, delivered by different people, including, naturally, the subject of the tapestry.

Many of the overlapping features and explanations can help us understand disorders which compromise the development and success of individuals and which can lead on to mental ill-health and antisocial behaviour if understanding and appropriate support are not provided as early as possible.

There is at last recognition of the importance of early intervention to offset later difficulties, linked with recognition that early evidence of significant problems worsens the prognosis. The tapestry allows us to understand that if there is evidence of early problem threads woven together with a number of coexisting risk factors, known as co-morbidities, then the greater the potential for later developing risk factors to weave increasingly tangled real-life tapestries.

Knowing how to intervene early with support within the home and for the individual is more helpful than dismissing all problems by saying that the child will grow out of it or waiting until the child fits more serious sets of criteria, which may be certain to damage his or her future potential and possibly stigmatise the child for life.

Despite increasing acceptance of the importance of early intervention in developmental disorders, many children may have been under a watching brief for years, if picked up at all, and then possibly placed on waiting lists for assessments and support for years. It is very common to hear a mother describe how she was treated as if she were neurotic by health advisers for her early concern, then subsequently treated in the same manner by educationalists, whose definition of 'early' varies depending on which school system they are in and how they target their resources. The first school may consider it alarmist to worry about a 5–7 year old. On transfer they may hint at problems for the middle school, which considers it alarmist to worry about a 7–8 year old. When concerns are passed on to secondary school, it might consider it alarmist to worry about the 'babies' of the big school. This can go on through to early adulthood.

If problems emerge more openly in school as the child reaches 7 or 8 years of age – for some sooner some later – there could be at least an 18 months' wait for an initial assessment. Meanwhile, the increasing frustration of the family will intertwine with increasing difficulties of the child, affecting self-esteem and resilience to cope with the difficulties. Finding help within the system can be extremely difficult with many families kept at arm's length for years by paperwork and delaying tactics. Once a child's behaviour totally collapses, the mother is likely to be brought back into the frame again for blame, the easiest but certainly not the wisest explanation.

For many, despite significant problems, support may never arrive during childhood, leaving the problem to arise in more severe forms in late adolescence or early adulthood, by which time academic failure, failed relationships and traumas arising as a function of the underlying unrecognised problems confuse issues and become the prime candidates blamed for causing all of the individual's difficulties.

Many families have found themselves numbed by helplessness to support their child as they exist in waiting mode, watching matters worsen. In time, parents of children whose problems have developed into behavioural difficulties can become desperate, weary and distant, just as the child reaches early adolescence and when even children without difficulties need maximal guidance and engagement with the family.

In the past and within the current process of assessment of children, a number of problems can arise which prevent appropriate and early diagnosis of these interwoven disorders and then cause delay in putting programmes into place, if they are provided. These can range from a lack of recognition through limited training, a refusal to recognise what others confirm, through to erroneous and/or inadequate assessment, diagnostic and referral procedures and inappropriate and/or inadequate interventions offered too late. Overly intellectual arguments and an over-focus on detail can be used to dismiss the value of any intervention for children in a system which threatens the job security, ability, integrity and even rationality of its professionals if precious resources are overused.

Meanwhile children can be left unsupported throughout childhood. Greater parental awareness as early as possible of the importance of developmental and family tapestries will empower families to help themselves in a changing world in which the knowledge base is not the sole possession of professionals with limited resources.

Without a doubt, the failure to recognise problems early, blame the mother tactics with no support, advice or education and the restrictions on the nature of the support once recognised lead to an increase in secondary psychological and psychiatric problems in the population, and overall increasing crime linked with these problems, affecting the children of these children, their wider families trapped in the tangled tapestry. The toll on the individual has no price tag, lives can be ruined by long-term distress and failure, the loss of their potential often total. Society then reaps the benefit in terms of an increased need for mental health services, the effects of crime and the massive loss of potential.

I have suggested that it could be helpful to create one's own practical tapestry in order to understand a child's difficulties and needs. This can be formed by considering three essential issues:

- nature of each thread – hyperactivity, obsessions, motor problems
- severity of the problem – use scale of your own choice
- timing of onset of each problem thread.

Tapestries of positive features, which help to offset difficulties, can also be drawn up as part of a positive intervention tapestry.

Summary

I have used the metaphor of the tapestry to discuss issues at various levels:

1. As a general artistic perspective of how unique people and their perceptual processes are woven into the natural world.

2. To illustrate the interweave of science and art in the development of people, their representations and emergent developing stories.

3. As a method of discussing how instinctive infant skills interweave with others through communication, to help us develop representations of our shared environment and make connections with other people.

4. As a base to explore the intertwining nature of specific developmental disorders such as autism and ADHD, which are seen as mutually exclusive in the current sets of criteria, raising diagnostic assessment and intervention issues.

5. To unpick the essential processes within interventions which lead to the formation of interconnected memories and cognitions, in turn leading to the development of better social engagement, academic learning and problem solving skills.

6. To weave tapestries which depict failing systems.

7. As a pragmatic framework within which individual cases can be described and supported and simple enough to be used by any parent in a number of ways. For instance,

    (a) to describe and chart family histories and child development to better inform interventions

    (b) as an opportunity to explore contexts and interactions for the child

    (c) to develop an understanding of the effect of co-morbidities and severity issues

    (d) to help provide a tangible base to monitor and evaluate interventions more precisely.

Finally, reweaving tapestries is not easy. It requires dedication, positive thinking and confident management through education, comprehensive assessment and appropriate support. Some of our children will never be independent in their lives but we can vastly improve the quality of those lives. The lives of others may be transformed.

Tapestry kid

 # Jack

Reason for referral

Jack was referred for a psychological assessment given a history of distractibility, overactivity and impulsivity; his family history of attention deficit disorders (ADD) and Asperger syndrome increased the heritability risk factors for Jack.

Family history

Jack and Rory are two brothers, aged 3 and 7 respectively. (Rory is discussed separately in the next tapestry kid section.) They have an aunt with Asperger syndrome and their father was highly active as a child and has problems with attention. Their mother can confuse word order sometimes. The boys' maternal grandmother suffers from depression, is a workaholic and can't sit still. The boys' paternal grandfather has problems with organisation, planning, managing finances, understanding time and holding down jobs. He also has a vocal tic.

Developmental history

There were no noted difficulties during the pregnancy, although Jack is reported as being an active infant in the womb. He was born approximately two to three weeks after his due date. Jack coped with feeding and sleeping without any problems and although he was overactive, he did not cry excessively. He was easy to cuddle, would reach out to be picked up and easily engaged with objects of interest in his environment, sharing this experience with others.

Speech and language developed on time and Jack started to walk at the age of 1 year. He proved to be very active and was described as an extremely energetic little boy following his assessment at the local child development clinic. It was also noted that he was difficult to engage and remained fairly distractible. It was noted that Jack's drawing was immature for his age but this was not felt to be related to any inherent clumsiness. His mother reported that in her opinion her child is not clumsy but 'in too much of a hurry sometimes and tends to bang his head playing over and under things'.

Jack has had difficulties with relating to other people and tends to be aggressive, rough and rather unpredictable in groups. After an operation when he was 2 years old, Jack had to be held down as his stitches had come apart because of his excessive running about. Being held down in this way traumatised him and his mother said that it took some time for him to recover.

There is clear evidence of Jack's overactivity and impulsivity. He takes risks, moves quickly, and puts himself into dangerous situations before he can be stopped. For instance, his mother reported that she need only turn her back and move towards the kitchen and he is pulling chairs and glass tables out to stand on in order to get the key to wind up the clock. His mother has to ensure that the top bolt is on the door, as he will simply run out of the house; he is quite fearless.

Jack has a fascination for things mechanical and is very keen to know how everything works. When he was 2 his mother reports that he had a fascination about boilers and upon arrival at his Nana's one day he looked past her and his first comment was 'You've got a big boiler, Nana!' On one occasion his mother found diagrams for the central heating. On showing these to little Jack 'he squatted down to look at them, realised what they were, jumped up and squealed with joy, ran around in circles, and then carefully studied them for days.'

Jack will insist on touching, smelling and tasting a whole variety of objects in order to learn about them. He remains distracted by fans, fire extinguishers, extractors, drains, locks and sounds. He will actually wake up in the night, very distressed, telling his mother to stop the fireworks in his head and to stop the noise. In large groups of people he will shout: 'stop the noise', 'it's too noisy', 'be quiet'. Jack will also grab at people while being wheeled about in his buggy, and will run away without any fear of the road. Jack also enjoys spinning around and looking at machines which spin around.

Jack is very difficult to manage given his impulsivity and his desire to engage in damaging activities. For instance, he will tear off wallpaper, draw on the walls, put toothpaste all over the beds and clothes, and disrupt board games being played by the other children at home.

Professional involvement

The local paediatrician has recognised that Jack's levels of activity and associated aggression and disruptive behaviour are excessive for his age, and he has been referred to a local psychiatrist.

Within school, despite his young age, Jack already has an individual education plan (IEP) and is on Stage 2 of the special needs procedures. The school within its IEP has noted a number of problem areas, particularly Jack's inability to wait and to share, his unpredictable behaviour, which includes biting and kicking without warning, his poor eye contacting, his total lack of co-operation when upset, and his tendency to ignore adults and refuse to answer in certain situations. Variability of fine motor control was mentioned, and concerns about putting everything in his mouth.

The nursery school is clearly concerned that Jack can rarely sustain attention for more than a few minutes without adult support, except if he is playing with water, with which he is fascinated. As a consequence he has been having one-to-one support since nursery school.

Jack's parents are extremely concerned about their child's future. They recognise him as a delightful little child who can be very anxious, and worry about him having no friends. He will talk incessantly, and the topic of conversation becomes 'deeper and deeper'. His mother wants him to be a happy child who can fit in with his world and be successful.

Test results
Jack's chronological age when tested:
3 years 9 months

British Ability Scales (BAS II)

UPPER LEVEL CORE SCALES

	Percentile	*Age Equivalent*
Verbal Comprehension	46th	3 yrs 10 mths
Picture Similarities	34th	2 yrs 10 mths
Naming Vocabulary	99th	8 yrs plus
Pattern Construction	3rd	2 yrs 10 mths
Number Concepts	1st	Below 2 yrs 6 mths
Copying	1st	3 yrs 4 mths

UPPER LEVEL DIAGNOSTIC SCALES

	Age equivalent
Recall of Objects Immediate Verbal	3 yrs 10 mths
Recall of Digits Forward	2 yrs 7 mths

CLUSTER SCORES

	Percentile
Verbal	95th
Pictorial Reasoning	3rd
Spatial	7th

Discussion

From this assessment we can see that Jack has a highly discrepant profile. Despite his overactive and impulsive behaviour and the need to have breaks to complete the test, he focused well on some items and was clearly challenged by others. The overall profile is typical of an ADHD/Asperger child.

Jack's Naming Vocabulary score – using pictures to elicit naming – was very highly developed, reaching an age equivalent above 8 years at only 3 years 9 months. By comparison Jack had significant problems with number, auditory short term recall, drawing and visual spatial skills to create patterns. He was poorly motivated to engage in written activities. Jack's Verbal Comprehension was just age appropriate and we would expect higher given his vocabulary. The nature of this comprehension task involves pragmatic language skills, which are often problematic in this particular group.

Jack's Verbal cluster percentile score is very high but it is unlikely to translate into attainments if the other areas – Spatial and Pictorial Reasoning involved in Number Concepts and Picture Similarities – are not addressed immediately. Many children with a profile similar to Jack's are not supported, as their brightness is the only aspect noted, the idea that other problems may exist and prevail being dismissed. Later, as we know, these problems can completely destroy the bright potential.

Despite his unusual fascinations and poor reciprocal and communicative skills, which place Jack on the autistic continuum, he was able to play very nicely in a symbolic way, which may be related to his high verbal intelligence. In a child's tapestry, the level of ability thread is important, as children at different levels with the same threads in other areas will differ in how they behave. This thread can totally change the weave of the fabric!

The local paediatrician referred to features of the learning environment in which Jack responded well. I also found that he responded well to brief intense one-to-one and this indicates a need for such support to provide a structure and feedback at the point of performance – within school and at home.

Conclusions and recommendations

There is strong evidence from this assessment and history that Jack is a child with a significant ADHD and I am of the opinion that he falls into the category of children whose ADHD overlaps with Asperger syndrome. In this group the accent is on speedily providing support before behaviours become fixed and exacerbated by the interwoven threads mentioned by the local paediatrician, 'a downward spiral in which undesirable behaviour leads to a bad reputation and poor self-esteem'.

The increasingly problematic ADHD behaviour including being a danger to himself, alongside over-reactions to emotional events and his convoluted conversations often on dark themes, indicate that Jack is at risk and needs an intensive multi-modal intervention plan put into place immediately. I hope the following recommendations are helpful:

Jack needs a Statement under the auspices of the Education Act 1996.

He requires ongoing medical support and advice on a trial of medication at some stage to manage the ADHD, which is pernicious. It would be helpful to educate the school staff in these disorders through literature on ADHD and Asperger/autistic continuum disorders. The local authority has responded well to this child's needs. Once in mainstream he will need a facilitator and a teacher trained to work with children with autistic spectrum and ADHD.

Jack needs to be seen by a speech and language therapist; if no one is available locally there are a number of excellent independent specialists who can provide programmes of work for semantic- pragmatic problems. Jack would benefit from being involved in some of the commercially available communication programmes undertaken daily in school with a group of children. It is not too early to introduce Jack to computers and to programs which will aid the development of his literacy, numeracy and written expression. Indeed, given his emerging profile, although it is early days, he may become a child who needs a computer to produce work which matches his intelligence.

Tapestry Kid

Rory

Reason for referral

Rory was referred for a psychological assessment given the early recognition of problems leading to professional involvement.

Family history

See Jack's family history in preceding section.

Developmental history

There were no noted difficulties during the pregnancy; Rory was born following a normal delivery. As a baby he was very 'good' and a watcher of people. Rory developed language on time and walked at 11 months. He proved to be a child with some co-ordination problems but could not be described as clumsy. When very young Rory would prefer to flick leaves and string rather than play with toys, and later tended to draw maps. At pre-school Rory looked as if he wanted to play with other children but stayed on the periphery. He would lie on the floor under chairs, making 'peculiar' noises. He felt under pressure in groups and did not like to join in party games.

Rory reacted badly to changes and transitions, was a dreamer and reacted to too many people. Once he started in school he was variously described as a loner, obsessional, unpredictable, eccentric, imaginative, creative, joy to work with one-to-one, and distractible.

Rory could not cope with groups of children and would 'go rigid' out of the blue at which times he was 'not available' and could not speak. He has a black and white sense of justice and becomes particularly angry if he sees injustice on the playground, often intervening and finding himself in trouble.

Professional involvement

While at nursery school Rory was seen by the educational psychologist, who suggested that he stay behind for a year. There were many expressed concerns by various professionals. The early concerns related to his odd behaviours, his poor motivation and limited concentration. Once in school, he produced little written work but was able to retell complex stories and to remember the details for a long time.

His teacher referred to him as unpredictable and said that Rory had problems coping with a larger group of children when the new intake arrived and that he was unable to sustain co-operative play without 'exuberant eccentric behaviour'. His behaviour in games was described as disruptive and hazardous.

Rory was referred two years previously to the emotional and behavioural support service, which reported on his obsessions (such as with shiny paper), his inappropriate modes of communication and behaviour in social groups and his tendency to become over-focused on certain interests.

Assessment by the local community paediatrician a year previously found Rory to be a child with 'some difficulty with co-ordination, attention control and planning albeit at the mild end of the spectrum'.

The local educational psychologist then assessed Rory and found him to be a child with excellent verbal skills alongside only average skills in visual motor activities. His attainment scores did not reflect the level of his ability and his spelling fell behind his skill in reading. The psychologist concluded that Rory was a child of above average ability who had a lively and interesting mind. His poor co-ordination and associated poor pencil control was mentioned with support suggested. It was felt that drama and social skills groups would also benefit Rory.

Currently Rory has been shifted back on to Stage 2 of special needs and receives an hour of support twice a week in a group of five children.

His mother remains concerned that her child has a learning difficulty, which is interfering with his progress.

Test results
Rory's chronological age when tested:
7 years 8 months

Wechsler Intelligence Scale for Children (3rd Edn UK) (WISC)
VERBAL SCALE

	Score
Information	10
Similarities	18
Arithmetic	7
Vocabulary	14
Comprehension	18
Digit Span	8

PERFORMANCE SCALE

	Score
Picture Completion	14
Coding	10
Picture Arrangement	13
Block Design	11
Object Assembly	12
Symbol Search	8

IQ AND INDEX SCORES

	Score	Percentile
Verbal IQ	121	92nd
Performance IQ	115	84th
Full Scale	120	91st
Verbal Comprehension Index	128	97th
Perceptual Organisation Index	116	86th
Freedom from Distractibility Index	86	18th
Processing Speed Index	94	34th

British Ability Scales (BAS)
RECALL OF OBJECTS

	Percentile
Immediate Verbal Recall	7th
Immediate Spatial Recall	58th
Delayed Verbal Recall	82nd
Delayed Spatial Recall	62nd

Test of Irlen syndrome

Rory shows clear evidence of Irlen syndrome.

Wechsler Objective Reading Dimensions (WORD)

	Percentile	Age Equivalent	Wisc III UK Scaled Score
Basic Reading	90th	9 yrs 7 mths	14
Spelling	19th	7 yrs	7

Discussion

Rory is a charming little boy with verbal giftedness, dyslexic problems and evidence of Asperger syndrome as part of DAMP syndrome (see below) which is defined in part by the ADD component. His tapestry of difficulties, as I like to call these interweaving developmental disorders, needs to be recognised and he needs supporting in the first instance by the provision of a Statement of Special Educational Need.

The presence of social communication and obsessional behaviours within Rory's family history make it less surprising that he presents with the same features. From an early age there is evidence of 'oddness' and unusual reactions to other people. He has sensitivities to people and before he was ever expected to engage in written work, his behaviour was seen as odd enough to warrant professional involvement, which, to its credit, the local education authority (LEA) brought in.

Subsequently Rory faced even more problems when he was faced with work within school, as his poor motivation for writing came to the fore.

Children with the tapestry of attentional deficits, motor co-ordination and features of Asperger syndrome have been noted by Ehlers and Gillberg (1993) who refer to DAMP syndrome – an acronym for Disorders of Attention and Motor Perception. The former two sets of features have been formally recognised locally by the paediatrician.

From my assessment it is clear that Rory is a highly intelligent child (as reported by his local psychologist) who presents with 'praxic' problems. Furthermore he has a specific spelling problem, offering non-phonic spellings for simple words, which is surprising given his IQ and his reading ability as tested on WORD. For instance, he spelt 'things' as 'theings', 'right' as 'rithte' and also mirror wrote some letters. It would appear that Rory is using his excellent visual skills, expected in the autistic continuum/ADD group, to read; his high score for Picture Completion reflects this ability to note visual detail.

It is also important to note that Rory's better visual skills came into play in the Visual Memory tests on the BAS. He scored poorly when simply asked to recall verbally a stimulus sheet of pictures but dramatically improved after he had been given the opportunity to hold and spatially place the picture cards.

As we can see, despite a delay, his verbal recall was much better after this spatial activity, in which he did very well. This tells us that his memory processing can be improved by the use of visual or kinaesthetic approaches.

Rory will also have problems presenting information in the written mode, and would be helped by the opportunity to present his work via a word processor to prevent him becoming increasingly frustrated, especially given his level of intelligence. We can then expect an upsurge in any repetitive behaviours raising concerns in school.

It was evident that Rory had Irlen syndrome and I have advised the family to have a further diagnostic check. He responded extremely well to acetate coloured sheets, which removed the distortions.

Conclusions and recommendations

Rory has experienced difficulties which can be fitted into DAMP syndrome and which relate to attentional deficits, motor difficulties and Asperger syndrome. He also has a specific spelling problem. Rory presents with Irlen syndrome, which relates to perceptual distortions. Rory learns through the visual, the kinaesthetic and the novel; he will respond well to computers. Given his gifted verbal profile Rory needs enhanced project work with his written presentations created through a word processor.

Rory would benefit from support for his specific spelling problem and computer programs can augment the work undertaken by the class teacher. I would advise that group social communication programmes are also put into place.

There may be some benefit in a trial of medication which addresses the obsessional behaviours and Rory will need to see a specialist for this purpose, if the family choose to take this route.

Given the significant scatter within Rory's profile, his gifted verbal reasoning and poor attainments, his very poor motivation in written work given the Asperger problems and his specific learning difficulties (SpLD), I would recommend that he be provided with a Statement of his special needs.

Chapter Two

Brief cross-Atlantic history of two spectrum disorders

Autistic spectrum disorder and attention deficit and hyperactivity disorder

In the United States and Europe over the past century or so, a strong literature has emerged related to the recognition and understanding of behavioural presentations such as ADHD and autism, which are the main focus of this chapter. Other work across the world including Sweden, Australia and New Zealand has further contributed to our rich knowledge base.

Clusters of behaviours have been recognised in stereotypical form throughout history through descriptions of particular personalities. There is clear evidence of the inherited nature of such clusters, which in turn interweaves with the total environment, including not only multiple environmental features, but also interpersonal interactions.

Classification systems have shifted from their initial role as effectively a social census of illness and disorders, to systems which are designed to help various professionals understand the problems brought to them in their work. Two main systems, the World Health Organisation's (WHO) International Classification of Diseases (ICD), mainly used in Europe until recently, and the American Psychiatric Association's (APA 1994) *Diagnostic and Statistical Manual of Mental Disorders* (DSM) have evolved over the past century, to include, revise and remove various named disorders. It is important to understand this evolution, the nature and differences between these systems in the past as they underlie the diagnoses which may be given to a child (see Appendix 1). Rigid adherence to a system or different ways of viewing the same problem could underlie the many confusions faced by parents when their children are not diagnosed with what appears to them obvious.

ADHD

Descriptions of behaviour considered to mirror ADHD first found their way into the *Lancet* when George Still (1902), a British paediatrician, referred to children he had identified as having 'volitional inhibition'. He also referred to them as passionate, lawless, impulsive and overactive. However, he also referred to 'curious' traits such as: solitariness, complete lack of natural affection, sullen manner, repetitive behaviours, pica (cravings to eat inapproptiate substances), motor problems, crossing social boundries, self-injury, odd gait and 'twitchings'. Punishment failed to work and 'unusual surroundings' provided a temporary cessation of symptoms (Still 1902). He recognised the significant inherited nature of the disorder as well as evidence of acquired nervous system damage.

Autism and Asperger syndrome

Two boys born in Austria around the same time, Leo Kanner in the late 1890s and Hans Asperger in 1906, were to focus their professional attentions on clusters of behaviours which they described as 'autistic', meaning self-oriented, derived from the Greek word '*autos*'. The conditions were recognised as essentially biological.

Kanner had moved from Vienna where he trained in medicine to Baltimore in the USA; Asperger remained in Austria. Neither knew of each other's work but both produced papers within a year of each other, in 1943 and 1944 respectively. Kanner's work was written in English while Asperger's work was written only in German, which limited its international recognition.

Kanner's 'children' were extreme in their distance from reality, the stereotypical expression of Kanner's autism describing the children as 'mute and aloof' (Kanner 1943). The children failed to use language to communicate with other people, they could not interact normally with others or with their environment from birth and demanded everything should remain the same in their lives. Kanner considered that the children had 'inborn autistic disturbances of affective contact' (Kanner 1943). His profile for autism is shown in Appendix 1, Table 1.

They were children in their own world, cruelly isolated from the other planets in the universe within which they had to travel throughout their entire lives, but not from the push and pull of the various forces. They engaged in repetitive and stereotypical activities in an apparent desire to reduce their sense of confusion, achieve sameness and take some self-control, if desire existed at all in their minds. These children also showed evidence of trancelike behaviours and many were hyperactive and impulsive. They could also become highly volatile, descending into rage reactions. The striking feature related to their inability to reciprocate appropriately with people.

Asperger (1944) described a very similar but less obviously 'in their own world' group of people whom he also regarded as having 'autistic psychopathy'. He referred to clumsiness and odd behaviours but the group had developed language and was felt to be as cognitively impaired as Kanner's group. The defining shared feature or outcome of their behaviour was the inability to make connections with people, at varying levels of severity and of various forms. The use of the term 'autistic' to reflect self-orientation holds within it an essential paradox – the failure to make connections with others also contributes to the failure to develop a sense of self in the very beginning, through the development of the essential interactive tapestry, a sociable blanket to snuggle into. The overused term 'low self-esteem' needs to be reconsidered in this light.

In the 1970s, Lorna Wing and Judy Gould embarked on an important population study in Camberwell, South London. It was established that autism existed on a continuum – Kanner had also remarked about illness appearing in different degrees of severity. The range of presentations of disability extended from profoundly physically and mentally handicapped to the able, highly intelligent people with subtle social impairment nevertheless representing a learning disability to the individual. Wing and Gould (1979) found an overlap with learning disabilities with a shading 'into eccentric normality'. Many other coexisting features were noted and the overall picture was found to depend on the particular pattern seen within the individual. It was also noted that some children shifted along the continuum over time, the pattern changing subtly.

Wing and Gould (1979) recognised three types of social impairment: the classic Kanner *mute and aloof* group; the *passive* group and the *active but odd* group which more closely resembled Asperger's group, although at the time they were not aware that Asperger had also written about such a group. They later added the *over-formal stilted* group.

In time, Wing would coin the term 'autistic spectrum' to reflect the greater complexity over the continuum. She first wrote about Hans Asperger (1944) in 1981 and set the condition within the autistic spectrum (see appendix 1, Table 9).

This insightful and wise British psychiatrist published a paper in which she described 34 cases that fitted the Asperger description and extended the boundaries of diagnosis in relation to disorders with a core deficit of poor reciprocity, by incorporating this group within the autistic spectrum, where it has remained. Gradually, an awareness of Asperger's descriptions began to dawn in the UK. It took until the late 1980s before Wing's work led to the translation into the English language (Frith 1989) of Asperger's paper. It was the mid-1990s before it began to reach the consciousness of a significant number of professionals, but Wing and Gould's (1979) work had already raised awareness of this same group – the active but odd group within autism. Controversy has been linked with the various diagnostic criteria for Asperger syndrome, each of which defines subtly different 'types'. These are set out in Appendix 1.

Deficits of attention in the Asperger group, implicating the central nervous system, were described by Asperger (1944) himself; Kanner (1943) had already considered that there were central nervous system problems within autism. In the 1940s an outbreak of encephalitis led researchers into hyperactivity disorders to consider that *all* such behaviour must stem from brain damage. This thinking prevailed within this research and led to the term 'minimal brain damage'. Over time it became clear that many children exhibiting such conditions had no obvious brain damage and so this term was replaced during the 1960s by 'minimal brain dysfunction' (MBD). During the 1970s it was found that this dysfunction was linked with the efficiency of the message system within the brain involving neurotransmitters.

Meanwhile, in the USA, Barkley wrote his first text on hyperactive children in 1981, which heralded a prolific decade of intensive research into hyperactivity disorders in the USA. The various name changes reflected changing opinions about the nature of the disorder as more research was undertaken, and various types of focus, i.e. names reflecting cause, symptoms and process.

The term 'attention deficit hyperactivity disorder' (ADHD) focused on what was then considered the core deficit in ADHD – attentional problems. There was an increasing recognition in US research that these problems, which seemed to have attentional features at the core, were shared with others who did not meet the criteria for hyperactivity but whose difficulties could nevertheless cause great distress for the child and family.

Research revealed a significant number of children who met the criteria for attentional problems and impulsivity, but not the hyperactive criteria. A separate group was found to have attentional problems without either impulsivity or hyperactivity and the third group, constituting the highest risk and the most likely to be recognised, with a ratio of four boys to one girl, is the group with all three symptom clusters. (The formal diagnostic criteria are in Appendix 1, Table 2.)

In accordance with the WHO International Classification of Diseases, a core group of researchers in Britain recognised ADHD symptomatology as we know it in the hyperactive form (Taylor *et al.* 1986), although ICD–9 focused on an all-pervasive 'hyperkinesis' at that time. A child had to be *constantly* restless to be given this label by paediatricians and psychiatrists. The prevalence rate amongst 7-year-old boys using this more conservative measure was 0.5 per cent–1 per cent (Taylor and Hemsley 1995). The general opinion was that unless children met the very strict hyperkinetic criteria, they did not 'have' a hyperactivity disorder despite meeting many other criteria which overlapped. The focus was on the *extreme* overactivity and left a number of children, recognised in the US system, in a no man's land in Europe.

Furthermore, the earlier WHO classification systems of ICD–8 and ICD–9 were not operational definitions, although many have used them as if they are. There were no rules guiding practitioners how to use what were effectively snapshot guides.

Barkley (1997) discusses how a rift developed between Europe and the USA in relation to ADHD, with the Europeans continuing to consider hyperkinesis as relatively rare and frequently linked with very low IQ and 'evidence of organic brain damage', (Barkley 1997, p.6), while in the the USA the spectrum widened to include children who could not be described as 'hyperkinetic' but who met the DSM–IV criteria for what became known as ADHD. Barkley notes that in Europe, by contrast, these same children are viewed as having a:

> conduct problem or disorder because of their often hostile, defiant and belligerent nature. It is viewed as a behavioural disturbance believed to originate largely in poor parental management of children, family dysfunction and social disadvantage (Barkley 1997, p.6).

The name 'attention deficit disorder' (ADD) had become well known as an acronym, and was therefore retained, despite the findings during the 1980s of a number of researchers which indicated that 'attention' was *not* the core problem. 'Attention' relates to a multiplicity of skills and it was becoming clearer with more focused research that the difficulties seemed to be related to the motivational state and to response consequences (Barkley 1997) which affected certain attentional skills:

> Children with a pattern of ADHD behaviour did not respond in the same way to alterations in contingencies of reinforcement or punishment as did normal children. Under conditions of continuous reward the perfor-

mances of children with ADHD were often indistinguishable from those of normal children on various laboratory tasks, but when reinforcement patterns shifted to partial reward or to extinction (no reward) conditions, children with ADHD showed significant declines in their performance. (Barkley 1997, p.8).

During the 1980s Barkley hypothesised that ADHD children had deficits in relation to rule-governed behaviour, using the language of behaviourists such as B.F. Skinner.

When I searched the literature in the mid-1980s to find reference to the behaviours I had observed in special facilities and in the highest referred group of pre-school children within the community, it was the minimal brain damage/dysfunction term which was commonly used. Although researchers such as Eric Taylor in the UK had focused on hyperkinesis, most of these children did not meet those very strict criteria, and most returned from special-ist hospital departments without a diagnosis and a way forward from long-awaited specially arranged assessments.

Parents complained that their outwardly normal children, mostly boys, seemed to 'have a connection missing' and consistently reported on their impulsive behaviour, inability to listen or understand rules, frequent clumsiness and inability to control temper outbursts. All the children, mainly boys and rep-resenting the highest referred group to child guidance at pre-school, had no sense of urgency or normal understanding of time. They had to be chivvied along all the time to meet deadlines and parents found that they had to help a child to get dressed long after the expected age of independence in such tasks. This was not because they could not manage such tasks, although a number with coordination problems would get the order of things wrong and couldn't fasten laces and buttons. These were the children who looked as if they had put their shirt on *after* their jumper. Many became embroiled in something else and then lost track of time and couldn't shift, or became panic stricken when they realised they were late, becoming more agitated as people confronted them, which they could not tolerate.

Some of these boys in the highest referred category were highly overactive and hurt themselves in numerous accidents through risky behaviours. During the early years parents felt they needed to wear roller-skates to keep up with their children.

Parents would say things like 'He's intelligent – so why won't he listen? Why can't he understand the rules like his brothers? Why can he do it one minute and not the next? What's the *matter* with him?'

I was struck by how many of these children had problems perceiving social cues, clues and rules. In severe cases they also gave out the wrong cues and clues which led to negative reactions from others, in turn affecting the intertwining interactions. I used the term 'poor transactional mediators' in psychological reports during those years as these particular children appeared to have problems mediating information at many levels of functioning. There were enough with a history of difficult births and prematurity to justify asking permission to undertake research with the local hospital, which was refused.

Many had problems with sleeping patterns, such as finding it impossible to get off to sleep late at night, then could not be roused the next morning, dog tired and yawning all day in school. Others also had a poor sleeping pattern, which presented as dog tired in the evening then awake really early in the morning.

Procrastination was common and many parents reported that the children could not tolerate any change to their routine. They could also take a long time to orient to new situations but this was subtle, the child's internal struggle to extract meaning from the environment before they could settle and focus remaining unseen.

Ear, nose and throat (ENT) problems and high temperatures were also such a recurrent theme that efficacy of the central auditory processing system was clearly implicated. Some had experienced at least one convulsion. A few were obviously clumsy and some were noticeably odd in their mannerisms.

At that point I had also spent some years in a large London, UK project as part of a university-based research team looking at mother-baby interaction, its ultimate collapse brought about from an initial withdrawal of funding in 1979. A biblical plague of disasters descended on us all from that time which prevented the work from being completed and published.

My interest was in the processes of reciprocal interaction and synchrony. There was a strong literature in this area at the time, which had grown out of theories of how attachment develops in children. Biological models were not generally incorporated into the thinking, which focused on psychodynamic issues, but the idea of a *tabula rasa,* a child whose behaviour and development was entirely dictated by interpersonal environmental experiences, was no longer accepted.

Within the interpersonal sphere, the idea of the dynamic between the parent and the child, each bringing their own contribution to the social scenario, lay at the root of theories of reciprocity and was highly compelling. I began to map my observations in the research into reciprocity in early human relationships onto my observations within the community (see Chapter 5 on the threads of social engagement).

Hobson (1993) saw the fundamental problem within autism as a deficiency in the psychological co-orientation between people, the stuff of reciprocity. He felt that this process required mutual engagement and mental co-ordination between people.

Parents whose children could not engage with them or the rules of their lives through extreme hyperactivity became increasingly interested in a parent support group set up in the UK to try to help the numerous children with hyperactivity disorders, including those who did not meet the strict 'hyperkinetic' criteria and who could not gain any support as they were seen to be outside the criteria. This included the hyperactive autistic children for whom the professional focus was on the defining feature of autism – the failure to reciprocate, which was often seen as the cause of the hyperactive behaviour rather than another strand in the tapestry.

The focus for the hyperactive child group was on management strategies for difficult behaviours and the still recognised allergic reactions in many children to certain foodstuffs. Over time it became clear that certain foods and colourings and flavourings within foods could aggravate the hyperactivity and this led to demands to know what we were eating through labelling, an important issue. Eliminating colourings and flavourings from medicines, food and drink has made a difference to many children's lives.

As with many other methods seen as beneficial to individual children, many held onto the wild hope that maybe diet was the sole cause of the problem and that a special diet would be the cure. Many children were placed on strict elimination diets, more and more foodstuffs eliminated if the problems remained, in a desperate search for the key to open their child's world onto their own.

Despite many years throughout the 1980s of a strong focus on diet alone in the UK to manage these problems, it did not prove to be a cure. The resounding failure of dietary interventions alone to cure hyperactivity problems, at that time, led to the baby being thrown out with the bathwater. The idea of dietary intervention has been thoroughly dismissed by many in the world of ADHD and autism when 'cures' were not found and so all the important contributions of such interventions for specific children were dismissed. However, there is evidence in some children of compromised brain or gut systems linked to poor metabolism of certain enzymes in certain types of food – casein and gluten –

with a consequent glitch in biochemical and neuroregulatory systems (Whiteley *et al*, 1999).

Within ADHD the focus was on the malfunctioning of the neurotransmission system, and the intervention of choice has been medication which focuses directly on the faulty transmitters. In numerous research studies involving hyperactive children, the resounding evidence was that Methylphenidate (Ritalin) had the strongest effect in relation to reducing hyperactivity and improving focus, and the overwhelming evidence of improvement in precisely the targeted area – 'focus' – in large-scale research within the hyperactive groups led to a rejection of the value of dietary intervention.

Given the DSM criteria for ADHD, these research studies would not have included any children with a Kanner type pervasive developmental disorder, although Chapter 3 will discuss the hidden overlaps that would inevitably have occurred. It is quite possible that the tapestries of many children who seemed to benefit from reducing certain foodstuffs or eliminating certain preservatives from the diet would not have met criteria for inclusion in the research which dismissed its value.

Furthermore, the results of large-scale studies which reveal clear effects of medication compared with the 'no effect' of dietary intervention studies mean nothing to the parents of a child who reacts badly to a medication but whose various forms of hyperactive behaviour at home at the very least reduce when certain foods are not given. The fine detail in the huge research tapestries is made up of individual children, which this book seeks to emphasise.

I retained the opinion that we should set aside the idea that one was seeking a cure. Food elimination procedures might not cure, but if such interventions reduced the exacerbating effects of certain foods in certain children, we should obviously retain this important intervention as part of a tapestry of interventions for the unique child. In the last few years the work at Sunderland University, in north-east England, has led to the recognition of the value of a casein- and gluten-free diet for many children affected by autism and bowel problems.

Research grants were dramatically reduced during the 1980s in England, the value of academic work somewhat disregarded politically and professionals in all spheres being restricted in their work. This severely limited professional development and prevented new thinking from emerging. The Children Act 1989 also placed an emphasis on 'protection' of children rather than 'prevention' and, given greater demands on professionals to meet surface targets with decreased resources, a helpless, punitive system emerged with little trace of science and creativity, not to mention compassion and integrity.

By comparison, research was not curtailed in the USA. Researchers in the field of ADHD undertook a significant amount of work. Having set out the spectrum of difficulties they were able to explore the underlying components of ADHD, Barkley (1997, p.8) coming to consider that 'response inhibition and motor systems control were more reliably demonstrated and appeared to be specific to this disorder'. Other researchers, for instance Pennington and Ozonoff (1996), began to look at executive functions mediated by the neurotransmission system in the brain within the fields of both autism and ADHD.

As the consultant psychologist involved in setting up the first facility for adolescents with Asperger syndrome in the UK in 1993, I observed the presence of a variety of ADHD-type behaviours which could be described as executive dysfunctions, in most of the group who came for assessment and placement, each child obviously unique in their cluster of presenting features and having a diagnosis of Asperger syndrome. The spectrum extended from more obviously socially and language impaired and eccentric to more obviously overactive, but each shared reciprocity problems and executive problems, albeit each unique child's tapestry woven slightly differently. The extended spectrum of subtle social impairment, overactivity and conduct disorder were not referred or were not accepted in the facility. However, the *relevance of the overlap* within the tapestry at all levels of severity is the focus of this book. My interest was less on *the* core deficit, a sort of Holy Grail much sought after within university departments, and less on whether a child fitted this or that list, but more on the interweave of threads and clusters of threads which I saw in the real world, how the mechanisms worked and if this knowledge could improve support.

On 12 December 1994 and 24 January 1995, questions were asked about the recognition of ADHD in the British House of Commons to the Department of Health and the Department for Education. In reply the Department of Health said that ADHD was identified under the term of 'hyperkinesis', which meant that only the 1 per cent with a hyperkinetic disorder would be recognised, and stated that ADHD was covered by procedures outlined in the Code of Practice, which relates to educational special needs in the UK. However, by denying the existence of ADHD, an education authority could easily over-ride its responsibilities within the UK Code of Practice. In the USA, very specific laws (the Individuals with Disabilities Education Act (IDEA)) driven by Children and Adults with Attention Deficit Disorders (CHADD) were set down in relation to ADHD.

By the mid-1990s, there was an increasing recognition of ADHD in England but a reluctance to accept the concept, which prevails, as noted by Barkley (1997), and a real lack of understanding about what the term identifies in individuals. The prescribing of medication became the sole focus and the bone of contention, providing a justification for not recognising the problems experienced by a significant group of children. Media coverage was negative and became non-existent within a culture which had become more comfortable blaming, but not supporting, parents, in particular mothers, for children's problems.

Many local education authorities responsible for providing support for children chose to adopt the same thinking. As time passed and the overwhelming research over decades from other countries became public knowledge in the UK, LEAs could no longer publicly argue against its existence as a behavioural cluster – although many did to parents and still do. They came to regard it as a medical condition, which they will not recognise unless a medical practitioner has done so, thereby shifting the focus and the onus of responsibility.

This sort of disclaimer is not unique to ADHD. It has been used *ad nauseum* within LEAs over decades for many disorders, including autism and dyslexia, leaving parents totally perplexed either by a total lack of reference within reports to a condition they considered their child to experience or by being blatantly told 'We don't recognise it'.

At the time of writing most medical practitioners are new to these disorders and of those who recognise the problem, some will send questionnaires to schools to make a diagnosis. Unfortunately the many hidden agendas can compromise objectivity and questionnaires may not be completed as honestly as possible. This is most unfortunate given the robustness of the standardisation of questionnaires such as the Conners (Conners 1986) and Achenbach's Child Behaviour Checklist (CBCL) (Achenbach 1986; Achenbach and Edelbrock 1988) and the extraction of valuable information as part of a comprehensive assessment, which can help ongoing evaluation. In turn, if the uncertain medic relies mostly on subjective questionnaire information which is not truthful, diagnostic errors will inevitably occur. If the child also sits still in the clinic instead of swinging off the lights, sliding off the chair, standing in his mother's handbag or constantly fiddling with the blood pressure monitor, and his mother says he can sit and watch TV or focus on his particular interest, he will be seen as perfectly normal.

The sole reliance on the medical profession to diagnose ADHD puts pressure on them and can also marginalise the psychologists who are employed to determine a child's needs. At the time of writing many local health authorities in Britain are setting up specific clinics to address the assessment issues, but this is still limited.

The British Psychological Society (BPS) set up a working party in 1995 to look into the issues becoming increasingly recognised in relation to ADD. I contributed to the advice given to the working party and their deliberations led to a publication entitled *Attention Deficit Hyperactivity Disorder (ADHD): A Psychological Response to an Evolving Concept* (BPS 1996).

Over the same period of time the nature of Asperger syndrome has been increasingly recognised. Cynical systems inevitably cry 'latest fad' rather than recognise that whatever 'it' is, understanding rather than dismissing the problem will increase our success in intervention work. No professional can honestly say that we have made great progress in our methods of intervention over the past few decades. Figures for outcome in autism make appalling reading, with very low rates of independence in adulthood (Rutter and Bartak 1973).

ADHD in its hyperactive form is well recognised within youth offending (Farrington 1994). The presence of language dysfunctions is also very high. Rising crime rates, younger children in trouble, soaring prison numbers and record-beating mental health statistics are deeply depressing at the present time.

A growing body of parents now aware of the nature of various conditions are finding themselves confused: 'Can he have more than one?' asked one mother, having recognised that in her son's case he displayed features of a number of disorders. The high co-morbidity – co-existence – amongst these disorders is increasingly well recognised and the arguments about differential diagnosis have not answered parents' queries. In many cases it is not possible to ascertain whether one disorder came before another and whether that implies that the first caused the second. Nor is it possible to consider that the existence of one condition is enough to explain the rest. This can lead to proponents of just one approach rigidly following a single path for many years, possibly blaming the family if the interventions 'do not work'.

Since the BPS deliberations in 1996, LEAs in the UK are setting up their own responses to ADHD and through the National Autistic Society (NAS) and media coverage there is a greater awareness of Asperger syndrome, although many are confused by the 'autistic' label, expecting the child in question to 'look' the part of the eccentric individuals when for many the same problems are hidden behind a veneer of normality, just like ADD, the inattentive ADHD without hyperactivity. It has been argued that this group is especially vulnerable.

There is a slow recognition of the overlap of disorders in ADHD and autism on both sides of the Atlantic, although many still consider the disorders to be so discrete that opinion tends to settle on the problem relating to the 'wrong' diagnosis being given in the first place. Recognising interwoven processes should help us to intervene to alter the emerging image.

Furthermore, is it not likely that it is the interweave of each specialist's perspectives in various countries which most likely reflects the total gestalt, and have we not simply been through the infancy of our own professional development in these areas, in which we focus on separate perspectives, on fragments, and not the whole? Perhaps we now need to weave together the threads of our own social communication, just as infants do.

Tapestry kids

 # Miriam and Rachel

Reason for referral

Miriam and Rachel were referred for psychological assessment at the age of 10 years, given their history of hyperactive, destructive behaviour.

Family history

The twins' maternal grandmother was highly active as a child. As a teenager she had what her mother (the twins' great grandmother) described as a 'breakdown.' In my conversation with the great-grandmother she said that her adored daughter had started to talk 'gobbledy-gook' and was highly agitated. So severe was her condition that she has remained to this day on medications, had many inpatient stays and has been diagnosed as suffering from various psychoses.

The twins' mother was not protected from her mother's various psychoses, was abused by her mother and stepfather throughout her childhood, and placed herself in care to escape the abuse. She was an intelligent and sensitive child who swore she would raise her own children entirely differently and always protect them. She loves order and symmetry, and attends to detail, with excellent powers of memory. She likes to see the washing pinned out 'exactly' on the line, in order of size.

The twins' father was impulsive and irresponsible, leaving the mother to raise the twins on her own.

Developmental history

There was a blood incompatibility with the twins and their mother and they were born very prematurely at 26 and a half weeks gestation. Miriam was a very low birth weight and Rachel a low birth weight baby. They were not expected to survive. They suffered from the multiple medical problems now well recognized in the very premature infant population. These severe life-threatening problems included intraventricular brain haemorrhages; the twins needed blood transfusions, and operations on internal organs were necessary.

The twins were transferred to a specialist hospital in London and ultimately came out of the special care unit at 16 weeks. Not surprisingly, they were soon back in with a variety of problems including bronchial difficulties. Miriam developed an asthmatic condition, which persists. The next two years were spent in and out of hospital.

There were no units for ongoing specialist mother and baby support after the twins returned home and their mother was not made aware that the girls would have developmental problems and were more likely to go on to have associated behavioural problems.

Both twins sat up at 13 months and walked at 2 years of age. Miriam in particular, the smaller twin with the most medical problems, was clumsy and poorly co-ordinated, and had a hand tremor.

The girls did not engage in joint attending and did not pretend play. They developed their own private language, which could be heard when they were alone together. They were aloof and indifferent in the presence of others during the first two to three years. Eye contact was fleeting and they would look at others when others looked away. It was this passive staring behaviour which a local psychologist witnessed on an early visit when the twins were two and a half years old. She referred them for early placement in a special school.

Photographs of the very young twins show their expressionless look repeated numerous times. One photograph of the twins when they were three years old, at a party of same-age twins, shows them together, eating, a favourite pastime. There are no expressions, and no sign of the girls interacting with others or each other. The other children by comparison are engaged in animated interactions with each other.

The twins' mother felt her daughters seemed to have no understanding of reality and she was able to give numerous examples of unusual interpretations and actions. The girls would 'argue black is white'. Illogical arguments could emerge from 'nowhere' and result in escalating friction in the family making the children increasingly difficult to manage.

Other behaviours were not difficult to manage, but confusing to the family. At a school race Rachel was winning and her mother proudly stood near the finish line with a camera at the ready. She called out to her daughter to run but Rachel turned round and stopped to have her photo taken – as the winner passed her. On one occasion Miriam ate the goldfish and years later wanted to know if it was still there in her stomach.

Once in school the girls were given speech therapy but this was reported to be significantly delayed and disordered. Miriam was still having speech therapy at the time of the assessment.

There were intense fascinations for environmental stimuli such as spinning things and bright shiny things. The girls could hear noises, such as the sound of a plane approaching, long before others heard them. They were drawn to tiny lights such as the light on a stereo player. They hated change and insisted on sameness in daily activities. They would also pick up on detail which was often used to cause arguments, as the children became older and resentful of each other. On one occasion their mother had bought them two bicycles. She knew how they would explore joint toys to ensure one was not getting something different or better than the other. Despite a thorough check of the bikes to ensure absolute sameness, the girls managed to spot a tiny detail that was different, which led to a catastrophic reaction. Miriam and Rachel also had special items that they liked to hang on to all the time.

The twins engaged in highly repetitive forms of behaviour, which included rocking and repeating words and actions, including increasingly aggressive actions, over and over again. Their behaviour took on an ever more bizarre quality with the girls imitating each other and others and laughing for no obvious reason. They would smear faeces and draw all over the walls. On one occasion Miriam painted her sister.

Once the girls began to walk they became hyperactive. They would also spin themselves round and would do this on their knees. They were risk takers and at the age of eight years Miriam suffered a head injury requiring stitches to the top of her head.

They engaged in frequent catastrophic actions once walking and hyperactive. They soon started to attack each other and, as they grew, began to break windows and other things in highly impulsive outbursts, which would usually be about nothing in particular or a tiny detail of no relevance to most. The children would explode after school, a rather typical pressure-cooker effect of frustration and confusion, combined with behaviours formed into entrenched habits and triggered by the presence of each other. The mother had recognized that they needed to be educated separately as they would easily wind each other up. However, she could not raise them separately.

This mother was accused of causing her children's problems through MSBP-type abuse. The children were said to be perfectly normal.

Psychological assessments shown to me reported moderate to severe learning difficulties, and a similar pattern of difficulties for both twins with Miriam, as expected, presenting with the most severe problems.

Test results – Rachel
Wechsler Intelligence Scale for Children (3rd Edn UK) (WISC)
VERBAL SCALE

	Score
Information	4
Similarities	5
Arithmetic	1
Vocabulary	4
Comprehension	7
Digit Span	2

PERFORMANCE SCALE

	Score
Picture Completion	1
Coding	6
Picture Arrangement	5
Block Design	1
Object Assembly	4
Symbol Search	8

IQ SCORES

	Score	Percentile	95% Confidence Interval
Verbal IQ	66	1	61–74
Performance IQ	59	0.3	55–71

INDEX SCORES

	Score	Percentile	95% Confidence Interval
Verbal Comprehension Index	80	9	64–88
Perceptual Organisation	57	0.2	53–70
Freedom from Distractibility Index	52	0.1	49–67
Processing Speed Index	83	13	76–96

British Ability Scales (BAS)

Word Reading Age	7 yrs 10 mths
Spelling Age	8 yrs
Immediate Visual Recall Age	Below 5 yrs

Test results – Miriam
Wechsler Intelligence Scale for Children (3rd Edn UK) (WISC)
VERBAL SCALE

	Score
Information	5
Similarities	4
Arithmetic	4
Vocabulary	3
Comprehension	2
Digit Span	1

PERFORMANCE SCALE

	Score
Picture Completion	1
Coding	5
Picture Arrangement	1
Block Design	1
Symbol Search	8

IQ SCORES

	Score	Percentile	95% Confidence Interval
Verbal IQ	63	1	59–71
Performance IQ	50	< 0.1	46–63

INDEX SCORES

	Score	Percentile	95% Confidence Interval
Verbal Comprehension Index	64	1	59–73
Perceptual Organisation	50	< 0.1	47–63
Freedom from Distractibility Index	58	0.3	54–83
Processing Speed Index	81	10	74–94

British Ability Scales (BAS II)

Word Reading Age	6 yrs 11 mths
Spelling Age	7 yrs 3 mths
Immediate Visual Recall Age	Below 5 yrs

Discussion

The test scores indicate significant learning difficulties in these twins and agree with previous assessments.

Miriam's scores are lower than Rachel's as expected, given her very low birth weight and greater problems after her premature birth. The pattern of learning difficulty is similar in both twins, with verbal skills better than performance skills. Both girls show the same peak in terms of processing speed and this is an indication of better skills in visual tasks with no language component.

Both girls are very pretty and look entirely normal. However, in a short space of time it became clear that they were not normal in their social use and understanding of language, but could give a very good impression to a non-specialist.

They have significant pragmatic problems, and their history, in terms of development of their language and the nature of some of their communications, would lead one to expect such difficulties. Generally, Miriam appeared to be more agitated and to present with more word finding problems in all of the tests requiring any verbal output. She needed constant repetition in most instructions and these had to be very clear and concise.

Even then she had considerable problems repeating and modelling behaviours which I modelled for her. For instance, in the Coding subtest, although ultimately she was able to achieve a reasonable score in this, she needed a significant amount of priming and conditioning before she could understand the activity. Her perceptual difficulties were very obvious in this test. Despite my instructions to Miriam, and the filling in of a number of items to start her off, she still proceeded to do the wrong thing.

With Block Design, Miriam said 'It's too hard' and wanted to give up fairly early on, but then decided that she liked the blocks and went ahead to attempt to complete them, but made tremendous errors.

Miriam made some bizarre connections in the jigsaw-type Object Assembly test. In a puzzle of a girl, she had no understanding of how to put the body pieces together and put the girl's hand next to her neck. When she stood back from it she was able to understand what she was supposed to do, but her own internal construct was lacking.

Miriam was frequently literal and easily confused by language, and was also confusing in her responses. She told me during the assessment that she was going to Spain on a holiday. I asked if she was flying, at which Miriam laughed for a long time.

In the Picture Arrangement test Miriam missed the point of every single item. In this subtest a series of pictures are set out on cards which a child must rearrange to make sense of what is happening. Most are social stories.

Given her significant problems with understanding sequence, cause and effect and the 'cues and clues' within social contexts, I was not surprised that Miriam had problems with this task. She simply described what she saw in each picture without making any connections and missed the crucial point every time.

Despite Miriam's exceptional problems she achieved a better score than her sister for Arithmetic. Her performance was very rote and she failed rapidly once reasoning and understanding of the language in the set problem was required. However, her skill in such tasks as she has managed to learn will give an impression of better ability to the non-specialist.

Miriam's working memory was very poor and she could not repeat a series of two digits backwards, expected of a child from the age of three years. This fundamental inability to hold certain types of information in memory and then manipulate it was evident throughout the assessment. It will considerably affect the way she consolidates anything she has learned and will interfere with learning within a social context, including basic interactions.

Rachel's profile was very similar to Miriam's, although she clearly has the edge over her sister and will present and function as verbally more able.

She was much more able to complete the Picture Arrangement task, but the same pragmatic problems arose again. Even when Rachel was able to put cards in a correct sequence, she could not interpret them correctly. Her stories did not make sense and she tended to miss the main point. Rachel also demonstrated considerable perceptual motor problems.

In discussion with the twins' mother she described many odd forms of communication. Some of what she described was immediate and delayed echolalia, odd logic and features expected within semantic pragmatic disorder such as not appreciating the position of the listener, not giving the listener enough information and then becoming furious if they could not make themselves understood. She also reported blurting out swear words on returning from school without understanding what they were actually doing. Over time, as they understood that this was wrong, it seemed to give them some kind of perverse pleasure to blurt out these words.

The twins were highly impulsive and hyperactive in the clinic setting. They demonstrated attentional problems throughout and these were interwoven with language and perceptual motor difficulties.

Assessments on the Achenbach CBCL and the Conners' Continuous performance test further confirmed the existence of clear attentional deficits threaded through the developmental tapestry of these children.

Conclusions and recommendations

Miriam and Rachel are twins who were born very prematurely with very low and low birth weight respectively. They present with a tapestry of neurodevelopmental impairments and features which fit with childhood autism. Sub-clusters of features fit criteria for ADHD and also semantic pragmatic disorder and developmental co-ordination disorder. It could be argued that they also fit oppositional defiance disorder but in my opinion this is better viewed within the context of autism and the language disorder. The diagnosis of Asperger syndrome using the Gillberg scales would not be out of place. Their hyperactive behaviours have reduced over the years and this is entirely as expected especially for girls. The underlying attentional and impulsive behaviours remain.

In my opinion the twins need to be educated within a school which specialises in autistic spectrum disorders or one which would be willing to train staff to help the twins fit into a social world. The school will need to have occupational therapists and speech and language therapists available to work intensively and extensively with the twins, and the interventions of therapists, teaching staff and home need to interweave. There are an increasing number of communication programmes which can be used with children demonstrating autistic spectrum/ semantic pragmatic language disorders.

The speech and language therapist needs to organise ongoing activities for the girls and these will need to include activities focusing on attentional, metalinguistic and paralinguistic skills.

The paediatrician has recommended a trial of Methylphenidate for the twins to address their impulsivity and this would need to be monitored and evaluated alongside their comprehensive educational programme.

The occupational therapist needs to help the twins with their perceptual motor skills including vestibular and proprioceptive skills. They need to be helped with their understanding of themselves and others in space.

The twins' mother urgently needs support within the home for these children. She will need outreach support from the specialist staff working with children with autistic spectrum disorders and associated language disorders, attentional and motor impairments.

Daily monitoring and regular evaluation should see these children making progress in the next few months, given appropriate support. However, it may be necessary for them to attend a residential school if they are unable to learn or change their impulsive and aggressive behaviours despite the above input.

Chapter Three

Causes, triggers and the interweave

A chip off the old block

(An Asperger father referring to his son)

All human physical traits and behaviours start through the interwoven process of genetic inheritance; the nature of human genetic transmission and the nature of the tapestry of the human brain are the same across the globe. History and common sense tell us of the perpetuating cycles of certain personalities which turn in extended families over generations, the inheritance from one to another not always directly a pawn's move, from parent to child, but often a knight's move from a one-step-removed family member.

In some cases there are remarkable cases of relatives who never met or even knew about each other seeking out exactly the same kind of specialised work experience or showing the same talents. Identical twins separated at birth also provide us with evidence of remarkable similarities, despite entirely different forms of socialisation. Such clearly inherited traits are represented by the canvas of the tapestry.

We are usually proud to talk of relatives successful in unusual areas in whose footsteps we follow. It is also commonplace to refer to physical features which dominate through families or which appear from time to time, such as unusual eye or hair colour, facial features and expressions, mannerisms and so on. As part of weaving family tapestries I ask parents if their child reminds them of anyone in the family or if there are stories of relatives who appeared to behave in a similar manner; this can open up a rich and fascinating seam. Any of us will find repeating family types in our history – and maybe a few ADHD or Asperger relatives.

The idea of genetic inheritance has taken a back seat in recent decades, given fears of eugenics. Ironically, in an effort to prevent the singling out of people because of their genetic inheritance, models have become entrenched in which problems within the child have been solely blamed on the environment (the nurture vs nature debate in simplistic terms) and 'the environment' has been solely regarded as our upbringing. This is erroneous.

No account has been taken of the myriad of repetitive processes emanating from basic genetics which could be altered by one tiny alteration in a myriad of environmental factors that are nothing to do with upbringing. The upbringing or teaching also interweave but come later.

Fortunately, new research and technology are now able increasingly to open a skylight into how and when basic processing stitches alter direction or colour, to change the whole tapestry. These changes can be detected in utero and as our knowledge base increases, we will be better equipped to understand what has interfered with the developmental process. In some cases an apparently normal child will be born very early and this very prematurity will lead on to multiple medical problems which can grossly affect development.

It is the *interweave* of processes propelled by just a few genes which make up human tapestries. This interweave starts rolling after conception.

There is increasingly powerful evidence that the observable clustering of behaviours within the tapestry disorders relates to a genetic potential for developing them, the warp and change in the DNA thread sometimes occurring through damage caused by medical conditions, infections or metabolic disorders. Examples include viral infections such as rubella, biochemical abnormalities such as phenylketonuria (PKU) and congenital syndromes such as Noonan syndrome which can be recognised by physical abnormalities from birth.

The inheritance of clusters of warped gene function on particular chromosomes and linked to the production of various neurotransmitters (and there are many) such as dopamine is also an interwoven process and the metaphor of the tapestry is useful at this level of explanation.

Increasingly, studies within autism research, ADHD and other disorders such as Tourette syndrome are finding faulty neurotransmission system threads suggesting faults in the cells of the embryo brain which hold the basic plan for the brain tapestry. Clusters of these overlapping disorders occur within families. It is common to find evidence of family members' various presentations of ADHD, autism, speech and language problems and dyslexia. Males are more likely than females to develop problems. Variation in presentation and severity will depend on the other threads in the unique person tapestry.

Trevarthen (1998) comments that the timing of such faults within the unborn infant's brain is critical, suggesting that the earlier they occur, the more damaging they are.

As we push out the boundaries of understanding of how best to intervene with the development of autistic children, Bachevalier (1990) has proposed that there are two groups of autism, Type 1 and Type 2. He suggests that Type 1 relates to the most debilitating form which may involve a genetic warping at such a stage in embryonic development that there is little room for significant change of the basic canvas, while the Type 2 genetic warp will have occurred at a stage when the main problems arise in the neurotransmission system or in the neurochemical threads, which can then be more easily rewoven, both medically and behaviourally, to improve fundamentally instinctive motivation to attend to appropriate stimuli in the environment.

There has been a rapid rise in our knowledge about the workings of the brain that maybe will lead to recognition that even very early damage could be detected and rectified – or, better still, prevented.

The important issue is how we weave new awareness and knowledge with action plans for prevention, detection and intervention – as early as possible. The increasing recognition of autoimmune disorders, the high prevalence of survival of the very premature infant, obstetric complications as well as immature gastrointestinal systems which link with allergic reactions to nonhuman environmental assaults, are well recognised now amongst specialist clinical groups.

The cellular immune system links with the process of neurotransmission and recent research points to 'the possible involvement of cell-mediated immunity in the aetiology of autism' (Messahel *et al.* 1998). The involvement of neurotransmitters such as serotonin and dopamine in autism and ADHD has been observed for some years and more recently there is research to confirm opioid peptides as 'chemical messengers of the neuroimmune axis' (Scifo *et al.* 1996). The link between such peptides and autism is the subject of fascinating cutting edge research.

Comings (1996) refers to the polygenetic mode of the inheritance of disorders such as autism, ADHD, Tourette syndrome, language problems such as stuttering, sleep apnoea, anxieties, phobias and obesity. He also proposes that oppositional defiance disorder (ODD) and conduct disorder (CD) are involved in the same inherited tapestries. Each person within a family could present with a different expression and be additionally affected by environmental triggers over time. He reports that the inheritance of such disorder occurs in a polygenetic manner, as part of a spectrum of disorders, and the gene variants are additive in effect causing problems with the balance of dopamine, serotonin and other neurotransmitters within the brain (Comings 1996).

Furthermore, Comings finds that particular neurotransmitters, serotonin and dopamine, are involved in 'the nerves and muscles of the intestine as for the nerves of the brain' (Comings 1996, p.171). Both of these chemical messengers, their actions dictated by our genes, are implicated in our tapestry disorders on the basis of significant amounts of research in both autism and ADHD spectrum disorders. Comings refers to gastrointestinal problems such as irritable bowel syndrome and reports on genetic links with these disorders and our tapestry of ADHD, autism and tics.

We are only just beginning to understand the complex dynamic neuronal functioning which interweaves with gene potential in contact with the nonhuman, as well as the human, environmental effects. This interweave incorporates a multiplicity of chemical and electrical responses to sensations as it sends and receives information at cellular level. Our future understanding of the aetiology of inborn disorders will come from this rapidly advancing brain research. Timing and nature of the most efficacious treatments will follow to replace the current hit and miss methodologies.

Tangles or missing parts of this genetic tapestry can cause havoc to the representations of the tapestry and the point at which this occurs is thought to be crucial. It is felt that certain interwoven parts of the brain relate to activity which is date stamped. Not until the individual reaches a certain stage in their maturation will these connections activate. There is also the possibility that certain propensities for later difficulties require a trigger in the environment as the child develops.

In turn these difficulties can lead to significant illness and developmental problems presenting as ADHD and autistic spectrum disorders and the co-morbid conditions such as sleep disorders.

Many a slip 'twixt cup and lip

The period between conception and birth should be an easy time for a baby, with few demands, regular sustenance, warmth, comfort, and a calm environment. Unfortunately, this is not always the case. Many factors can contribute to early warping of the neurodevelopmental system. If damage to a father's sperm has occurred, for instance, as in rare cases of interference by chemical agents, this will obviously damage the DNA of the infant. A mother's illness can interfere with a child's development and various problems can emanate from the effect of certain medications on the unborn infant. There may be many difficulties during the pregnancy including bleeding, threatened miscarriage or miscarriage of a twin. Within autism and ADHD research, there is a higher rate of such known difficulties. Although this may not indicate cause, such difficulties may at least serve to tangle an existing tangled genetic tapestry. In some cases they will indicate cause.

Inherited and acquired pre-birth risk factors can be compounded by complications including prematurity and anoxia at birth. The more premature the infant the more likely that the child will have difficulties related to the functions of the frontal lobes, which will not have developed in utero. The 'tapestry twins', at the end of Chapter 2, Rachel and Miriam, were not quite 27 weeks when they were born. They went on to have brain haemorrhages and other serious medical complications, which affected their later development and led to obvious autism and ADHD. Recent research has shown clear links between the very premature infant and later attentional and social awareness problems (Hepper *et al.* 1995).

We need to develop a much greater understanding of the needs of extremely premature infants whose brains are not fully formed at birth, with the frontal lobes, which mediate executive functions, still to be laid down. For the premature infants who may also suffer from organic brain damage around the time of their births or subsequently while in special care, problems related to frontal lobe function will be compounded. For instance, Pennington and Bennetto (1993) reported on the executive function problems in premature infants who suffered from intraventricular lesions like our tapestry twin girls.

There is increasing recognition of Asperger syndrome presentations amongst children with hydrocephalic conditions. Hydrocephalus results from an abnormal accumulation of cerebrospinal fluid in the ventricles in the brain. This condition is not hereditary but relates to abnormalities before birth (congenital) or to trauma to the brain during or after the birth.

Technology is advancing to a stage where we can detect neurological abnormalities within the unborn infant (Hepper 1995). During the 1990s and at the present time many parents have been blamed for disorders if they cannot be explained, given the lack of knowledge and a refusal to accept that some things are inherited and some things are caused by medical conditions.

Warped imagination and the tainted perceptions of suggestible professionals, combined with limited understanding, have led to suspicion which can lead to false accusation, as in Munchausen syndrome by proxy (MSBP), in which mothers are said to have made their children ill for attention. In a number of cases children have had real medical disorders, albeit rare and complex in some cases, but which include outcomes of presentations of autism and ADHD. These are actually ignored given the powerful MSBP agenda as the 'cause', and the influence of rigid classification systems of the notion of differential diagnosis – something else caused the problem and the notion that some conditions take precedence over others. Unfortunately, MSBP has never been validated in such a way and it is the powerful suggestibility of the phenomenon which leads some professionals and courts to believe that once MSBP has been suggested, even just a whisper, nothing else explains it.

The hypothesis of MSBP has no logic and depends on witch-hunt thinking to operate. If people 'admit' they made up or caused a problem, then they are guilty. If they do not admit it, then they are in denial. It is most unfortunate that features of very serious, very real and very rare mental conditions have been so recklessly applied ad nauseum to the actions and statements of honest and caring parents. It is also intriguing that the phenomenal rise in these accusations has coincided with the phenomenal rise in the incidence of autism and ADHD since the late 1980s.

While the UK continues to deny there has been any increase in numbers, Japan has recognised them and linked the rise with vaccine. It has changed its vaccine programme accordingly. California has recently charted the rise in presentations of Kanner type autism. The figures do not include Asperger syndrome or wider tapestry presentations. The California Department of Developmental Services found a 273 per cent increase in presentations from 1987 to 1998. In February 2001 it was reported that:

> It took over 25 years, from the inception of the establishment of California's developmental services system in 1969 to 1994 to have 5,100 persons with autism in the system. Remarkably, between 1994 to 1999 we DOUBLED the number of cases by adding an additional 5,100 new children in just five years! Most disturbing of all is the fact that in 1999, 2000 and the first half of 2001 we will add at least another 5,100 cases this time in just 2½ years!
> (FEAT DAILY NEWSLETTER February 2001)

California also estimated that taxpayers would spend $2 million for each child for a lifetime of care.

Purely environmental models – usually inferred as meaning nurture – have not generated robust explanations of behaviours applicable to the considerable population of children with quite specific developmental disorders and methods of interventions based solely on such models soon hit brick walls when the methods do not work for certain individuals.

Part of the problem with current explanations is that we know that DNA which holds the information about a person can be compromised by extreme environmental interference which includes certain medications for certain people. Knowing this general information can then lead some workers to feel justified in considering that nothing is inherited or damaged through non-human environmental interference. Any child disability, if accompanied by the presence of a mother who apparently fits a profile, is disregarded. The lack of logic and wisdom is startling. The general awareness is applied to specific cases often with little evidence. Therefore all inexplicable problems – within their frame of reference – *must* be caused by the parent. Mother, in particular, is blamed for everything. Thankfully, brain research and new technology are providing the positive proof of inborn difficulties of brain processing and problems from non-human environmental effects. Training of staff at the coalface with our vulnerable children and families needs to focus on these areas of knowledge. Brave researchers and clinicians are also asking questions about vaccines and/or other pathogens in the environment responsible for the dramatic rise in autism. From my own observations since the late 1980s I have considered that it appeared to be medically vulnerable children and those with allergies such as asthma and eczema and other medical problems who seemed more inclined to react to vaccine. It is some years now since I shared this observation with Dr Wakefield, who mentioned finding the same.

When I naively wrote to Great Ormond Street Hospital for Sick Children in London in the late 1980s about my observations of a cluster of autistic children who lost skills around 18 months, with such vulnerabilities, there was no response.

Out of synch

Researchers working on the faulty brainwaves leading to dyslexia have found that auditory and visual problems, which can later be revealed within autism, ADHD and dyslexia, originate in cells within specific mediational circuitry of the brain. There appears to be a problem with the timing of both fast auditory responses and visual perception of shape, form and movement through the auditory and visual pathways within the thalamic region of the mid-brain.

In work on the visual system, within the lateral geniculate nucleus, the magnocellular structures, involving larger cells and tracking processes faster, and the parvo-cellular system which involves smaller cells and slower processes, did not work in synchrony with each other. This mistiming appears to be linked to perceptual distortions even though the child may have perfectly normal vision. Irlen (1984) has pioneered the use of colour through overlays and lenses and for some as yet unexplained reason, the colour and the wavelengths within them can rectify this problem as long as the lenses or overlays are used.

In the 1970s Paula Tallal, working at the Rutgers Center for Molecular and Behavioral Neurosciences in Newark, New Jersey, USA, found that rapid changing acoustic components of speech, as in rapid consonant sounds, caused problems for people with subtle language problems. If certain 'fast' sounds are missed, then whole meanings can be misinterpreted through partial or distorted auditory representations. Rosen and Galaburda (1994) found the auditory equivalent to the out-of-synch visual system, as an asymmetry in the medial geniculate nucleus.

An eight-year longitudinal study in which the brain activity of 36-hour-old infants was tested, the children followed up over eight years, has found differences in the brainwave patterns of the newborns which were linked with later dyslexia (Molfese 1999). Hearing has been considered and this could be linked with the rhythmic faults, the mistiming which interferes with attention and processing of sound.

In an interesting study of 6- to 12-year-old children inpatients, the children were given music therapy to establish if it made a difference to the neurotransmission system within the brains which in turn affected the immune system and in turn, recovery. They established that the children who had received music therapy produced a chemical, IgA, which protects mucosal membranes and plays a strong role in defence against upper respiratory tract infections. It was concluded that music therapy could help boost the immune system (Lane 1992). Other studies with adults have found an increase in melatonin, the 'sleep' hormone, when exposed to the rhythm of music therapy 30 minutes a day for 5 days a week. Rhythmic auditory timekeepers such as metronomes were also found helpful to improve gait in stroke victims learning to walk again. From the recognition of these auditory difficulties, in particular through the experiences of children who either fail to hear certain sounds or are hypersensitive to sound, often putting their hands over their ears, as many autistic and ADHD children do, auditory integration training was developed.

The difficulties discussed here are related to glitches in auditory and visual perceptual processing in the brain. The immune system may be implicated and the fundamental glitch seems to be at the biochemical level. Hearing and vision can be perfectly normal alongside these out-of-synch processing problems. Restoring the balance is clearly essential.

Head trauma

I have assessed many children with the interweave of social reciprocity problems, executive problems, ADHD at different levels of severity and in some cases with either a traumatic delivery affecting the head or treated head injury in the history. Head injuries through falls or car accidents can result in similar problems. The incidence of such events with hyperactive or clumsy risk taking children is very high and can lead to ADHD type problems of an executive nature, if nothing else. A number of the tapestry kids have had head injuries and I always ask for information on such injuries in the pre-assessment question-naire to parents.

These then exist as hidden disabilities. Even amongst those described as suffering from a *severe* head injury, 90 per cent suffer no obvious physical dis-ability. In the UK alone 170,000 people are living with the effects of a head injury (Headway June 1999). Comments made by families coping alone include 'Now that he looks better they think everything is back to normal' and 'It's a Jekyll and Hyde situation, one face for us and another for the rest of the world' (Headway June 1999).

Some parents have found that their children have responded well to cranial osteopathy, especially if they experienced a difficult birth.

I have found that the incidence of perceptual sensitivity amongst this par-ticular group is very high. Colour can remove or improve these distortions, which can be associated with headaches and migraines. For many, the problem mainly affects reading and an appropriate coloured overlay can solve the problem. For others, including many with severe ADHD or autism or those with a head or brain injury, the distortions can affect their total perception of the world. One male student thought he had been hallucinating for most of his life. When he put on coloured glasses the 'hallucinations' went away.

Evidence of executive dysfunction within the head- and brain-injured group is well recognised, with head injury groups describing ADHD-type clusters of behaviour problems such as impulsivity, disinhibition, distractibility, volatility, poor working memory and poor organisational skills. In the numerous people with closed head injuries who leave hospital after a quick X-ray such problems are rarely recognised. Even the families of children with a fractured skull are not likely to be directed to specialist groups who can help them cope with their child and their child cope with this disability.

In those risk-taking ADHD children who find themselves with closed head injuries because of their actions, the problems compound. I have found this in many people and there is confirmation through research (Gerring 1998). The researchers tested 99 children who had experienced moderate to severe closed head injuries and who were followed up for a year. Through interviews and rating scales to construct pre- and post-morbid diagnoses – before and after the accidents – they found that the number of pre-accident ADHD children in the group was four times higher than in the control group.

It is also becoming clear that we need greater understanding of the needs of extremely premature infants whose brains are not fully formed at birth, the frontal cortex which mediates executive dysfunctions still to be laid down. For the infants who also suffer from organic brain damage around the time of their births, problems of this nature are also documented and likely to be compounded. Pennington and Bennetto (1993) reported on the executive function problems in premature infants who suffered from intraventricular lesions like the tapestry twin girls.

Theories of autism

The interweave of behaviour and of hypothesised underlying processes within both ADHD and autism is becoming increasingly clear. The fundamental communication problems ranging from subtle to extreme in this combined group are invariably not understood, especially if children appear normal and alienate others over time by their angry responses to their misconstructions.

Confusion about causality exists within each of these groups, for various reasons, but this can arise when researchers and practitioners work to different levels of explanation. This matters because the tests relating to these different explanations can be used in diagnosis and a child could suffer from a rigid expectation that he or she should or should not meet a particular criterion or pass or fail a particular test to meet diagnostic criteria. For instance, within autism, there are differences of opinion as to which level the glitch occurs at.

At the cognitive level of explanation researchers refer to Central Coherence Theory in which a child fails to see the whole gestalt, just the detail (Frith and Happé 1994), and the Theory of Mind (Baron-Cohen 1990, 1995) in which it has been proposed that children with autism cannot infer what others think, as they fail to recognise that other people have minds of their own.

Others consider it to be more appropriate to consider the underlying executive processing problems at the level of planning, organising and remembering, shifting from one context/perspective to another and putting plans into action in the various contexts (Pennington and Ozonoff 1994).

Concerns about the validity of such theories centre on the separation of mind from body, and the failure to take bodily expressions of emotion into account which relay information about our psychological state (Aitken and Trevarthen 1997; Reddy *et al.* 1997).

Bailey (1996) refers to the need for an 'integration of perspectives' within autism. He refers to autism as a syndrome which clusters together and for years we have focused a searchlight on different aspects of the disorder, referring to Theory of Mind, Central Coherence Theory, executive dysfunctions and so on. Problems have arisen with each theory given the nature of the original plan – to find a single testable feature for autism, which is shared by no other disorder. Bailey (1996) proposed that the searchlight beam should be broadened:

> The challenge now is to provide a better integration across the different levels of research in order to gain an understanding of the causal mechanisms that lead to autism and the abnormal processes that underlie the clinical features. The objective is no longer completely out of reach but success will depend on conceptual, as well as technological advances and on the bringing together of different areas of expertise in order to provide a concerted attack on the problem. (Bailey 1996, p.117)

The interweave

New ways of thinking about developmental disorders are dynamic. While we expect no miracles, and know that some 'golden children' may always 'straggle the rocks of life', our understanding is allowing us to seek balance in out-of-synch systems which we thought were fixed forever.

Sewn into the dynamic tapestry, the *interweave* allows the unique person-picture to emerge, as dynamic neuronal threads weave with the fixed genetic canvas and repetitive processes weave the environment onto it from the moment of conception. Our own emerging awareness will lead to dynamic interventions which breathe normal life, structure and colour into the developing story. As disturbing as it is, if there is a growing population of children with autism whose systems have been compromised by iatrogenic processes, we have a profound moral duty to investigate and report honestly.

If we discover that concerns of mine and others are correct, obviously the 'cause' must be stopped immediately. Furthermore, for those who have been affected, given the greater opportunity for change in the early years of life, the more urgent the need to understand how we can intervene to reweave those unique child tapestries.

Tapestry kid

Lorelei

Reason for referral

Lorelei (aged 6) was referred for an independent psychological assessment to ascertain the nature of difficulties experienced since infancy.

Family history

An elder sister is dyslexic.

Developmental history

Lorelei was born four weeks early in distress. She was delivered by ventouse extraction which left a large bruise on her head. After five days in the special care unit given breathing difficulties. she was allowed home. Feeding and digestion were normal. A few days after coming home from the special care baby unit, Lorelei began to suffer from severe baby eczema, which required hospital attention and 10 months' cortisone treatment.

At 8 weeks Lorrie reacted very badly to her first immunisation. Screaming fits ensued and became regular. The family has struggled to cope with these and to find remedies to help their daughter over the years since that time. Lorrie developed a highly anxious demeanour after this time and the screaming fits occurred in situations of change, amongst crowds at the shops, for instance, to the extent that her mother stopped taking her. She would scream when visitors arrived and would be inconsolable. Lorelei became tactile defensive and would quieten only when left alone in her cot.

In the 'first year' section of my developmental questionnaire, Lorrie's mother wrote: 'The worries over health changed over the first year to worries about her behaviour. She disliked being with other babies/children. She hated shopping and would scream constantly. She disliked being comforted.'

She wrote: 'At the start, Lorrie's health problems of eczema and initially being in the baby unit were my main worries. As these abated it became apparent that the "screaming fits" which appeared after the first inoculations were also problems. When they occurred it was not possible to find a way to calm her or to know what had caused it to start and I felt helpless and upset at not being able to comfort her and stop the distress she was feeling.' All reasoning goes during the screaming fits and Lorrie is pale and exhausted, 'like a rag doll' after them.

So severe were the reactions to pertussis vaccinations that it is now on Lorrie's medical notes that she must not have them. Her parents took their little daughter to the Dolphin clinic from the age of 10 months and after six months of using a holding technique she said 'Mummy I love you'.

At the age of 4 it was established that Lorelei had developed Kawasaki Disease, a health problem which is linked to a failure of the immune system. She has had two bouts of this, which is unusual, and is under the care of a major London teaching hospital. Heart problems were found following these episodes.

Lorelei did not chuckle or laugh as a baby but enjoyed rough and tumble as time passed. She began to use single words at 10 months and went on to join words at the appropriate time. Teachers at school have noted poor eye contacting skills, but the piano teacher has realised that Lorrie is nevertheless 'taking it all in'.

There is little empathy and when Mummy was ill Lorrie showed no real understanding or instinctive concern, instead just asking who would look after her (Lorrie).

Just beginning to understand about jokes, Lorrie has learned one about a dog and a telephone. To interact she has proved skilled over time at 'doing funny things' like odd walks. Parents said she can be 'like a clown'.

Lorelei walked at 14 months and has fine motor problems, proprioceptive difficulties and she still cannot ride a bicycle without stabilisers. She has a rather odd gait and 'people have commented' about this.

Lorelei has always had particular fascinations for animals. She 'has always hated dolls'. At the age of 3 years her parents found all her dolls hidden under the bed. She has now given them all away.

She did not engage in normal pretend play but has engaged in repetitive role play of pretending to be an animal. Lorrie will use certain themes from the TV, mainly to do with animals although Bob the Builder has now been incorporated into the games. She will 'add more and more characters'.

The noise of groups of children made Lorrie afraid. On one occasion when parents took the children to see *Postman Pat* at the theatre, she became hysterical when the 'lights went down and children started calling out'. Her mother said it was as though she could not cope with the 'shock of something new'. There was an intense dislike of being with other babies or children and Lorrie avoided children at nursery. At the age of two and a half she 'threw herself from the top' of a slide when a baby began to crawl up behind her.

She appeared 'awkward' as she remained alone, uncertain what to do in groups of children. Parents said 'It's like the spontaneity is missing'. They would say 'Play, Lorrie' and she would answer 'What shall I play?' A child has apparently said of her, ' Oh Lorelei doesn't like people'.

Her parents feel that this is a major concern for them. As Lorelei has always 'shied away' from children they feel she has missed out on normal play and social-ising.

Over time Lorrie has developed a desire to play with others sometimes, and this is often achieved through the skill of getting others to join in with the games she likes based on the theme of animals.

She is now felt able to play normally one-to-one but struggles and has difficul-ties mixing with peers in a larger group situation.

The 'screaming fits' which began after the first immunisation have been described above. These 'fits' shifted to occur amongst people and when faced with change and with environmental confusions or sounds. Sometimes these reactions were so bad that little Lorrie would 'froth at the mouth'. In a panic state Lorelei will become hysterical and 'cannot be calmed by reason'. If she is outside of the home she is able to control these reactions but instead she often 'freezes and withdraws' into what has been described as intense shyness.

Parents have had to learn how to help their vulnerable daughter cope with change. They give her advance warning, try to prepare and gently coax her before any changes occur. 'Even then', they said, 'she can react out of proportion to any sudden change'. From infancy there were intense fascinations for certain noises such as the washing machine spinning and toilets flushing and from discussion it would appear that baby Lorrie was *afraid* of these noises. Over time the focus has continued but the concern is now formalised through language with Lorrie fearful that there may be flooding or an overflow problem.

Intense interests in certain themes have been evident from early in life with an obsessive interest in animals. Lorelei will want to play at being a particular animal each day in school and this play is rigid and repetitive. A nose twitch has been noted which parents feel is Lorrie unconsciously imitating a mouse. Parents cannot take their child 'out for a treat' as she overreacts to crowds, noise and change. She was upset when taken to Chessington Zoo, in theatres and at the school play.

Professional involvement

Nursery school teachers reported that Lorrie was 'the shyest child they had ever seen'. Teachers have reported poor eye contacting and one teacher queried Asperger syndrome. Lorrie would turn her chair away from other children and instead choose to face the wall when she first started school. She would stand next to the wall outside at playtimes. When her mother asked her why she did this she said 'Well, the wall needs a friend too sometimes'. During the school play Lorelei looked 'very wooden' and tense and was lethargic afterwards.

The health visitor expressed concern and referred Lorrie to the Communication Clinic where she attended at the age of 3 years 3 months. A report was completed by a consultant in community child health and a speech and language therapist.

It was noted that the family had been working on ideas from a book on autism called *Hope for a Cure* and had found a transformation in Lorrie since they began to use these methods. On the Reynell, Lorelei achieved above average scores for receptive language and could use a wide range of grammatically correct utterances. She 'has a good vocabulary for her age' although 'limited' expressive language was heard.

It was written: 'Lorelei is reported to use language to express a full range of communicative intent' with the family, from the history taken from parents at that time, but she had problems with peers and unfamiliar environments. It was reported that she presented as shy with unfamiliar adults and 'was very wary of being watched'.

It was concluded that Lorelei had no developmental problems but was 'a very shy child who has some obsessional features to her personality'. It was felt that the methods used by parents had been 'helpful to develop Lorelei's personality'.

Test results
British ability scales (BAS II)

Average T Score	50
Average Range	43–56
Average Percentile Score	50

CORE SCALES

	T Score	Percentile	Age equivalent
Recall of Designs	54	66th	7 yrs 7 mths
Word Definitions			
Pattern Construction	70	98th	10 yrs 3 mths
Matrices	56	73rd	8 yrs 3 mths
Verbal Similarities	59	82nd	7 yrs 10 mths
Quantitative Reasoning	72	99th	10 yrs 3 mths
	48	42nd	6 yrs 1 mth

EARLY YEARS

	T Score	Percentile	Age equivalent
Picture Similarities	66	95th	8 +

Diagnostic Scales (Memory)
Auditory

	T Score	Percentile	Age equivalent
Recall of Digits Forward	63	90th	11 yrs 9 mths
Recall of Digits Backward	56	73rd	7 yrs 4 mths

VISUAL

	T Score	Percentile	Age equivalent
Recall of Objects Immediate Verbal	60	84th	8 yrs 4 mths
Recall of Objects Immediate Spatial	52	58th	
Recall of Objects Delayed Verbal	74	99th	
Recall of Digits Delayed Spatial	51	54th	

Lorrie has an excellent auditory rote memory, and this quite likely supports her in the recall of verbal labels more than her spatial recall when visual stimuli is presented. Working auditory recall is discrepant from immediate rote recall, and falls at the average level.

Achievement Scales

	Score	Percentile	Age Equivalent
Number Skills	119	90th	7 yrs 10 mths
Spelling	102	55th	6 yrs 7 mths
Word Reading	103	58th	6 yrs 7 mths

There are significant (0.05) discrepancies between achieved and predicted scores in Reading and Spelling, reflecting a dyslexic profile.

CLUSTERS

	Standard Score	Percentile	Confidence Interval
Verbal	133	99th	124–140
Non verbal	106	66th	97–114
Spatial	108	70th	97–118
GCA	119	90th	112–125

Average Standard Score = 100
Average Band = 90–110

COMPARISONS WITH GCA

	Difference	Significance
Verbal Reasoning	14	.01
Nonverbal Reasoning	13	.01

BETWEEN CLUSTER COMPARISONS

	Difference	Significance
Verbal v Nonverbal Reasoning	27	.01
Verbal v Spatial	25	.01

There are significant (0.01) discrepancies between Verbal and Nonverbal Reasoning scores and the GCA.

There are significant (0.01) discrepancies between Verbal and Nonverbal Reasoning cluster scores and Verbal and Spatial scores.

Wechsler Intelligence Scale for Children (3rd Edn UK) (WISC)
PICTURE ARRANGEMENT
Age Equivalent to 7 years 10 months

Wechsler Objective Reading Dimensions (Word)
READING COMPREHENSION
Age Equivalent to 6 years 3 months

DISCO (Wing 2000)
Lorelei meets the ICD-10 criteria for Asperger syndrome and the Wing (1981) and Gillberg and Gillberg (1989) criteria for Asperger syndrome

which includes categories relating to Nonverbal Communication skills/Speech and Language use and to Motor skills.

Three wishes

To have a thousand pets
To live on a farm
To collect mice

Conners Scales

Non-significant scores for Attentional problems
T score of 85 for Anxiety (Significant = above 65)

Discussion

Lorelei is a charming little girl who presented (as others have described) as 'very shy'. During the assessment she was able to demonstrate excellent cognitive skills mostly above her age. There were nevertheless discrepancies, which hint at underlying difficulties.

The Verbal IQ score of 133 places Lorrie into the superior category of intelligence but is discrepant from scores in relation to Nonverbal Reasoning and to Spatial Ability. Whilst these latter scores are still above average, the disparity between these and the verbal skills will create internal confusions and frustrations. The fact that Lorrie is so intelligent bodes well for the future and must be nurtured through an appropriate educational placement and curriculum, but her anxieties could easily increase without understanding and interventions starting at this stage.

Throughout the assessment Lorrie was compliant but very quiet with a tense demeanour, no gesture and very limited facial expressions. When I made amusing comments she did not laugh and had not really been part of the interaction.

In Picture Similarities, which has a ceiling of 8+ which Lorrie reached, she showed excellent skills in pattern matching but was less certain when people were depicted. She failed to match obvious smiling faces in one item.

Despite excellent Verbal Reasoning shown up in Verbal Similarities, Lorrie had problems with inferring meaning when presented with a set of four pictures and asked to match a describing sentence. She correctly matched just 5 out of 10 pictures in an Early Years test. In the test of Picture Arrangement Lorrie was able to pass a number of the items, but took the longest time. She also tended to miss interactions and in some cases got items right but had misconstrued or missed the point. For instance, in an early item, one card depicts a couple walking along with a picnic and a spotted dog is walking with them. In another the dog reaches up and eats the chicken leg obviously sticking out of the basket and in another they show obvious shock and horror when they open their basket to find no food. Lorelei placed the cards in the correct order but described the story as 'they're taking the dog for a walk, he jumps up and they have a picnic'.

Lorelei also presented with various vocal tone changes and parents have commented that she can be 'like an actress'.

In certain items Lorelei showed signs of becoming 'stuck' in relation to problem solving and remained silent instead of telling me that she was stuck or that she had finished.

Lorrie sat throughout with her toy bear. She liked to talk about animals and when I asked her for three magic wishes the choices were all animal related.

Despite excellent cognitive ability, Lorrie's achievement scores in relation to Reading, Reading Comprehension and Spelling were below expectations. She also struggles with Quantitative Reasoning even though her written number is above her age.

The intellectual assessment indicates that Lorrie is verbally gifted with a score which places her at the 99th percentile. Although her cluster scores for Spatial and Nonverbal reasoning fall into the average range they are significantly discrepant from her verbal ability and this will cause confusion for Lorrie. Achievement scores are also below expectations. Children who are so bright will also use many personal strategies to help them cope and also to disguise problems which they may be unable to cope with. This acts as a double-edged sword especially if others do not understand. The very bright child who is able to disguise cognitive difficulties but who reacts emotionally to confusions will nevertheless still struggle to cope emotionally, and this is exacerbated by a lack of understanding and support in others. The hidden handicaps are all the more disconcerting in such cases.

Lorrie has shown unusual interactions and styles of responding to both adults and children, intense fascinations and motor difficulties since pre-school. She has developed a fearfulness for stimuli, which is ordinary, and also for stimuli which excite other children. Indeed, even children and the excitement of other children has made her fearful. Her early years have been significantly affected by undisputed reactions to vaccine and there is a growing awareness that some children develop autistic spectrum disorders and compromised immune systems from such reactions, which interweave with pre-existing allergic reactions.

It is not possible to say whether Lorrie's emotional responses to people, to change and to the wider environment, her repetitive behaviours and narrow interests would have developed if she had not reacted to vaccine but there is nothing in the family history which indicates a higher susceptibility to ASD. From the evidence it would appear that there has been a tapestry of problems including being four weeks premature, a difficult birth and severe eczema which rendered Lorrie more medically vulnerable. This group, from my experience (the more medically vulnerable child with allergies), seem more likely to react to vaccine which in turn can result in a variety of problems at varying levels of severity.

There have been unusual interactions with peers, gauche body language, inappropriate expression, stiff gaze behaviour, limited use of gestures, pedantic use of language and an odd vocal prosody. Anxiety interweaves with semantic pragmatic problems invariably recognised on the autistic spectrum.

Lorrie's high intellect and her parents' focused and unstinting efforts and the school recognition make up a very positive tapestry which has helped Lorrie achieve what she has achieved so far and which will be necessary in the future, improved, it is to be hoped, by increased awareness and more focused interventions.

Conclusions and recommendations

Lorelei is a highly intelligent little girl with intense and unusual interests, anxieties, motor and social impairments which fit onto the autistic spectrum and meet the criteria for Asperger syndrome. She has difficulties of a semantic pragmatic nature which increase anxieties, and literacy development is more delayed than expected.

The determination of whether a child has an autistic spectrum disorder depends on close examination of a child's family and developmental history, looking out for particular cognitive and behavioural features and clusters of features and other qualities/impairments which form a child's unique tapestry. Differential diagnoses are also taken into consideration before a diagnosis can be determined.

Lorrie's verbal giftedness interwoven with some impairment in motor skills, poor social awareness, extreme emotional reactions to everyday things, a focus on narrow repetitive themes and problems with cognitive shifting and orienting to new situations is the stereotype of Asperger.

I consider that early intervention can change the tapestry considerably and if a child's difficulties and development have been compromised by vaccine it may be that even more positive change can be brought about than in more 'fixed' states through severe brain damage and a strong history of family autism, say. In Lorrie's case, positive change has been achieved and this bodes well for the future. It does, however, indicate that it is crucial for those around her to understand her difficulties and apply appropriate strategies.

The family need to explore interventions for allergy induced autism and liaise closely with the school to put in place appropriate interventions and evaluations.

Despite better skills now emerging, Lorrie's history cannot be ignored and will come back to haunt her if support for underlying difficulties is not given.

I would like to make the following recommendations:

- Education for staff and family can be easily achieved through accessing the now not insignificant number of books on this subject. The Internet also provides a rich vein of information.

- Liaison between home and school and sharing of ideas is vital if effective interventions are to be put into place and to work.

- Winslow produce social packages such as Social Use of Language, Social Stories and Comic Strip Conversations which need to be implemented within the school. See References.

- Lorrie needs to be part of pragmatic processes designed to help her understand social scenarios, which lead to problems. Pictorial prompts will help Lorrie to absorb the information. Practise and role-play and activities occurring within groups will also reinforce the message. This must be done within the mainstream setting given Lorrie's profile now, her age and her successful integration in her small private school.

- Direct teaching with respect to social awareness will need to be conducted with staff and family explaining to Lorrie how groups operate. It requires the parent formalising all the instinctive skills, which are not normally identified. These processes will interweave with others developed through Social Communication packages.

- Lorrie needs daily input and a constant awareness of others who can gently guide without making Lorrie seem different. Class and group-based activities which will help others helps reduce this possibility.

- Emphasis needs to be placed on learning certain skills such as improving Lorrie's ability to listen to others as part of more focused engagement with people in interpersonal relationships; she also needs to develop an ability to express confusion to others in order to reduce internal anxieties and emotional explosions. Parents will be a source of good advice to the school, and can help them to understand how to introduce change to Lorrie and how to interpret some of her nonverbal behaviour.

- Motor skills can be improved through activities which can be found in packs now on sale through companies such as Winslow.

- Activities mentioned above cannot be bolted on and 'taught' every week, say. They need to be understood by all staff working with Lorrie and seamlessly interwoven into her home and school day and night.

- Consistency of methods across these contexts is important.

- Lorrie will be helped if school and parents can arrange a meeting in which they plan, using the above as a framework, to improve specific skill deficits and ensure that all staff in all contexts can help Lorrie to fit in with her social world.

- Evaluations to establish progress are crucial to fine tune the programme. These need to involve: daily home–school links (phone or book) which focus very precisely on the targeted problem and how Lorrie coped on that day; weekly more formal discussions and three-monthly formal written evaluations. Off-the-shelf programs, tailored to suit Lorrie, provide evaluation forms etc.

- Computer programs to improve basic literacy skills may be salient for Lorrie and she would need to access such activity daily for at least 20 minutes on Spelling and Reading. It is important that Lorrie takes control of this activity for herself.

- The Allergy Induced Autism project at Sunderland University run by Dr Paul Shattock OBE is a useful contact to explore through some simple tests, whether Lorrie would benefit from certain interventions.

- The use of Efamol has been recognised as helpful for some children who present in a similar way to Lorrie and this could be trialled.

Chapter Four

Definitions, descriptions and disorders

Real life is complicated. The more we look at behaviour, the more we find that simple explanations and descriptions are elusive. Checklists of behaviours designed to clarify our thinking can create greater complications. Although there are obviously the classic or stereotyped cases, the variability and spectrum nature of behavioural disorders requires flexibility by those responsible for diagnosis *and* provision of support.

The metaphor of the tapestry may appear to be complicating matters all the more by weaving together multiple overlapping spectra. However, I consider that this metaphor allows us to understand this natural interwoven effect of behavioural development, recognise how various threads of behaviours can coexist at varying levels of severity and provide us with another way of perceiving the unique child in order to ensure our systems, including families, are able to put in place appropriate support as early as it is needed. It is also intended to show how some similar clusters of behaviours could be given different names – leading to different treatments and causing confusion.

For example, this can happen easily happen through:

- variable research focus
- influence of certain groups of professionals
- different training between and within countries
- increasing parental awareness of unheard-of conditions and support in other countries, which seem like those experienced by their child.

In this chapter I have set out a number of currently diagnosed disorders and their pivotal stereotype features. For instance, ASD refers to autistic spectrum disorder and the pivotal feature is described as poor social reciprocity and obsessional behaviour. There is also some detail about the nature of the name for disorders, which can cause a lot of confusion. For instance, some relate to the name of the person who first saw the cluster of symptoms, others are descriptions of the first recognised symptoms, and others relate to the suspected underlying cause.

Many parents can believe that a 'disorder' relates to a specific medical cause, linked to a very specific part of the brain or body. Many do not realise that the disorder or syndrome is actually a reference to a clustering of observed features and the name it is given could just be of the person who first wrote about that cluster. The features could be associated with neurodevelopmental processes and it is this grey area which allows for controversy. Different types of professionals can perceive the same cluster of symptoms but go on to use different terminology.

The current diagnostic criteria for these disorders are given in Appendix 1 to show the variability as well as the similarities. Other professionals, seeking a causal explanation, may choose to bark up an entirely different tree as they are locked into determining causality and have differing views about what has caused what they see.

There are many interweaving features which compromise development, and which need to be recognised to understand the child's problems properly.

Unifying causal theories relate to underlying problems at the genetic and biochemical level. Coexisting presenting disorders are called *co-morbidities* and can include psychiatric and psychological disorders such as sleep disorders; mood disorders such as depression; anxiety disorders such as panic attacks; behaviour disorders such as oppositional defiance disorder; learning disorders such as dyslexia; motor disorders such as the dystonias and dyspraxia; communication disorders such as semantic-pragmatic language disorders and nonverbal developmental disorders; tic disorders such as Tourette syndrome; perceptual disorders such as Irlen syndrome.

Most individuals with ADHD will have one or more co-morbid disorders, and these may be partly shared with the ASD group, indicating that the ASD group also has co-morbid disorders and that some of the threads within each disorder's tapestry of factors and features may not be unique to one disorder.

Many children may not receive comprehensive assessments or the wrong questions may be asked, or behaviours misunderstood, leading to no recognition of the problem and no help. Many will be given a thorough assessment but rigid adherence to black and white checklists and the current elimination of one 'disorder' if another is present, for example ADHD if autism is present, could limit understanding. This over-focus – while important – can often mean that we fail to perceive the whole gestalt and ignore interweaving difficulties which are not looked for in the main presenting disorder, and then forever work with only part of the tapestry.

There is a need for professionals to be more flexible, using the notion of the spectrum (Wing 1996) as we understand more about the nature of the interwoven threads underlying all behavioural presentations. From such a perspective we are in a better position to create a tapestry of the enormous amount of research undertaken in disparate areas. This position has been reached appropriately, as knowledge has increased. Like the developing young child, we now need to assimilate this information which allows us to see both the wood and the trees, to provide richer forms of support for our children.

The long search for the Holy Grail, the single dropped stitch at one or other level of explanation leading to a disorder, has ended. While we may find a unifying biological cause at a DNA or biochemical level, people weave their own unique and beguiling tapestries in interaction with their unique environment – only in part related to interpersonal relationships. Birth injuries, allergic reactions and others are all 'environmental'.

Why autism and ADHD?

ADHD, as a description of a cluster of neurodevelopmental problems, can and does interweave with autistic spectrum disorder and the severity of its presentation depends on the number and severity of coexisting conditions and other circumstances. The overlap relates to shared dysfunctional brain processes. Those without autism on the ADHD spectrum are still grossly affected by a breakdown in relation to the same types of processing and management of moment to moment events in life (Barkley 1995) as are children whose difficulties extend into autism.

The social problems of most ADHD children without autism are not appropriately understood or recognised as they exist in subtle form and in many cases can hide behind apparent social awareness, apparent better understanding. This is made worse when ODD, rages and threatening social behaviour are present, preventing the recipient from understanding or even wanting to understand what lies behind the tirades. Inappropriate reactions of others add more threads to the problem tapestry.

Co-morbidities – which mean other problems that can coexist with ADHD (Biederman 1996) and autism (Wing 1998) – are well recognised but great confusion occurs when people try to blame one condition for all of a child's problems. This can then lead to just one type of provision, which may be very limited and focused on a thread rather than the overall picture. If the child does not improve as expected this could result in removal of any support or family blame. The metaphor of the tapestry is suggested to allow us to consider the rich complexity of brain processing and behavioural presentations through a simple and respectful fretwork. These are living, moving, abstract forms. Through accepting and understanding the complexities we are poised to apply more efficacious forms of support to each thread depending on a range of factors, including severity.

The often reported diagnostic uncertainties and treatment response confusions for many on these spectra could be reduced by considering the interwoven nature of various spectra. Could an understanding of the autistic spectrum help professionals working with ADHD and vice versa? I believe that it could. Although limited, epidemiological studies in both the autistic and ADHD populations recognise the overlap of these behavioural presentations (Ehlers and Gillberg 1993).

Our systems need to be more flexible, to put the child at the pivot to provide support early which has a better chance of making a real difference, and it may be useful to look at the value of using the necessarily very strict criteria for research purposes for practitioner interventions. They were never intended to be used so strictly for casework and the *Diagnostic and Statistical Manual of Mental Disorders* (APA 1994: see Appendix 1) clearly states the importance of clinical judgement.

The research departments of overworked teaching hospitals, whose main focus of work is research and whose brief is quite different from that of the community practitioner, will inevitably eliminate many who exist on the spectrum and whose needs for support are just as great.

Waiting lists of at least 18 months before a child is even seen for the first appointment are the norm, which is very frustrating for families and professionals. In the UK there have not been the resources to provide wide-ranging support attached to hospital departments, as has been the case in the USA. Furthermore, local professionals have always been discouraged from referring 'out' to specialists, the local area being expected to perform this function without the knowledge. Local clinical initiatives and collaborative training need to be interwoven more consistently with specialist research departments and international perspectives, for an interplay of understanding.

Without such an interweave, children will be affected by the misperceptions of educationalists when ADHD and autism are mentioned. Within the world of education management, there can be a cynicism which denies *any* behavioural condition in a child, other than describing it as just that – a behavioural problem, with little support. There can be usually extraordinary attempts to prove that the behaviour is 'within normal limits' over many years, local systems adhering to rigid ideas as to how many children should present with problems and extending the notion of normal limits accordingly.

Unfortunately such rigidity is not helpful to communities and can lead to short term savings and huge longer-term expense. Energies would be better directed at working positively together toward new discoveries and early dynamic interventions.

Some of the practical problems within ADHD and autism, for instance, include the label of ADHD as another name for 'naughtiness'; in the UK the cluster of problems recognised as ADHD has been dismissed as 'an American condition'. Unless there is something I do not know, we all have the same brains wherever we live in the world, and these clusters of warped processes relate to brain function and are not a superficial construction.

The perception of Asperger syndrome, as an autistic spectrum disorder, is often regarded as 'just' a behavioural problem or the latest fad. It is remarkable that many intelligent professionals will dismiss the very clear cluster of neurodevelopmental problems on the increase in our societies.

There is also the erroneous expectation that all children on the autistic spectrum should conform to Kanner's (1943) description of extreme autism and appear mute and aloof, or the condition as a form of autism will be dismissed. Similarly, the stereotypical ADHD child is expected to spend his entire time skidding about on skateboards.

Tourette syndrome is considered to be very rare and erroneously solely defined as barking out swear words incessantly. Genetic researchers have independently linked Tourette with ADHD and also with autism.

Dyslexia has suffered very badly with local education administrators openly saying 'We don't recognise dyslexia', leaving parents stunned by their bright child, struggling to read and spell. Parents are often told that as the LEA does not recognise the problem, nothing can be provided. Although families have a legal right to appeal against such decisions (different systems are in operation in different countries) many will be unaware or will not have the resources to fight.

For many who work as researchers and clinicians exclusively in either field, there is often no recognition of the other condition as co-morbid; instead, it will be more likely regarded as a differential diagnosis. Similarly, for those who toil away in separate fields looking at behaviours which commonly coexist, for instance semantic-pragmatic disorders, attachment disorders, tic disorders and reading disorders, there may be a tendency to claim a causal ownership of *all* the presenting problems. For instance, a child with ADHD, language problems, obsessions and reading difficulties, if he or she is given any support, will most likely be provided with support according to the ideology prevalent in the local area and the available resources, a single feature being highlighted.

It may be decided, in the UK for instance, that a child has not 'got' ADHD because he can sit still and he can pay attention sometimes (reflecting a lack of understanding of the nature of this disorder). Or has not 'got' autism because he can make eye contact sometimes and doesn't have a very special ability. 'He does have a problem reading, but he's not "got" dyslexia because his language – therefore his "intelligence" – is at the same level as his reading ability.' But if dyslexic, most children will have language problems at one or another level which could mask their intelligence. If there are also unrecognised co-morbidities such as ADHD and dyspraxia, the development of a child's intelligence will be affected over time. There may be an attempt to blame the family, depending on ideology, but if nothing can be found it may then be concluded that he clearly has difficulties with understanding and using language and so that explains why he appears to be ADHD, to be obsessional and to have problems reading. This conclusion could lead to the child, if he's lucky, being placed on a waiting list for speech and language therapy, possibly along with another 100 or so hopefuls from a group of schools, with each professional having to fight the child's corner for the support. It could take years to get to this point with a further wait of at least a year to decide what is to happen. Once receiving the therapy the child may *actually not progress*; this points to issues which will be explored in Chapter 6.

Given the real-life limitations of resources, the 'it doesn't grow on trees' argument is rife. Therefore very strict criteria are applied. Inevitably, the child whose language problems are less obvious will not be a high priority for such support or for places in units. One solution must be to weave additional new knowledge and interventions into our systems.

With greater knowledge, those at the coal-face with children will be able not only to home in to the defining feature but also to recognise the interwoven threads. We would then all need to work together to provide what we collectively know to be crucial which is intensive, fine-tuned early support pertaining to each problem behaviour, before the tapestry becomes even more tangled.

'Can he have more than one?' (Mother of an ADHD/ Asperger child)

Research in the USA (Biederman *et al.* 1991, 1993) has clearly demonstrated the high incidence of co-morbidity in populations of children who meet ADHD criteria (80 per cent) and informs us that some children can have a number of coexisting disorders. Poorer outcome is predicted for those with a number of additional disorders, especially if they appear early and are severe. Given these predictions, intensive early intervention is clearly imperative in such cases of tangled tapestries.

Increasingly there is evidence of an overlap of presenting features in the ADHD group: 50 per cent of the ADHD population are reported to have social skills problems; 50 per cent to have emotional immaturity; 30 per cent to present with immature gross motor development; 60 per cent to present with immature fine motor development; 30 per cent with sleep disturbances; 20 per cent with enuresis; 15–25 per cent with a learning disability such as dyslexia and 15–30 per cent with anxiety/depression; 10–20 per cent present with 'mania' (Biederman *et* al. 1991).

Within the 'manic' group 80 per cent were reported to suffer from depression and a very high proportion develop conduct disorder and oppositional defiance disorder. Many in this group may find themselves with a stigmatising diagnosis of bipolar disorder later in life and this may be better understood and remediated if the interwoven social communication disorder were recognised in childhood and if the benefits of quite specific forms of support from both sides of the Atlantic for what appears to be the same group were recognised. This group represents some of the 'poor responders' to stimulant medication for ADHD, with behaviour problems often escalating. As their behaviour can be extreme with very early onset – before the age of 4 in some cases – they must be targeted for thorough assessments and linked tapestry interventions which are likely to include highly focused and intensive behavioural methods and alternative medications. Thorough psychological assessments should provide clues as to whether the ADHD child is actually on the autistic spectrum and understanding this may be more appropriate than considering the child to be 'manic'.

Considering many who present in the UK with the overlap of Asperger syndrome and ADHD, the 'mania' and the ODD are well recognised parts of the condition and are managed in particular ways. Emotional reactions to environmental confusions or failure to recognise certain emotions in others are understood as part of a social communication disorder using the autistic model and may link with glitches in the mediational functions of the amygdala. Howlin (1998) reports that Baron-Cohen, using PET scanning, has found that young adults with autism tend to use the pre-frontal lobes rather than the amygdala to process emotional and social stimuli which suggests at the very least an adaptation in the tapestry over time. Given that both the ADHD and the autistic group have well recognised overlapping executive dysfunctions (see later discussion in this chapter) which are mediated by the pre-frontal lobes, this particular group may well be seen to be doubly disadvantaged neurologically if larger studies confirm these findings.

It may also help us to understand the impulsive and passionate responses so well known within Asperger syndrome and noted by Still (1902), which result in an apparently highly emotional response when most people hardly respond at all through to no emotional response when there should be. Combine an emotional approach to interpretations of the world with the stuck state of responding obsessively to fragments of the world, not shifting to develop a wider representation or perspective and we have a highly anxious, perseverating individual who cannot move on.

With greater public access to information through technological advances, parents are able to read about different disorders and can be uncertain as to which label best suits their child if he or she is complex. The mother in our subheading said 'Can he have more than one?' after seeing two separate specialists and being told he met the criteria for both separate conditions. The answer is: 'Yes he can.' Indeed he might fit criteria for a number of disorders which overlap and in time we will find more precise definitions as we push back the boundaries to remediate earlier and earlier. In many cases different countries may actually be talking about the same disorder, but may not have asked the right questions of the study group to enable us to check appropriately. The same underlying neurochemical processing might be implicated, but different studies, especially when they occur in different countries, will easily perceive the same issues from different angles and use different terminology, despite a greater consensus across international systems.

Some would argue against using any labels, saying that the increasing confusion reflects the greater need to describe needs, which was a pivotal issue in the drawing up of the special needs procedures in Britain in 1981. Unfortunately, without an understanding of the failing processes underlying description of behaviour, we have failed to understand and support appropriately. Such apparently respectful attitudes all too easily lead to children not being helped at all. Advancement requires that we incorporate perceived knowledge from various sources which we then weave into our systems for greater future advancement. With a greater understanding of underlying processes, the use of labels can be more focused to provide the help and make positive change.

It is important to know that criteria lists are not set in stone. They reflect the most recent understanding of the problem but inevitably different countries and cultures look at the same behaviours and terminology may differ. The list is by no means exhaustive and just aims to cover the typical conditions co-morbid with ADHD and autistic disorders.

The nature of the descriptions vary depending on a variety of factors; in some cases the different descriptions actually describe the same disorder but with a different focus and emphasis. Many families can be confused by the names and sometimes anxious. The history of methods leading to how disorders are named takes us back to the beginning of time.

The many nomenclatures that have developed over the past two millennia have differed in their relative emphasis on phenomenology, aetiology and course as defining features. Some systems have included only a handful of diagnostic categories; others have included thousands (American Psychiatric Association 1994, p. xvi).

Emphasis has also varied dependent upon whether the main objective was clinical, research or statistical settings.

Clusters of disorders

Certain disorders are named after the first person who recognised the problem and a family may think their child has something quite different from a previous diagnosis when in fact a look at the actual criteria will reveal the overlap. Or they may find that a particular specialist focuses on only one aspect of the child's tapestry of disorders – such as the motor skills – resulting in a diagnosis that may lead practitioners to ignore other features. Here are a few clusters of disorders and the emphasis leading to the name:

Disorders named after those who first described certain features and/or clusters
Asperger syndrome, Gilles de la Tourette syndrome.

Disorders named after descriptions of the first recognised features
autism, attention deficit disorder, tic disorders, dyslexia, semantic-pragmatic disorder, anxiety disorders, obsessive-compulsive disorder (OCD), oppositional defiance disorder and conduct disorder.

Disorders which describe clusters of problems and imply causality
Dysexecutive syndrome, developmental co-ordination disorder, dystonia, dyspraxia.

Disorders named after clusters of recognised features and given an acronym
ADHD, ADD, DAMP syndrome (disorders of attention motor and perception), OCD, ODD, CD.

Differential diagnosis

Differential diagnosis relates to the recognition that there are different explanations for the presenting problem and reflects the desire to find one pivotal feature. For instance, if it is established that problems which may appear to fit ADHD did not emerge until the child entered school, assessment needs to be sure to include assessment for reading disorders in case there is a dyslexic problem which is wholly responsible for the child's problems. This would then be the differential diagnosis for what was masquerading as ADHD.

However, it is entirely possible that another child's ADHD may not have been caused by the frustration given the dyslexia. A closer inspection of the child's history may reveal that there were unrecognised problems before the child entered school. The ADHD then becomes co-morbid with dyslexia and the frustration will aggravate the problems. Simply applying weekly support for one problem is not going to meet the need in such cases. In severe dyslexic children many years of reading support may result in little improvement. In these cases there will be co-morbid conditions which can help us understand additional interwoven processes which are preventing the child from benefiting from the support which helps most children with just this problem. Research by Biederman (1997) reveals that possibly 30 per cent of children with presenting ADHD also have specific learning difficulties like dyslexia.

One young woman with severe dyslexia came to me for an assessment. She was in her twenties and met the criteria for Asperger syndrome and ADHD. When we read a text she focused obsessively on each tiny segment of a word. This procedure is commonplace when remediating for dyslexia. Through a focus on the separate parts, both the sounds and the look, the whole word, then sentence then meaning *emerge* like language initially, after much repetition. But this woman, being both dyslexic and on the autistic spectrum, had never been able to make that mental leap in reading. Each week she travelled for a double intensive work session in reading. She had moved on from a reading age of 6 years to 7 years over the previous two years and was understandably proud but totally confused as to why she made such slow progress. She worked laboriously on each segment, sweating over the effort. She told me that after 'ploughing' through one page, 'You breathe a sigh of relief – then you turn it over and there's another load!' She was seeing only the intense detail.

We now know enough to tell us that we have to recognise the interweave of disorders and move quickly, early, intensively and for as long as possible with an appropriate tapestry of support. In the past, we would give support for a six-week period, focusing on what seemed to be the most obvious problem, and then stop, in order to provide the same support to others. As soon as the support stopped, especially if it only focused on one part of the problem, the child's difficulties could return and in some cases escalate. There is increasing awareness that piecemeal support does not work.

There are therefore dangers inherent in the overuse of differential diagnoses as opposed to co-morbidity, which recognises coexistence. If a professional decides that the problem is in the family relationships or more likely to be a language disorder, a motor disorder or a reading difficulty and targets support in one area, it could take some time before it is realised that the cluster of problems has not dissipated with just one focus for support, by which time there could have been a lot of wasted time and resources, and problems could easily have worsened.

In a cynical world, an argument can be made to support anything and everything and so if resource providers do not feel inclined toward the disorder in question they can easily dismiss it with a wave of the hand, instead arguing for a differential diagnosis which may offer the child nothing and blame the family. There is a considerable amount of research which clearly sets out the prevalence of such co-morbidities, but so far the autism and ADHD combination has not been well researched and it is likely that other disorders such as ODD and OCD may include people who could also fit onto the autistic spectrum with ADHD, and their difficulties may be much easier to ameliorate if the underlying autistic features and the attentional features are recognised.

The more co-morbidities there are in a child's tapestry, the more help the child will need. Furthermore, the earlier a child presents with a number of co-morbidities, the greater urgency in terms of support. In particular, if a child starts to show autism, ODD and/or CD behaviours before the age of 5, whatever the underlying cause, rapid support needs to be put into place. This turns on three issues: the very early evidence of such problems is indicative of their severe nature and potential for tangling is all the greater; the earlier a child can be given appropriate interventions and the greater likelihood of a better response; early support is infinitely easier to put in place for social systems and much cheaper.

Within the tapestry of coexisting disorders are likely to be glitches in the workings of common brain pathways, which create fundamentally similar underlying problems, expressed in various ways. Furthermore, these problem threads can tangle together into clusters of defining features ranging from shared cluster features through to those varied expressions which are currently used to recognise separate disorders or syndromes.

Hyperactive children – whether diagnosed autistic, Asperger syndrome, ADHD, Tourette syndrome or DAMP – are more prone to risky behaviour and not considering the consequences of their actions, which could result in many accidents and blows to the head. These in turn can cause considerable problems and currently only groups who work with head and brain injuries understand that a serious blow to the head will result in a variety of problems even if current methods of casualty-based assessment show nothing.

The ubiquitous neuropsychological problems manifesting themselves after such traumas have been called the 'dysexecutive syndrome' as they relate to problems which we have believed are related to the central executive. These behaviours are also found among children with autism and ADHD who have not experienced such head traumas. In the children with early evidence of such behaviours, if their risky behaviour leads on to more head traumas we can expect a serious compounding of their difficulties. So many children with hyperactive and/or risky behaviour hurt themselves so regularly they become known to the casualty department. One child I assessed had a tapestry of language, motor, perception and ADHD problems. This combination led to falls because he was clumsy, because he was hyperactive and acted rapidly before he thought, and because his distorted perceptions led to magical thinking and risk-taking behaviour. For instance, after hearing the lyric 'I believe I can fly' he was found hanging outside his bedroom window.

One teenager with Asperger syndrome who was cavorting around the house after a house move, bumped into a precariously positioned wardrobe, which knocked him over and out. When he came to, he staggered to the top of the stairs and fell down them.

Risky behaviour leading to swollen heads and fractured skulls or car accidents leading to unconsciousness are higher in these groups. Often the child is in the road before anyone can stop them. One of our tapestry kids hurtled down stone steps as a toddler and ended up smashing his head against a stone wall, another had run into the road and under a car before his parents could grab him. He was unconscious for days. One child fell backwards out of his seat at a circus. He landed on his back and head and was knocked out. A number of parents have noted a loss or deterioration of speech and language following such events. In older children the volatility and impulsivity is obvious and complies with expectations in relation to the dysexecutive syndrome found in people after head or brain injuries and felt to relate to the pre-frontal lobes. People who experience serious blows to the head invariably present with executive dysfunctions regardless of which part of the head was hurt and whatever other problems there may be.

Many children with such disorders engage in head banging. One Asperger youngster said he found that heading a ball seemed to put his brain back in gear. Many children and adults with these disorders mention that their brains don't seem to be working as they should and so they bash their heads as if to restart a broken radio.

Knowing about the common threads as well as the differences and the tangled effects can help us to describe and manage them more efficaciously. The level of severity varies across time in relation to each feature and to the nature of the cluster of features, the context and other aspects of the individual, demanding dynamic modes of assessment, diagnoses and ongoing evaluation.

Developmental disorders

I have outlined the defining features of the most well recognised overlapping developmental disorders – not all of which are listed in DSM or ICD – with some thoughts on evidence for the interweave. The diagnostic criteria are set out in Appendix 1.

Autism

Defining feature: inability to engage in appropriate reciprocal regulating inter-action with people together with rigid thought patterns; repetitive, obsessive, routinised behaviour; a resistance to or fear of change and often catastrophic emotional responding. Inability to interpret language and social clues and cues in the environment leads to increasing distancing from people and traditional forms of recall and learning.

Asperger syndrome

Defining feature: as above but can use language, sometimes in unusual and complex forms. Problems at varying levels of severity in terms of language pragmatics; understanding and/or manifestation of 'social' clues and cues such as voice prosody, gesture, body signals or posture. There are invariably motor co-ordination/planning problems and executive dysfunctions/ attentional problems at varying levels of severity. Tics are not uncommon within the Asperger group and both verbal and nonverbal peculiarities are expected.

Hyperkinesis

Defining feature: grossly excessive motor activity. Many very young autistic children present with very high levels of hyperactivity and many hyperactive children who appear normal in that they seem able to engage with others, go on to develop problems which can place them on the autistic spectrum.

Attention deficient and hyperactivity disorder (ADHD)

Defining feature: impairments in regulating behaviour, involving thought, action and speech compromised by variable motivational and attention shifting and sustaining skills and in some cases by motor hyperactivity and impulsivity. There is increasing research evidence of clinical observations which find social impairments in this group, some of which fit the autistic criteria. There is also evidence of severe motor co-ordination disorder in a proportion of ADHD children and a recent study found this to be 4.9 per cent with moderate disorder at 8.6 per cent (Kadesjo and Gillberg 1999). They also noted that the children with the combination of ADHD and developmental co-ordination disorder (DCD) were more likely to have Asperger syndrome, school problems and poorer outcomes, 'particularly delayed reading development'.

Semantic-pragmatic disorder

Defining feature: deficits in comprehension, semantics and pragmatics of language with no problems with syntax. Invariably found in autism. Underlying cognitive confusions despite giving a good impression of understanding and ability. Children with this problem will blurt out inappropriate comments, fail to take turns in conversations and start a topic with insufficient information so that the listener cannot understand. The children also take things very literally. A failure to interpret basic emotional clues and cues correctly, the social nuts and bolts in the expressions, gestures and actions of others can also coexist.

Dyspraxia/developmental co-ordination disorder

Defining feature: marked impairment in the development of motor co-ordination. An inability to engage in appropriate motor reactions. Significant motor planning problems which include perceptions and judgements within space affecting action. Its coexistence with autism and ADHD is well recognised clinically (see ADHD section). Specialists in the field also refer to a cluster of difficulties which will be recognised as defining features for other diagnoses. Poor articulation; limited concentration and poor organisational skills; heightened sensitivity to sensory information e.g. differences in noise and changes in lighting; motor stereotypies; being 'unable to form relationships with other youngsters – appears isolated in the class group'. (Madeleine Portwood 1999).

Tourette syndrome and tic disorders

Defining feature: inability to inhibit inappropriate motor and vocal reactions. Inability to stop twitching, jerking or engaging in other odd simple/complex motor/vocal mannerisms such as throat clearing, at different levels of severity. Although it is known for the blurting out of repetitive swear words or rude gestures, these do not need to occur for this diagnosis to be given and indeed occur in only about 30 per cent of the affected population.

The high rate of ADHD – at least 60 per cent – found to coexist with Tourette syndrome, has led some to refer to Tourette as ADHD with tics. However, there are a small proportion of people who do not meet the ADHD criteria.

Recent research has found that the rate of Tourette syndrome (8.1 per cent) in a population of children with autism 'far exceeds that expected by chance' (Baron-Cohen et al. 1999).

These authors also noted the shared features of echolalia and palilalia, certain types of obsessive-compulsive behaviour and also abnormal motor behaviours.

Dyslexia

Defining feature: failure to develop reading skills as expected given age and intelligence. Underlying processes are felt to be phonological leading to significant difficulties deciphering word forms. The condition can extend to specific spelling problems, specific arithmetical problems and specific writing problems. The higher rate of reading problems in a population of ADHD children with developmental co-ordination disorder has been mentioned.

Irlen syndrome

Defining feature: perceptual distortions in print and in the environment. There can be evidence of poor depth perception, migraines and overlaps with seizure disorders and epilepsy, which can include reactions to lights and associated self-injury. Children with dyslexia, with ADHD and with autism are more likely to experience these distortions. I have found a high incidence of the problem in children who have experienced a closed head injury.

Associated medical problems

In some cases a child has a recognisable medical problem which can disguise and confuse if problems similar to those found in Asperger syndrome and/or ADHD are noticed – implicating shared warped processes.

Dysexecutive syndrome

After a head injury, there is recognition of the dysexecutive syndrome at varying levels of severity, which implicates the functioning of the frontal lobes. There can be disturbance of attention, increased distractibility, but no problems working along routine lines. New tasks pose great problems. There is impairment in the supervisory system which exerts an executive function (Shallice 1982) that is also felt to be analogous to the central executive component of working memory.

Kawasaki Disease

Kawasaki Disease is linked with a breakdown of the immune system which 'attacks itself', leading on to very serious health problems. The presentation of Asperger syndrome is also found in this population.

Hydrocephalus

In this serious neurological condition there is an accumulation of cerebrospinal fluid in the ventricles of the brain, with an increase in the pressure inside the head. Most children require a shunt to relieve the pressure. The condition is found at a rate of 1 in every 1000 children. Children can also acquire this problem after intraventricular haemorrhages and meningitis. About 40 per cent of premature infants experience intraventricular haemorrhages, including the tapestry twins Rachel and Miriam, but not all of these children will develop hydrocephalus and of those who do, in many it will stabilise and there will be no need for a shunt. There will, however, have been an impact on neurological development.

While there are many types of learning difficulties experienced by this group of children, often differing with each child, many present with semantic pragmatic disorders, attentional problems, Irlen syndrome and Asperger features (Blakemore-Brown 2000). Raising awareness of how people with Asperger syndrome can be helped, in turn helps those with hydrocephalus and the interwoven Asperger features. Southampton University is involved in research with the Association for Spina Bifida and Hydrocephalus (ASBAH) which appears to be confirming the clinical picture.

Dystonia

Defining feature: a neurological movement disorder, which causes muscles to contract and spasm. Primary dystonia can begin in childhood and cause an abnormal foot inversion, an awkward gait and contractions of many different groups. Blepharospasms cause involuntary muscle spasm of the eyelids; facial muscles can also be affected leading to grimacing and facial distortions.

Torticollis involves involuntary neck turning which can lead to extreme pain.

Dysphonia affects the muscles which control the vocal cords and can result in wavering or halting speech or even a breathless whisper.

Writer's cramp is triggered during writing or the performance of other fine motor activity. The hand and finger muscles contract or extend. There are links with gastro-oesophageal reflux when the sphincters in the digestive system do not contract properly. Symptoms can include throat clearing. Research has focused on the basal ganglia, the part of the brain governing movement.

Cluster disorders

A number of researchers have publicly recognised the clustering of features or disorders within the empathy disorders, which has led to more descriptive terms which highlight those features.

DAMP syndrome

DAMP syndrome pulls together the clear recognition of a cluster or tapestry of disorders of attention, motor and perceptual processes (Gillberg 1992). Asperger syndrome has been found within this population, implicating inter-woven neurodevelopmental processing of attention, motor and perception in turn linked with the development of social awareness at varying levels of severity.

Same disorder – different name

Some professionals have suggested that one disorder is actually the same as another, i.e. Tourette syndrome is essentially ADHD (Comings and Comings 1988; Spencer 1995) and this is an increasingly interesting issue, as we become aware of the way different countries perceive similar clusters of disorders. When I first attended a CHADD conference in 1995, I realised that many children described as ADHD in the USA would be described as Asperger syndrome in the UK. Many children described as Asperger syndrome in the UK are closer to the ADHD picture. Essentially, this arises as different researchers focus on different aspects of interwoven problems and as we look in much greater detail at the threads of disorders but not at overlaps with other disorders or the interweave of them all.

It also arises from the understandable desire to find the nub of the problem and this results in definitions which refer to what is considered the pivotal issue, with all other features seen as secondary to it.

The following are examples of contenders for each other's name:

- Tourette or ADHD/dystonia/autism and Asperger syndrome?
- Bipolar or ADHD and Asperger syndrome?

- Mania or autism/Asperger syndrome?
- ODD or ADHD/Asperger syndrome?
- Asperger syndrome or ADHD?
- Social phobia or Asperger syndrome?
- Asperger syndrome or social phobia?
- Semantic-pragmatic disorder or autistic spectrum?
- Dyspraxia or developmental co-ordination disorder/dystonias/Asperger syndrome/DAMP?
- Dysexecutive syndrome or ADHD autistic spectrum?
- ADHD or dysexecutive syndrome?

Recognising the interweave should help to reduce parental confusion and enable practitioners fully to describe interwoven threads and explain to families that such difficulties arise as more and more details are amassed within separate departments focusing on pivotal features, yet inevitably finding other shared threads and given a lack of sharing of knowledge between departments, and between clinicians and researchers. This is compounded by the different perspectives of different countries.

I was also recently reminded that some practitioners are still using outdated terms such as MBD (meaning minimal brain damage) which I thought had been discarded long ago. This overarching descriptive term was used for many years to describe the ADHD and Asperger groups and while it might seem appropriate for some people, parents need to be told that it is an old term which has been little used since the late 1980s or so, as it implied there was something physically damaged in the brain. This has not proven to be correct. Although some children, sadly, have suffered actual brain damage, our understanding of these disorders tells us that we are looking at faulty processes and mechanisms which can be changed provided the support is early enough and focused.

When refering to the various classifications provided in Appendix 1 it needs to be borne in mind that these are not fixed, but are updated as more knowledge adds to our perceptions; nor are they devised by the same type of professional, hence the variation in terms of diagnostic criteria even within the same disorder.

The research and clinical knowledge base of each disorder is valuable and needs to be shared. From this the underlying interwoven processes and the

pivotal feature can help towards the development of more focused and efficacious individual tapestries.

A shift from the strict classification system categories

Recently researchers have confirmed clinical findings of what I call 'the tapestry' and consider that instead of the traditionally used categorical systems
(DSM–IV and ICD–10) perhaps a dimensional system may be preferable to
deal with co-morbidity issues, as they permit the description of multiple
symptoms present in one individual. This may be especially important in disorders in which the rate of co-morbidity is very high, such as Tourette syndrome
(Ozonoff *et al*.1998).

Leekham *et al.* (2000) have also referred to the need for a dimensional
rather than a categorical approach when classifying autistic spectrum disorders,
with a rigid approach to strict categories preventing individuals from getting
the help they need.

Howlin (2000) feels there is a pressing need for diagnostic instruments
which will reliably 'identify those individuals within the autistic spectrum
whose deficits are "milder", or more subtle, and yet still have a major impact on
their lives' (Howlin 2000, p.127). In particular reference to Asperger
syndrome, she goes on to say that a single instrument cannot be used in isolation to ascertain diagnosis. Instead, detailed information relating to many areas
of functioning, and as set out later when we build the tapestries of individual
children, is also required.

Definition confusion facing families

ADHD is used to define a group by its poor ability to focus, plan and regulate
behaviour. It was first noticed in groups of children with hyperactivity, hence
the original term. In the UK many children are still not supported with these
problems as there is a prevailing attitude that a child must be totally overactive
the entire time, as in hyperkinetic disorder, including the time spent in the
doctor's office, to receive this diagnosis.

Differences between the use of the ICD and the DSM have led to significant differences of frequency between countries.

ADHD exists on a spectrum and while history is littered with examples of
ADHD behaviour, the UK has been slow to recognise the spectrum nature of
this condition. In the UK during the 1980s and into the 1990s just a small per-
centage – roughly 1 per cent – of children have been recognised on this

spectrum, the defining qualifying feature being hyperkinesis. In the USA the figure is higher at around 5 per cent of the population.

Attentional problems were seen as cardinal, hence the name, and the term has become so well known that when more fine tuned research revealed other more salient common features the name was retained (Barkley 1997).

Increasingly, researchers in ADHD have come to recognise executive functions and self-regulatory behaviours which interweave with the apparent poor attention. Regulatory and motivation problems are at their most extreme in the child who fails to focus on anything. Children with head injuries after accidents and falls can present with similar problems and this is why careful evaluation is crucially important after such events. ADHD children are more likely to go on to suffer head injuries which then exacerbate the problem.

As we move along the spectrum and onto the autistic spectrum in which relationship problems emerge more clearly, the ability to focus on highly specific features and objects becomes clear, confusing those who think that if a child can focus on a particular thing for a reasonable duration of time, then they cannot fall into the ADHD category.

Although this group can focus on specific things these are usually inappropriate (e.g. hyperfocusing) and often relate to highly unusual features such as flickering lights and certain textures or an unusual hobby, TV programme or activity. Classic ADHD children will be restless, impulsive, taking risks without considering a plan and without considering the consequences. They will have poor temporal judgement, even if they are able to manage time using clocks, and be unable to focus on most things, although this will be variable across time. Their behaviour will continue over time, and not be a single occurrence when under stress, for instance.

A person with Tourette syndrome or a tic disorder may twitch, flick hair back in a repetitive manner and 'bark' or cough incessantly; many families just get used to it. A genetic disorder, I recall asking one set of parents if anyone in the family had similar mannerisms to their son who I was assessing. His parents shook their heads and said 'No' but Dad had a persistent shoulder tic throughout our discussion. It had become known as his 'nervous habit'. Tic disorders are usually diagnosed if the person has just motor or just vocal tics, while Tourette syndrome requires both.

Many people first develop an eye blink and this overlaps with the dystonias, in which eye blinking is a specifically defined condition. A simple vocal tic could be persistent throat clearing and complex vocal tics are often found within the Asperger population. These could include the blurting out of phrases inappropriately or echolalia, the rapid repetition of a word.

Research into Tourette finds an overlap with both ADHD and autism and it is likely that many people diagnosed with Tourette syndrome in one country would be diagnosed with Asperger or ADHD in another.

Developmental co-ordination problems and dyspraxia

The motor problems invariably found at one level or another within Asperger syndrome; those with severe dyslexia with problems writing, the muscular pains found in dyspraxia could all relate to particular dystonias and benefit from understanding more about research in this area. Many children with dyspraxia and social problems do not have the wider Asperger problem recognised, but some children, with the appropriate focus and intensive support from occupational therapists, can alter their presentation.

Motor skills incorporate an interweave of functions which overlap other areas of ability. They include perception and incorporation of what goes on around us and in turn this involves sensory, praxis and sequencing skills.

Sensory skills

Motor activities include: tactile awareness and kinaesthetics, the vestibular system and balance (in turn interweaving with the auditory processing system), an understanding of direction and our spatial awareness, and proprioception, linking our movements to brain signals which tell us *how* we are moving.

Praxis

This relates to motor planning activity. It involves the ability to plan and co-ordinate motor action – such as throwing a ball, catching a ball – interwoven with perception and imitation of simple actions, particularly those involving both sides of the body.

Sequencing skills

These relate to gross and fine patterns of motor activities and interweave with the above.

For a number of professionals and parents, the idea of autism is terrifying and they consider that use of the term should be avoided at all costs. If a child's social awareness can be fully resolved with support from the occupational therapist for the dyspraxia, say, then it would be right to avoid any thought of an autistic spectrum disorder. Unfortunately, given the interwoven processes at work, many of those children with significant dyspraxic problems do present with an autistic spectrum disorder which should not be viewed with fear and shock. With appropriate early support and recognition of *all* the difficulties – attention, communication, motor and perception – *the whole tapestry* – the child can be shifted along the spectrum, the threads of social clumsiness abating over time.

Many babies with apnoea and gastro-oesophegal reflux problems are found to have muscle difficulties which will have a faulty genetic message system. A history of such difficulties is common amongst those with later developing developmental disorders and there is a high rate of inherited and acquired neurological impairment through prematurity and so on (see Chapter 3).

Politics

There are also political considerations. Dependent on the area in a country, there will be a reluctance to use certain labels, which is partly driven by the available educational support. I have been told many times in the past in relation to tapestry kids, that if ADHD is mentioned children will not receive the support they need, the label of an autistic spectrum disorder favoured with the ADHD perhaps not even being mentioned. However, over time, both disorders have faced the same brutal treatment.

In other areas I have been told that if a child is diagnosed with either disorder there will be a risk that the family, particularly the mother, will be blamed for creating or fabricating the disorder. This is particularly likely if the child has a history of breathing and feeding difficulties alongside allergies – which we know coexist – hyperactive behaviour and bowel problems. Those trained in these disorders will know that there is a medically vulnerable subgroup within autism and ADHD with exactly that type of history. Some researchers have alerted us to the opioid-excess theory of autism (Panksepp 1979: Reichelt 1981, 1993, 1994; Shattock 1990; Wakefield *et al.* 1998) in which peptides disrupt neurobiological function. There is also the presence of gastrointestinal conditions and a high rate of asthma, eczema and allergies within the family. The strong presence of particular specialists in certain areas will also help to determine the recognition of particular disorders and perhaps the denial of others.

Generally, limited resources can lead to administrators discouraging professionals to label children, instead preferring to use umbrella labels such as MLD or SLD (moderate learning difficulties or severe learning difficulties), which traditionally have focused on one thread within the tapestry – a child's IQ level. While this thread is of importance in the tapestry, and particularly when determining provision, it is the pattern of scores within the IQ which matter, and even the IQ can be modified over time if interventions are focused and successful. Indeed, if nothing is put into place and children fail to progress, the IQ can effectively drop as the child fails to learn along with their peers against whom their score is measured in standardised procedures. This is particularly relevant to the pre-school group of under 4-year-old children with language and attentional impairments and overactive behaviour combined with obsessions and rigidity of thought.

Below are summarised some of the interwoven threads in overlapping descriptions of disorders – not an exhaustive list.

- Hyperactivity is commonly noted amongst young autistic children and the associated 'spacing out' as part of an attention disorder can interfere with even intensive facilitation programmes.

- Various features which we currently recognise as being executive functions are also shared within these groups.

- Sensitivities commonly found among the autistic group are also found in children with ADHD and Tourette syndrome. All become worse under conditions of tiredness and anxiety, further tangling the tapestry. The auditory sensitivities can improve when the focus of attention is appropriate. Visual sensitivities are often found to be Irlen syndrome and the distortions can be immediately removed by the appropriate use of colour. In the worst cases people think they are hallucinating and depth perception distortions lead to odd reactions and fearfulness about moving around in the world.

- Many consider a tic as a sign of Asperger syndrome. This group is defined by its eccentricity and while the interwoven tic disorder is more frequently found in this population, it is possible to have a tic disorder and not have Asperger syndrome.

- Tic disorders are described as ADHD and while the interwoven tic disorder can coexist with ADHD there are many people with tic disorders who do not meet ADHD criteria, but do have threads of executive dysfunction.

- Motor co-ordination problems including sensory glitches found within the autistic spectrum, particularly the Asperger syndrome group, define dyspraxia, are implicated in DAMP syndrome and are frequently found at fine, gross or both levels with the ADHD group. The finding of motor difficulties amongst the language impaired and the dyslexic group is also well recognised. Dystonias may be described in the USA with dyspraxia the term more commonly used in the UK, dystonias relating to the defining feature of extreme and obvious muscle abnormalities.

- Dystonias and tic disorders are often seen as part of Asperger syndrome.

- The language peculiarities particularly within the Asperger group define the semantic-pragmatic group and are frequently found in Tourette syndrome. Many with ADHD, dyslexia and dyspraxia also present with varying levels of severity of this problem.

- The nonverbal developmental disorder relates to the cluster of difficulties commonly described above.

Staged diagnoses

It may be helpful to use a staged approach to diagnosis, each stage modified dependent on the effects of the earlier treatment and intervention. This is not, however, a wait-and-see approach, which has left many pre-school children at risk.

The value of a staged approach is that one works with the tapestry as it is presented at the time, and does not wait for the child's disorder to fit into a particular classification. The family will be informed that the child's tapestry points to various features warranting various forms of support. The next major evaluation will determine how the interventions have worked and where the child fits at that point in time. Early interventions should ensure that serious errors are not made in terms of clinical intervention and educational placement. This approach, in which one *expects* to be able to reweave the tapestry, gives hope to families, provides them with an empowering role in the process and introduces the expectation that children with these disorders can change their hue over time.

Without this understanding, many professionals and parents may at the least find themselves confused as their child grows and does not conform to the expected pattern inherent in the original diagnosis. At worst parent and professional blame can be brought into the picture as anger and defensiveness take over. With the right interventions we would be *expecting* change, however minimal, and this staged approach would normalise the situation, make it more dynamic and less devastating for a family.

If appropriate interventions are applied, the entire tapestry can change: the 'autistic' child may respond very well to intensive work on communication and then present more like an Asperger or an ADHD child, at which point alternative interventions may be put into place. The ADHD child whose overactivity may have responded to medication may emerge as a child with Asperger syndrome who needs additional plans in the multi-modal treatment.

Combined tapestry programmes meet the need for multi-modal approaches, which are effective for both groups. This may involve medication but not necessarily. To best help each child we are concerned with unique behavioural presentations, which require comprehensive behavioural, psychological, educational and sometimes medical evaluation and treatment (Barkley 1995).

We are developing the knowledge to recognise which methods work for different groups and the challenge is now to recognise the tapestry and incorporate various strategies. Early intervention, ongoing evaluation and dynamic, flexible programmes are crucial.

Tapestry kid

 # Graham

Reason for referral

Graham (aged 7) was seen for a reassessment of his needs.

Family history

Graham's maternal grandmother could not read or write until the age of 15. She was impulsive, hyperactive, aggressive, violent, and antisocial. She has needed to take medication for various disorders and has violently attacked another individual, leading to her own incarceration. Graham's father regarded himself as a Walter Mitty character and needed assessment as a youngster. More recently, his nephew, Graham's male cousin, has been assessed and diagnosed with Tourette syndrome. American studies have shown that Tourette syndrome and ADHD are intimately linked and indicate that 60–80% of Tourette syndrome patients have ADHD. In the USA, amongst a number of medics, there is a strong opinion that Tourette is essentially ADHD with tics (Comings and Comings 1988).

Developmental history

Graham was late reaching developmental milestones, a socially distant infant who engaged in impulsive, self-harming behaviour (head butting the floor and the cot before the age of 9 months). His difficult behaviour escalated. Speech and language did not develop normally and when Graham became violent and aggressive towards his family they sought assessments in order to ascertain the nature of their child's problem.

Graham has met the criteria for an autistic spectrum disorder within which the pivotal problem relates to an inability to develop reciprocal social relationships appropriately. Associated difficulties which exist in individuals whose problems occur on this continuum relate to repetitive, obsessional behaviours. There are also strong overlaps with attentional deficits and these were also in evidence in Graham, leading to a trial of medication to improve the impulsivity, overactivity, emotional reactivity and obsessional behaviour.

Professional involvement

Speech and language therapy has been warranted and the family are having ongoing discussions and meetings with the school in order to secure appropriate long-term support for their child.

The neurologist is continuing to see Graham, who has required modifications of his medication given the autistic obsessional traits which coexist with the attentional problems. My understanding is that the focused medication for his poor attention is having a noticeable positive effect. The neurologist reports: 'Both his father and grandfather say that he is much calmer than before and is giving attention to things around him to the extent that he never did previously.' However, and as is commonly found, there has been an increase in the obsessional behaviour which has been well recognised in this child throughout; I understand that the specialist is in the process of trialling combinations of medications to reduce this obsessional behaviour as well as increase his concentration.

The family have also become much more aware of the nature of autistic continuum disorders and the associated behavioural problems, especially in children with poor communication generally, as is the case with Graham. They are supported by individuals from the National Autistic Society and I am pleased to see that this same group is now developing a national network of people who can support families who experience parenting difficulties with their handicapped children. These specialised groups are imperative in our society as their ability to understand and focus on the specific nature of the child's problem which leads to a breakdown in relationships is fundamental to any parenting programme with this group. A failure to recognise and/or understand such fundamental problems is likely to lead to misinterpretations of behavioural difficulties and possible blaming of the family, which in turn simply exacerbates the chances of any progress, as individuals will close down when blamed.

I have become increasingly aware that many professionals are on a steep learning curve with respect to their understanding of these disorders and it is necessary for them to make some paradigm shifts, which in turn will allow them to incorporate an understanding of fundamental developmental problems and their impact on relationships rather than assuming that the entire problem is one of relationships. As part of the process of understanding in order to support their child, Graham's parents feel that his needs would be best met within a language unit.

Test results

Wechsler Intelligence Scale for Children (3rd Edn UK) (WISC)

As a guide to interpretation a range from 8 to 12 is considered average with a full range of 1 (being the lowest score) to 19.

VERBAL SCALE

	Score
Information	8
Similarities	2
Arithmetic	2
Vocabulary	1
Comprehension	2
Digit Span	6

PERFORMANCE SCALE

	Score
Picture Completion	13
Coding	3
Picture Arrangement	2
Block Design	8
Object Assembly	8
Symbol Search	1

TABLE OF IQ AND INDEX SCORES

	Score	Percentile	95% Confidence Interval
Verbal IQ	70	2nd	65–78
Performance IQ	77	6th	71–87
Full Scale IQ	71	3rd	67–78
Verbal Comprehension Index	77	6th	72–85
Perceptual Organisation Index	85	16th	78–95
Freedom from Distractibility Index	66	1st	61–80
Processing Speed Index	58	3rd	55–74

British Ability Scales (BAS)

TEST OF VISUAL MEMORY

	Percentile	Age
Immediate Visual Recall	25th	Below 5 yrs

Graham's responses included a number of intrusions.

Wechsler Objective Reading Dimensions (WORD)

Graham read two words.

	Percentile	Age Equivalent
Basic Reading	18th	<6
Spelling		<6

Graham was unable to spell the sounded out letter forms.

Discussion

Graham presented as a more biddable child during this reassessment. His eye contacting was more appropriate and his concentration skills were improved. He demonstrated sharing by offering me a sweet, and instead of becoming angry during a challenging task (Coding) he said 'I'm sweating', and smiled, revealing the enormous difficulties this child continues to experience with visual motor sequential processing, strongly correlated with skills in writing, spelling and the development of reading.

As we can see from the scores on the WISC III, Graham still presents as a child whose overall difficulties fall within the moderate learner range. However, it is crucial to interpret his profile closely as there are considerable peaks and troughs, reflecting a specific learning difficulty as opposed to a global learning difficulty. It is interesting and important to note that on this occasion Graham demonstrated reasoning skills in the high average range, managing to tell me that the similarity between an apple and a banana was that they were fruit, and between a cat and a mouse that they were animals. Compared with these skills in abstract reasoning, he was unable to define words in the Vocabulary subtest, and couldn't cope with the Comprehension subtest within this IQ assessment. It is also worthy of note that the Comprehension subtest is undertaken towards the end of the whole assessment, and therefore the difficulties with concentration are likely to contribute in part to his problems in this area. Nevertheless, we still see the fundamental language difficulties inherent in the previous testing and this is also borne out in the poor score for Picture Arrangement, which despite being a visual test involves processes of sequencing and an understanding of social clues and cues and an ability to work out consequences. Graham was unable to understand the fundamental principles of this test despite a demonstration. It is also of note that in an attempt to place the cards in the correct sequence, he set them down in a right to left order.

In the Information subtest Graham also demonstrated other dyslexic signs relating to sequencing. As previously mentioned, Graham's visual motor sequential processing is very poor and the score for processing speed at 0.3 of a percentile is a strong indication that academic work and the expectation of the production written information will be an enormous struggle.

His difficulties in Arithmetic are not unsurprising given his overall profile, and it is frequently found that children with attention deficits and dyslexic problems have arithmetical problems also. This is in part related to the working memory, and in some cases to their ability to calculate. It is important to separate out these tasks as they are separate skills.

In the Digit Span subtest Graham's score was much better than the Arithmetic but nevertheless still far within the moderate learner range. It is important to know that he was well able to engage in the rote task of repeating digits forwards but unable to repeat digits backwards, again a task involving the working memory and the holding and manipulating of information. This skill normally begins to develop around the age of 3.

Graham's best skills, in terms of picking up visual detail and therefore not involving any visual motor or language skills, were clearly evident within Picture Completion, on this occasion and previously. These excellent visual attention to detail skills were evident in other areas also.

Within the Object Assembly subtest, Graham enjoyed all of the puzzles apart from the face. This is a fascinating finding as many children with a problem which exists within the autistic continuum have difficulties understanding and discriminating between various facial expressions. When Graham looked at the face he said 'That's horrible'. As the face slightly looks to one side he attempted to put the eyes central to the jigsaw, and then stated 'It hasn't got a middle'. Cognitive perceptual issues were thrown up within Graham's management of this task. He managed to complete another task which involved a jigsaw of a football, but this took 3 minutes and 10 seconds when only 3 minutes was given in total, leading to no score for this item. Only the first two relatively easy items were completed. Given Graham's age and the fact that the WISC begins at age 6, the overall score for his performance in that area is still within the average, albeit low, range.

In the test of visual memory Graham had difficulty holding information within his mind and it is important to note that there were a number of intrusions, i.e. he recalled objects which were not part of the stimuli array, which reflects a divergence of thought processing and possibly a problem discriminating relevant from irrelevant.

There were also some signs of perseveration on the Coding subtest, reflecting poor inhibition of responses. Graham's comment that he was 'sweating' revealed the effort that this child had to put into this work. I have seen a number of children with similar disorders to Graham who become totally enraged by their inability to write or engage in highly focused written tasks. One child of Graham's age, with a similar level of difficulty, picked up an iron bar and swung it around the room, screwing up his paper and kicking the table away. Before the presentation of the stimuli that particular child had been calm. From the way in which Graham met this particular challenge it would seem that the treatment programme is beginning to work.

In the test for basic attainments Graham was still at the two word level, managing to recognise one word ending and another word beneath a picture. Given his overall IQ the score in this area is at the level expected. However, as previously mentioned, Graham has highly significant discrepancies and needs to be seen as a child with specific learning difficulties, which much more appropriately describes his problems.

Conclusions and recommendations

Graham continues to present with difficulties in relation to a pervasive developmental disorder, attentional problems alongside poor visual motor skills, and executive dysfunctions. As Ehlers *et al.* (1997) report: 'The syndrome of deficits in attention, motor control and perception [DAMP] (Gillberg and Hellgren 1996), executive dysfunctions are present in many cases (Barkley 1990), children with attention disorders often have mild autistic traits (Gillberg 1992). Thus Asperger Syndrome appears to share some neuropsychological dysfunctions both with autism and with ADHD/DAMP.'

Graham typically presents with difficulties in terms of crystallised cognitive function, as shown in his weakness in vocabulary and comprehension, and this is linked with his language and attention problems. In order to see improvement the focus will need to be intensified in these areas which are highly dependent on learning experiences. Graham's developmental difficulties linked with his neurobiological status will affect his ability to consolidate information which exists within his learning environment.

Performance subtests, Block Design and Object Assembly, which are reasonably intact in Graham, measure what is called fluid ability, which appears to be related to basic reasoning. With better concentration over time I would expect these skills to improve also.

Generally, Graham conforms more to the autistic than Asperger category, given his relatively poor crystallised cognitive function linked with difficulties in terms of being influenced by context. Wing describes this as a failure to 'seek out experiences and make a coherent story out of them' (Wing cited in Happé 1994; Frith 1989 refers to this as central coherence). Those working closely with groups of children with pervasive developmental disorders and attentional deficits will know that the profile of the particular individual child can vary over time and also that we are at the cutting edge of a better understanding of these complex and intertwining developmental disorders.

Regardless of which labels are used, it is important that after each thorough assessment that child's specific problems are focused upon. In Graham's case, his problems are severe, despite obvious improvement through medical treatment, and we can now see clearly a specific learning difficulty running alongside a language impairment, in part related to semantic pragmatic problems and frequently found within the autistic continuum and attention deficit disordered groups. Graham will be best supported at this stage within a unit for children where the development of language and social skills is a top priority. Alongside this there needs to be a teacher who is trained in TEACCH (Treatment And Education of Autistic and Related Communication-Handicapped Children) methods for the autistic traits and who recognises the needs of this population, and a teacher who is trained in work with dyslexic children. It is hoped that the improvements with the fine-tuning of the medication will improve and that Graham's difficulties with impulse control and self-regulation will be reduced, and his ability to relate to other people increased. The parents' understanding of the disorder is likely to lead to better management of Graham within the home, but he still continues to present with challenges. He will still watch a video for long periods of time if allowed to and will rock in front of it. It is therefore important that the family continue to be involved with the National Autistic Society, and in particular their new group which aims to help parents with children with these difficulties.

Recognition of Graham's severe problems which relate to a pervasive developmental disorder, attentional deficits, an associated dyslexia and variability of mood, is imperative within the local system. Given this recognition, an appropriate specialist unit based education, support for the parents and medication, we should begin to see significant improvements in this lovely little boy. Without these forms of support and recognition of his problems, I fear the prognosis is not good.

Tapestry kid

 # Trevor

Reason for referral

Trevor (aged 4) was referred for a psychological assessment given long-standing concerns about his poor communication and hyperactive behaviour. He had already been seen by a number of professionals and is the subject of a Statement under the auspices of the Education Act 1996.

Family history

There is evidence of ADHD on the maternal side of Trevor's family, and an 8-year-old second cousin has just been diagnosed ADHD. Trevor's mother reports being very clumsy, and becoming easily bored once she has reached the top of each job she has undertaken. She is also highly organised and would organise conferences for 1000 people. Trevor's father has a highly specialised job and is exceptionally talented at repair work. Both had very supportive and happy family lives and are caring parents who have sought out all possible explanations for their son's problems. Now that they have discovered that a normal disciplinary approach, whilst appropriate for other children, can make children such as Trevor worse, as they do not understand it. Trevor has a brother with no history of developmental or behavioural difficulties.

Developmental history

Trevor was born normally at 37 weeks following an elective caesarean. He proved to be a baby who was difficult to feed, and he would cough and projectile vomit frequently. On one occasion he had to be hospitalised for dehydration. He suffered from many colds and coughs. Whilst feeding Trevor would sometimes scream for no reason 'as if someone had made him jump'. He did not naturally hold out his arms to be held, look in the direction of a point nor point to anything of interest – he still does not point things out. Trevor would scream excessively and 'move his fingers a lot'. He did not cry when his mum left the room and was not at all clingy.

Walking and talking did not develop on time and by the second year his parents began to worry about his development. By the age of 2 years he still could not speak and so he was given speech and language therapy. He began to use single words at 2 years 6 months and sentences at 3 years 6 months. He continues to stutter sometimes. Trevor walked at 18 months but still cannot tie shoelaces. He has just learnt how to ride a bike with stabilisers. He would fall lots of times because of his boundless energy and this has resulted in hospital visits with blows to the head. At two and a half he had a laceration to his eyebrow and at 3 years he needed stitches to his head.

There were no noted incidents of loss of consciousness or reactions to vaccinations. Trevor's colds continued and he had to have regular hearing checks given fluid in the inner ear and a possibility that he would need grommets. Trevor's play was highly active and unusual. He would line up a variety of items such as bells, little ornaments, small cars, dominoes, conkers or cards. He did not engage in symbolic play and has just recently become interested in acting out traditional stories such as *Sleeping Beauty* with his brother but is not interested in the 'latest fads'. In play with other children he has not been interested in play, always wanting to lay down the rules, issuing orders and unable to realise when others laugh at him. He thinks he is making them happy. Trevor is not able to read the clues which should tell him to 'back off' from situation. He will often move very close to other children and then start making peculiar noises or waving his arms. 'He won't say hello or look at them – just go off and do his own thing.' There have been incidents of aggression and Trevor will sometimes hurt children or animals but is sorry afterwards.

Change is upsetting for Trevor, and he will become quite cross if expected routines are altered. He is also oversensitive to light and sound and to too many people. Among lots of people he is very likely to become loud and boisterous and 'even more excitable'. Trevor will ask questions excessively and will become frustrated if he does not hear the answer he is expecting. It is clear that communication is extremely frustrating for Trevor. He will misconstrue circumstances and cannot understand 'I don't know'.

Trevor continues to be fascinated by collections of things. 'It used to be pebbles from the beach, then conkers, coins and cassettes – now bells, all sizes and he will not share them.'

Professional involvement

A number of professionals have seen Trevor. His health visitor referred him at age 2 years 6 months to the speech and language therapist who reported that his receptive and expressive language were delayed. He was then referred to the paediatrician, who found that Trevor had 'significant language, social, interactional and behavioural difficulties.' Ultimately, and after a period in nursery when he was found to have considerable problems, the paediatrician diagnosed his problems as autistic continuum. He had problems interacting with peers, presented with semantic pragmatic problems and continued to engage in repetitive and obsessive behaviours.

The occupational therapist found that he had problems with fine motor control and dynamic balance and he began an occupational therapy programme. Trevor was also given pre-school educational support and music therapy which he loved.

A consultant paediatrician assessed Trevor and felt that he met the criteria for ADHD with some ODD features. In assessment he was found to be easily bored, a poor listener and flitting from one activity to another. Appropriate medication for ADHD was prescribed.

Trevor was also seen by the local psychologist, who stated that he 'experiences significant difficulties and it is evident that he needs a high level of informed individual support in order for him to be enabled to access the curriculum and make progress in his learning and general educational progress.' A very comprehensive list of forms of support was included in her report. In the Aims of Provision there was a strong accent on communication, which is to be expected given Trevor's communication problems.

The local speech and language therapist reports:

> Trevor will require considerable adult support within the class-room, to explain and clarify information. He will need specific teaching and role models of how to use the pragmatic elements of communication and this will be more effective within his daily

contacts with other children. Trevor will require speech and language therapy input. This should take the form of monitoring his progress and close liaison with staff in his educational environment.

Assessment by an independent speech and language therapist reports that Trevor has 'persisting communication difficulties which are now presenting as a semantic pragmatic impairment co-existing with and exacerbated by inattention, impulsivity and hyperactivity.' She goes on to say that Trevor would find it 'extremely difficult' to learn in a large group or distractible setting and that he would 'certainly benefit from a small group learning situation'. She recommends weekly speech and language therapy intervention to develop Trevor's listening and attention skills using specific strategies, his semantic skills and subsequently his word recall and precise choice of vocabulary as well as his social use of language and his understanding and interpretation of situations.

It is evident that all professionals recognise the extent of Trevor's communication problems but despite this, his Statement merely lists provision in Part Three, the expectations falling entirely on the school without including reference to multidisciplinary support within Part Three. Under Part Five 'Non Educational Needs' we are informed that 'speech and language therapy is indicated'. Given that his communication is of pivotal importance in order to allow Trevor access to the curriculum and that failure mixed with poor communication will cause deterioration in his behaviour which will further prevent access to the curriculum, I cannot understand how the LEA can argue that speech and language therapy is non-educational. The unfortunate 'behind the scenes' recognition of his needs which is not so forcefully stated in formal reports either from the school or the speech and language therapist is not helpful to this child, their professions or our society. The gravity of such methods is slightly reduced given the widespread evidence of such practice across Britain.

Trevor's school report dated July 1998 was positive, his teachers stating that he had made progress, but I note in letters to the LEA Education Officer that Trevor's behaviour was so difficult to manage, including other children being badly hurt by Trevor, that his teacher had become very disillusioned and the headteacher was worried that other families would sue. Quite appropriately, the headteacher asked the local authority for full-time support to manage Trevor's very difficult behaviour.

Subsequent to this time Trevor was prescribed Ritalin, which made a difference to his violent and overly boisterous behaviour but this was also a cause of concern to the school. They report that he 'has lost his sparkle' and that it is difficult to manage his behaviour. I understand that the school has refused to give Trevor this medication.

There have been long delays with various forms of educational support and given the long struggle, perceived limited recognition of Trevor's neurobiological problems, and his slow progress, the family have explored other school options. They also feel that a mainstream school with large classes cannot meet his needs, even if they felt that Trevor was properly understood and supported. Other professionals, less tied to the education department, have said the same. It is clear that the school also recognises Trevor's needs but is placed in a very difficult position, as are the parents, with Trevor in between.

His parents have noted a return of the 'startle' response which they saw when he was an infant, with Trevor frequently looking round to the right in a ritualistic manner. They feel that this is because he is among large groups of people.

Test results
Wechsler Pre-school and Primary Scale of Intelligence (WPPSI-R)
PERFORMANCE SCALE

	Age
Geometric Design	4 years
Mazes	Below 3
Picture Completion	4 years
Animal Pegs	Non-compliant

VERBAL SCALE

	Age
Information	6 years
Comprehension	4 years
Arithmetic	3 years
Vocabulary	3 years
Similarities	below 3

British Ability Scales (BAS-II)

	Age
Picture Similarities (Using Pictures)	8+
Verbal Comprehension (Kinaesthetic)	5 years 1 mth
Block Building	5 years 10 mths
Pattern Construction	3 years 7 mths
Recall of Digits Forward	3 years 4 mths
Immediate Verbal Recall of Objects (Using Pictures)	4 years 7 mths

INTELLIGENCE SCALE

	Score	Percentile
Immediate Spatial Recall of Objects	35	7th
Verbal Comprehension	48	42nd
Pattern Construction	29	2nd
Picture Similarities	69	96th
Immediate Verbal Recall of Objects	44	27th
Recall of Digits Forward	38	12th

Discussion

From the history and my assessment of Trevor it is clear that he is a highly vulnerable 'tapestry' child, as I refer to those children with the combinations of ADHD and autism. During the assessment, I witnessed his behaviour without Ritalin, after taking Ritalin, with his parents and without his parents. I understand the school's comments about the loss of sparkle and Trevor's parents were able to see how he was affected in a learning situation. It is well recognised that it can take some time to fine tune the essential medications for such children so that they can learn and careful monitoring and liaison between school and home is obviously imperative so that this can be successful. I understand the family are also well advised by the psychiatrist.

Despite the difficulties between the school and Trevor's parents, their separate scores for his behaviour in various domains using the Conners Scales were highly correlated. Both sets of scores were highly significant for hyperactivity and asocial behaviour.

It was clear that his performance wavered off Ritalin and he made a humming sound or talked constantly during tasks. He also had a facial twitch. As he became bored and before a break and a Ritalin he was rapidly giving up. He was completely perplexed during the Immediate Recall task in which a child has to be shown a card of pictures three times and asked what he can recall three times. He couldn't see the point and said 'I already looked'. He was also less inclined to tell me what he had seen, missing the point of giving information, considering it enough to have looked. Despite these problems and the need to cajole, he was still better at this task with the pictures as a stimulus than when he was simply asked to repeat numbers.

After the Ritalin had taken effect and Trevor had had a break, he was better focused, stopped making the noises but was rather distant. His medication is now managed slightly differently to help create a balance. Trevor proved to be more able to recall information when it was presented in object form which he could handle, as in for instance the BAS II Verbal

Comprehension compared with the WPPSI Comprehension or when he was able to use pictures to help retain information, as in Immediate Recall of Objects compared with Recall of Digits Forwards.

Crucially, in terms of future predictions and to inform his IEP, Trevor was excellent at a reasoning task in which he had to match pictures according to a similar concept (Appendix 1 gives details of this important test). Comparing his ability to engage in this pivotal test of intelligence using spoken language for most of the WPPSI task or pictures and cards which he could handle in the BAS II test, he performed at 2 years below his age on the WPPSI task and 3 years above his age on the BAS task! He is also reported to be excellent and well motivated on the computer.

Clearly, the use of visual/ kinaesthetic stimuli is vital for Trevor to learn. Furthermore, his ability on this Similarities test give a strong indication that he is a child of above average intelligence whose ADHD and autistic continuum communication problems are significantly disguising and restricting his potential.

His spatial ability is not well developed whether making up a pattern using patterned blocks, recalling the spatial orientation of pictures or using motor skills in drawing, and this has implications for his academic development.

Understanding arithmetic is also poorly developed and is a typical problem for many children with ADHD and overlapping Asperger syndrome.

We can see that Trevor has a good grasp of general information. He also has a number of learnt phrases which can give an impression of better social understanding. It is very obvious from the history and the assessment that Trevor has enormous problems of comprehension and with the social use of language. Given his score for Picture Similarities, which gives us an insight into a child's ability to reason without the mediation of spoken language, it is not surprising that he becomes extremely frustrated with his own difficulties with motor skills, including writing and drawing, reading, doing sums, speaking and relating to others.

Conclusions and recommendations

Trevor has a recognised 'tapestry' disorder combining ADHD, autism and related communication problems. My assessment finds agreement between all professionals, parents and the school with regard to the extent of this child's problems but his Statement lists only the support which the school is expected to provide. I would like to make the following recommendations.

The recommendation for a placement within a typical mainstream school is fatally flawed. Trevor cannot cope within large groups of people and his above average reasoning prevents his placement in an MLD (moderate learning difficulties) environment which may provide such small groups and specialised teaching. Trevor needs to be taught in a distraction free environment. His confusions and anxieties will increase with the number of people around him.

Structure, routine and predictability are of key importance to Trevor and need to be planned as part of his IEP. Speech and language therapy needs to be provided within the social contexts within which Trevor communicates but it is also essential that staff are trained in modes of response and that he is also enrolled in a 'circle time' exercise and other social communication group-based programmes.

Instructions need to be short, with Trevor's name spoken at the start of each instruction. Try using the touch–talk–gaze approach which essentially involves gently engaging Trevor with a hand lightly on his arm, back or shoulder, ensuring eye contact when the instruction is given. Within class Trevor also needs the support of a facilitator who can develop a baseline understanding of his strengths and weaknesses and liaise with other staff members.

Regular liaison with Trevor's parents is imperative and this needs to take the forms of telephone contact, daily home–school book with Trevor contributing and a relaxed and flexible weekly meeting. Ongoing support and advice from the medical professionals involved with the management of Trevor's ADHD are vital.

Trevor clearly has a learning style which responds best to visual and kinaesthetic stimuli. He will be more able to understand language if it is presented in this way. Trevor responds well to computers and this must be seized upon. There are a number of early years forms of software which will inspire him. Trevor needs also to be given the opportunity to learn keyboard skills and to produce stories on the word processor.

From the information available to me a small, specialist school will be able to provide much of the recommended forms of input, whilst recognising that structure is a crucial component which needs to be created in Trevor's day, as he does not have the internal temporal and spatial judgements to cope with it instinctively.

The class will need to have coloured visual timetables which he can help to make and various 'signs' which can be moved around using Velcro.

I wish Trevor and his parents the best of luck in their sterling endeavours with their engaging little boy.

Chapter Five

The threads of social engagement

Dance of life

This chapter begs the use of artistic licence to focus on the area which is malfunctioning for children with autism – the ability to engage appropriately with people through instinctive interweaving patterns of sensory, communicative and attentional skills. It briefly discusses some ideas about processes and mechanisms in normal instinctive responding.

Processes which breathe life into artistic representations, in the widest sense, can be mapped onto the emergence of life itself and unexpected glitches in these instinctive processes can be linked with the mechanisms which lead to the development of poor life skills.

The use of *tempo* and *rhythm* in music, *pauses* in film narrative, *colour* and *pattern* in art evoke imagery and emotion in the perceiver, and these processes can also be seen as crucially important in human behavioural development, emotional regulation and social awareness. If they are crucially important, they should help us with the development and planning of interventions.

Weaving real life into the process of developing social awareness requires a balance of colour and pattern perception, hidden from view like the prism of colour in light, precise and delicate symmetries controlling and guiding our development. Natural rhythmic alternating passages and interludes are bound up in the heartbeat, talking and whispering, listening and looking, playing and crying, laughter and tactile responsiveness. Fundamentally artistic, musical, tactile and olfactory features determine how the natural world's symmetries, hidden from view, the waves of chemistry, biology and the electrical charges weave together within the brain to create a balance of action, emotion and cognition.

Our combined senses interpret these complex perceptions in fixed timetables and in turn whole synchronous life tapestries are woven, tailormade as dynamic and distinctively human outfits – donned in the dance of life. The weave which creates the unique people-pictures is the culmination, the expression of the weave of common threads, shared with all others.

Without this woven dynamic effect we have no person-picture, no rich representation of the social self, no dance of life.

As we share the threads and make each collectively conscious metaphoric leap through our interactions, our tapestries are woven even more richly through the incorporation of each other's differences. This behaviour occurs instinctively in normally developing children and interweaves with instinctive reactions from others in the immediate environment. A world without people is no longer our world and a child with no connections with people is forever consigned to poor constructions, isolation, withdrawing and avoiding and/or fighting, criticising, suspecting and aiming to defeat.

The non-verbal intertwining process of communication – paralinguistics and metalinguistics – leads to more than just knowing how it feels to be in someone else's shoes – it requires the ability to incorporate and assimilate an understanding of its *properties* (Barkley 1997). We learn the subtle properties of others from the earliest stages of our existence in the womb through an increasingly complex instinctive capacity to interact with the sensations around us.

Glitches in basic brain systems and/or in early development through genetic mis-wiring, damage through illness or birth injuries and viruses can prevent the reciprocal dance of life from even starting. Instead, for the most seriously affected autistic children, they pirouette alone.

There is a tradition in the field of autistic continuum disorders of looking at normal early infant development in order to understand better what goes wrong in autism. Researchers interested in normal development also look to the intriguing lack of the most instinctive qualities in autistic children, looking for clues about normal development. We are intrigued to understand the timing and nature of differential development.

We have long desired to establish the ideal weave of the early communication tapestry, in order to better plan and execute our early interventions in autism and related disorders of communication. Sadly, some children will have irreversible problems and our interventions can never be considered as cures, though some children may make considerable improvements. Our aim must always be to push at those limits.

In the population about which we are concerned, about children whose problems have been described and have perplexed us since time began, our quest is to establish the underlying fault lines which prevent them from engaging with an appropriate environment. I do not claim to be able to provide any answers, but would like to contribute some observations.

The engaging trio

During the late 1970s and 1980s I spent a number of years on university-based macro-analytic research on mother-baby interaction from pregnancy through to the end of the first year. I became intrigued by what seemed to be instinctive and enduring behaviours which are played out in a balanced manner. The possibility that these crucial behaviours were part of a set pattern, part of an instinctive unfolding of a natural tapestry, became palpably clear. I became fascinated by a number of issues:

1. The most frequent behaviours in my 28 normal dyads were talk (any vocal activity), touch/hold and gaze activity, and the essential clustering of these behaviours seemed important. The multi-modality issues raised by Kuhn and Meltzoff (1978) made a lot of sense.

2. There was a turn-taking and imitative quality about interactions including gesturing, head turning and head angling which agreed with Clarke-Stewart's (1973) findings of *alternation*. This seemed to find a resonance with all the rhythmic cyclical patterning of various natural features, i.e. the heartbeat, and fitted with Trevarthen's (1981) theories of the musicality and dance-like quality of interaction.

3. *Pauses* within the turn-taking events seemed crucially important. Grossman (1988) felt that such pauses in interactions were to allow for *assimilation* of information and it has been proposed that such pauses in interaction with infants may link with prosody in language and may be related to developing skills of *reflection*. Does gaze link with the development of prosody? Others have noted the musical elements inherent in smooth synchronous engagement (Trevarthen 1979) in order to achieve attunement (Stern 1985).

4. These simple behaviours, first as basic as eye gaze, clearly designed to draw the carer and infant together, were also part of reciprocal and repetitive rhythmic exchanges shifting from one perspective to another, pauses functioning within the cycles of looking at/looking away possibly for assimilation of information.

The third feature was verbal communication, the parent 'talking' to the little infant who would imitate: the development of a rhythmic discourse clearly emerging. Lots of natural and cultural games and humour were also interwoven. More recent work by Reddy (1991) highlights the intrinsic value of teasing within early interaction.

By the age of 3 months pattern perception has been consolidated, so a lot of work has been done before that time, particularly in relation to interactions with people (Hobson 1993). It is interesting to note that humans perceive patterns of angles and edges and naturally seek out novel information, but are particularly primed to respond to faces.

Holding, touching and certain motor movements such as gesturing also seemed to be part of the salient reciprocity tapestry, this occurring alongside looking at and looking away – how did all this activity weave a sociable blanket for the human infant to snuggle into?

Normally developing human infants seem to have instinctive repertoires of complex behaviours which still occur even in the absence of very attentive families, but obviously our potential is improved by having a sociable partner in this early social dance. If we can establish the ideal weave of the early communication tapestry, our early interventions can be better planned and executed.

Work by Clarke-Stewart (1973) highlighted the importance of alternations in interactions and Kuhn and Meltzoff (1988) discussed the relevance of the multi-modal quality of interactions. Fogel (1985) referred to the possibility that touch was linked with empathy and in a later study Fogel, Toda and Kawai (1988), compared Japanese and American mothers in interaction with their infants. Fogel saw a lot of complex gesturing in the Japanese dyads and also noticed that there were fewer clashes in communications within these dyads compared with the USA dyads. In other words, the pauses within the Japanese mother's communications were left open for the child.

In the small group of 28 dyads in which the behaviours of touch–talk–gaze were the most frequent, I observed turn-taking from moment to moment creating pauses within interactions and an observed frequency count of an alternating pattern of mother, then baby behaviour taking over – more obvious in girls. This seemed reminiscent of Clarke-Stewart's alternations. Touch–talk–gaze frequencies reminded me of Kuhn and Meltzoff's (1988) research into the importance of multiple modalities working together and Fogel's suggestions that 'touch' may be linked with empathy struck a chord.

I felt comfortable, from others' work and my own observations, that there was something salient about this multi-modal cluster of behaviours, its instinct for balance and order, creating harmony between people. It followed that if an infant showed no motivation or ability to engage in such activities or failed to do so through illness, the subsequent expected interweave could not occur, or not as intensely as they should. One mother of three children told me that her autistic child was obviously different from the others the moment he was born (12 weeks premature). He did not mould into her arms, instead he 'sort of slithered'. Eye contact was never established with anyone, he gazed at lights and patterns formed by sunlight through blinds. All the weaving baby-carer work of reciprocal touch, talk, gaze in multi-modal action simply never started.

Eye gaze is part of reciprocal and repetitive rhythmic exchanges shifting from one perspective to another, pauses designed within the cycles of looking at and looking away possibly for assimilation of information, as Grossman (1988) suggests. Autistic children have significant problems with eye-gaze monitoring (Tantam, Holmes and Cordess 1993) and joint attention.

The instinctive nature of these behaviours has shown us that normally developing children will continue to develop normally even in the absence of the ideal reciprocal action by the carer. Even in studies of terrible deprivation which do seriously affect the child, normal infants can soon return to normal with even a short time of normal and loving child-rearing (Rutter 1996).

This confirms that there are some children who simply do not have the skills in the first place, and if they lose them, it is as a result of a serious neurodevelopmental glitch or damage as they simply cannot be brought out of these states by normal loving and nurturing practices, no matter how hard we try.

Work by Reddy (1995) has highlighted the crucial importance of *humour* in human interactions and how infants as young as 10 weeks begin to engage in 'teasing' activities through turn-taking and looking at and looking away.

Most people alter their style of 'chat' when involved with a young infant and the pitch, tone and rhythm is universal to all languages – a human communication rhapsody to which all normally developing infants respond.

The normally developing baby responds by imitating the smile and the movements and can respond to a smiling face even if it is not directed at them (Trevarthen 1979). If a child gives out the wrong signals the instinctive imitative and repetitive reactions of others could begin to falter. Howlin (1998) reports on a study in which mothers of children with autism and their children were brought together with mothers of normally developing children. In a carefully designed study it was clearly demonstrated that when the mothers of normally developing children played with the autistic children, their mode of communication became odd and stilted, as had been noted with the mothers of the autistic children. When the mothers of autistic children played with the normally developing children, their communications were normal.

Holding and touching the infant seemed to be part of the salient reciprocity tapestry, possibly linked with neural motor mechanisms and circuitry involved with the regulation of emotions. Face-to-face interactions involving looking at and looking away show the infant *mouthing* imitatively and making pre-speech sounds. The infant needs time to *pause* to absorb information and not be overloaded with stimulation, but angling the head and visual focus may also help the infant achieve wider perspectives – physics specialists can tell us a lot about the importance of angles altering the perception of light and colour.

Unlike the chameleon, whose interactions with the environment can be *seen* by the way the skin colour changes (is the chameleon colour change equivalent to the perception and expression of emotion in humans?) human interaction with colour occurs only at neural level – we do not have the benefit of the swivel eye and others can't see our rainbow skin.

From the complex interactive geometry and rhythmic behaviours, normal infants regulate their own emotional system in relation to others in a reciprocal manner and the reciprocal human emerges. We know that humans respond to touch which links with emotional responding and Fogel, Toda and Kawai (1988) link this with empathy development.

There is increasing evidence that baby massage in premature infants helps the child to engage with the carer. The mother of a baby boy born six weeks prematurely, with a family history of prematurity, autistic spectrum and ADHD behaviours, decided to use baby massage while the infant was still in his incubator. She continues to use the special techniques and special baby oils now he is at home. She says he 'loves it', his whole body relaxing while she gently massages his head, arms and legs. She feels surges of love for the child as she engages in this activity.

Differences have been found in synchrony between term and pre-term infants, the cycles of interactive rhythms seen as homeostatic mechanisms which regulate the system and having implications for the development of communication and language (Lester *et al.* 1985).

The third most frequent feature in my work in the early 1980s was verbal communication, the parent talking to the little infant who would imitate, the development of a rhythmic discourse clearly emerging. Lots of natural and cultural games and humour were also interwoven.

The full-term infants in the Lester study who achieved 'synchrony' had begun to show dominance in mother-child interactions at 3 months whereas the premature infants did not show dominance at this stage, or later.

Ozofsky and Danzger (1974) felt that there seemed to be an interrelationship between visual, auditory and tactile stimulation and the concept of bimodal organisation was discussed. Kuhn and Meltzoff (1988) refer to the specific multi-modal delivery of speech. They highlight the importance of visual and tactile cues in the perception of auditorally presented information. 'By 18-20 weeks of age infants relate the speech sounds they hear to the ones they see being produced' (Kuhn and Meltzoff 1988, p.263). This is also interwoven within a 'complex system of affect'. Fogel et al. (1988) and Grossman (1988) suggest that we should consider the development of affect alongside the development of cognition.

It seems that specific informational cues (linguistic features) are more easily understood by specific senses (Kuhn and Meltzoff 1988). It follows that tactile experiences convey aspects of meaning which operate in concert with meanings conveyed by visual experiences during auditory stimulation.

Trevarthen (1998) has found that infants are visually focused on their carer for the first three months of life, after which time they shift interest to objects in the environment. It certainly seems that during these first few months, when the baby cannot move away from his or her immediate environment, the normal infant is primed to engage in crucial perceptual games with the immediate environment.

Engaging with another person requires the infant to have *appropriate* eye-contacting skills, which people with autistic spectrum disorders fail to achieve. Indeed, poor eye gaze, in particular gaze monitoring in the first year, is felt to be one of the very few behaviours which form a cluster with lack of pretend play and pointing to share attention which, in turn, can predict later autistic spectrum disorders (Baron-Cohen et al. 1996).

Years of work with children with early developmental disorders such as autism confirmed for me that the glitch in the neurological development of these infants prevented them from engaging in these fundamentally important activities. For the group of highly active, sleep deprived and constantly crying infants who could go on to be diagnosed with autism and/or ADHD, it is clear that certain rhythmic functions were not developed, but unclear whether this was inborn; intrinsic to the child before the first year after failing to demonstrate and practise the skills; or a combination.

Problems occur when infants do not appear to have inherited such instincts or may be too ill to engage with them, creating delays in parts of their development. Some vulnerable children undoubtedly suffer reactions to vaccine and this further compromises their immune system.

Many shrink away from tactile experiences and many have poor motor control and limited gestures. Most fail to shift from an isolated and egocentric way of interacting with the world to one of interactive play, imagination and representation, or rapidly lose early normal skills as described above at a particular maturational stage. They develop a basic misunderstanding of meanings within their own and others' actions, language and gestures. In severe cases this misunderstanding develops rapidly. The communication problems within autism are so incredibly entrenched, often associated with increasingly aggressive responses to our interventions, that these children have broken our hearts for decades as we search and search for the window of light into their minds.

At one end of the communication spectrum the autistic infant is very self-contained, quiet, interested only in focusing on visual detail, almost stuck on the natural physics of seeing edges and angles and details, which our brains perceive, but unable to make the metaphorical shift, the perceptual leap to *imagine* the connected wholes. Increasingly less inclined to share with others through eye contact, games, looking or pointing, they may develop early babble but this often fades and does not shift into more complex language, or children may use unusual word forms or seem precocious in their use of language.

Other children spend the entire first year screaming with a poor sleep pattern. They are often more medically vulnerable and possibly allergic. Even if they have the basic skills to engage with others, their ability to take advantage of their opportunities within the family and wider environment are grossly limited. If they are born with the instincts, and these inherited and universal human skills are not compromised by the effects of their illness, which they could be if they have viral infection, appropriate family input should allow the child to pick up after a difficult few months. However, it is increasingly clear that a small proportion of vulnerable children develop reactions which interfere with brain and gut processes. A specific gluten- and casein- free diet can, in many cases, reduce the terrible screaming fits and tantrums. Ongoing recognition of this significant problem is crucial and educationalists need to be made aware that biological glitches are interfering with the child's cognitive and social development.

It is clear that it is the children with inherited and acquired disorders who fail to engage with their environment appropriately and that intense and quite specific interventions are necessary.

Children with autistic spectrum disorders, autism and ADHD inherited or acquired through glitches before or at the time of their birth or through viral infections later have fundamental problems with the following: rhythm, eye gaze, shifting from one perspective to another, turn-taking, reciprocity. Most either fail to shift from an isolated and egocentric way of interacting with the world to one of interactive play, imagination and representation, or rapidly lose those early skills at a particular maturational stage. The instinctive sharing of meanings within their own actions and gestures in relation to others has not been triggered.

Within the ADHD group it is increasingly recognised that the same kinds of problems are interfering with successful engagement with the world, but further down the spectrum and 'milder', to human observation.

All of these ADHD children who can appear to be sociable have tremendous problems with self-regulation, shifting, planning, which are all frontal lobe tasks. Many have real problems with multi-modal processing. In fact they often cannot deal with dual channel processing. They can't engage in interpreting visual clues and cues while listening.

One 23-year-old student with a long history of inattentive ADD behaviour, such as daydreaming, was regarded as rather eccentric as a young child. She would not appear to listen to instructions and would dash into roads. As she grew she was always late through being engrossed and stuck in one-track activity, unable to shift. Her over-attention to detail within such times often led to her being totally overwhelmed and unable to structure the detail. A very intelligent and creative young lady, she was able to tell me: 'I can't listen and speak at the same time'. She had to continue her train of thought in speech even when others were trying to engage in normal reciprocal chat. In many cases this typical one-track communication was interpreted as rudeness, the person locked in a monologue, unable to listen. But individuals with the problem, ADHD or Asperger or both, are unlikely to be able to return to the thought if they break off, the memory lost forever, they think, and there is also an emotional drive for completion. This can lead to intense irritation with the other person, and a likelihood that the other person will avoid future conversations considering them rude and self-centred.

Many autistic spectrum/ADHD children consider others to be rude for 'interrupting' them! In one case this was amply demonstrated when a young man with Asperger syndrome told me that people were constantly interrupting him and were very rude. An 8-year-old would shout loudly 'Excuse me!!!' if his mother or I dared to try to interact with him while he detailed, in precise order, his special interest.

Thinking in general terms, and recognising the obvious importance of developing early reciprocal skills, it seemed possible to me that there was more than just a survival purpose linked with late walking of human infants. A mobile baby would not be able to engage in the early baby work previously described. I reasoned that maybe we need to have the fixed canvas of a non-mobile infant in order to weave the reciprocal processes leading to the development of *self*.

Prior to the invention of baby seats, push-chairs and television, infants would *have* to be held a lot more than they are in modern society, and would spend most of their first year interweaving with the rhythm of human processes, the feel and sound of the heart beat of the carer while held. The sensation of the human touch, to be incorporated into the tapestry, perhaps helped rhythmic motor processes.

In Trinidad in 1995 at a Lifeline conference I was invited on to Breakfast TV to talk about early development and parenting. Tongue in cheek I commented, 'Babies can't walk until they are 12 months old because they need to be held' and this comment seemed to strike a chord with the presenter. This small island community had seen the importance of very early intervention for later problem behaviour, and incorporated this into its conference.

Balance is important: we cannot hold a child constantly, and infants need the times when they can look directly at the carer for eye work, to participate in turn-taking and visual games. It is the *balance* which matters.

But, clearly, non-mobile infants will spend more time being held during their first year than at any other time in their life and if this can be tolerated it must have a function which may be linked with processes of human engagement.

Years of work with children with early developmental disorders such as autism confirmed for me that the glitch in the neurological development of these infants prevented them from engaging in these fundamentally important activities. For those highly active, sleep deprived and constantly crying infants who go on to be diagnosed with autism and/or ADHD, it is clear that certain rhythmic functions were not developed, despite the best efforts of excellent parents.

When we consider the interpersonal difficulties of children with Asperger syndrome and/or significant ADHD through a trawl through their histories we find a familiar picture. Many have often been found to be children who, despite good homes and caring parents, could not be easily held, had problems with appropriate eye contacting and did not respond to the salient aspects of their environment such as the language of others, the faces of others and certain rhythmic interchanges. Instead they either cry incessantly, possibly rock or head bang or seem oblivious to those around them. Toward the end of the first year they are most likely not to look in the direction of their parent's look or in the direction of a point. Many are excessively active and this itself poses problems. Many parents say they knew something was wrong in those early months:

> He lifted his head from the cot just after he was born. The midwife couldn't believe it. It didn't take him long to work out how to roll and then climb. I couldn't turn my back for a second. He was out of every harness I could find.

One family said: 'He just seemed to look through us'. A mother with experience of raising other children said: ' I knew from the moment I first held her. She just didn't seem able to mould into my arms.' ' I just couldn't catch her eye,' said one father. 'He never did anything except yell. My husband used to drive him round and round the block to get him off to sleep,' said one weary mother.

The mother of premature twins (see tapestry kids Miriam and Rachel at the end of Chapter 2) showed photographs of her infants at a party with non-expressive faces and a rigid, rather squat mode of sitting compared with other same-aged full-term twins at the party whose faces were angled at each other and whose body language was animated. Their mother said: 'They always looked like that – whatever I did. They weren't interested in anything but eating'. The twins had learning difficulties and ADHD, and their fascinating language and lack of social awareness fits on to the autistic spectrum.

The excessive criers with a poor sleep pattern frequently seem to be more likely to have medical problems and to be allergic, often to basic foodstuffs such as milk. Their constant crying inevitably interferes with their early reciprocal babywork but there is also increasing evidence that the allergic child may have or may develop bowel problems which can be linked with their later recognised autism or ADHD and that vaccine and other medications and other environmental interventions may play a part in the acquired problems of these children.

> He had lots of medical problems in his first year and never stopped crying. It turned out he was allergic to milk and he was much better after he went on soya milk.

Dietary interventions made a significant difference to this child's restlessness as an infant, but he nevertheless continued to have developmental problems. If his early allergies had not been recognised his problems could have been much worse.

Other parents report children who had developed perfectly normally during the first year and up to the 18-month point and who then suddenly stop speaking or their skills gradually fade. 'We just lost him.'

The quiet 'good as gold' babies who go on to develop autism are not generally ill but they fail to be motivated by social clues and cues which should lead them into social engagement and reciprocity. Such babies often lie happily awake for hours, staring at the twizzling mobile, their own twisting hands, the red light on the video or the shaft of light playing across the room, but fail to attempt to communicate their needs to their carers.

As time passes parents of children on the autistic spectrum notice that their child seems to pick up on unusual aspects of the environment and into the second year they notice the emergence of repetitive routines and intense and/or unusual fascinations and less interest in people. It is as if the natural drive toward the novel becomes totally focused in one specific area and change in all other things is not tolerated.

> The first word he said was 'Superstar' because he had one in his mobile and watched the TV programme over and over again.'

Young Jack, one of two little brothers (see end of Chapter 1), had an abiding passion for things mechanical. When he saw highly detailed plans, just looking at them made him leap for joy.

> As soon as his Nana opens the door he will look beyond her and say 'Ooh, Nana you've got a big boiler!' When he saw plans of the central heating he jumped up and down in excitement.

During these early years and through the interweaving processes, children begin to engage with others, wanting to share experiences, the *sharing* being the most important feature and having developed as part of the process of the development of self probably in the early months of life.

For those with little knowledge of autism, the clear lack of a desire to share in the Kanner group through to an inability in the Asperger/ADHD group, has often been blamed on the mother and the child's environment. So many times I have read 'the child was unstimulated', implying that the mother had failed it, when usually their families were excellent parents, going to any lengths possible to help and encourage their child.

We now know that autism and ADHD occurs in all environments and in the most extreme cases even highly intensive daily support as part of a 24-hour curriculum may not bring that child back to his parents.

Working as a researcher on the *Sesame Street* project when London Weekend Television was deciding whether to buy the programme in 1971, my patch was a very deprived area of London in which the families had to walk down flights of stairs to get water from shared water taps. I vividly recall one occasion when a small group of children and I were watching a *Sesame Street* programme in which the yellow Big Bird appeared. The mother of the child living in these poor and deprived circumstances was an alcoholic but the child was totally normal in the way in which she rushed to share the experiences which she had seen. She squealed: 'Mummy, Mummy, Mummy – come and look at Big Bird!' That deprived child may develop other problems but her natural instincts were intact, emerging in spite of her circumstances. Whatever else happened to that adorable little girl she would not have become autistic (Blakemore-Brown 1999).

By comparison many children with reciprocity problems, including the very hyperactive and impulsive, *fail* to share their experiences with others and will fail to understand what others need in order to understand them. As time passes they can become angry if another person fails to pick up their meaning, as if by telepathy.

Weaving images of the world: the metaphorical leap

Infants and young children receive a hugely complex array of sensory information, which they need to process, using their emotions, perceptions and cognitions. For many with autism, the threads of interacting perceptions are so poorly woven that they can fail to move on from the basic level of emotional and sensory responses to process and retain that information appropriately, often becoming highly anxious and confused about the world.

We know that our senses interpret information which, when scientifically analysed, is not as we ultimately perceive it. Light is made up of wavelengths, which produce a spectrum of colours through light slowing down and forming an angle. Richard Dawkins (1998) described how we perceive the 'cacophony of light' in white light. The vibrations of sound waves are processed by our brains and filtered, focusing on the most salient and the most relevant. Our perceptions create images of a virtual reality.

For the severely autistic child these complex behind-the-scenes perceptions are not interpreted and woven into reciprocal tapestries. Many autistic children remain fixed on perceiving angles, not making the shift. Fundamental levels of emotion are not woven positively to aid development; instead, they rise dramatically with no reasoning interwoven to provide a balance. Instead of gradually fitting into the world they find themselves in free-fall out of it. But in addition, their perceptions of sound, light and people can be intense and frightening. 'Stop the noise in my head' screamed one of the two little brothers. For many, they are simply seeing, hearing and feeling 'pure' reality, the threads without the metaphorical and imaginative reciprocal weave.

Many people with autistic spectrum and ADHD spectrum disorders have enormous problems 'shifting' perspective from their obsessive fascination with complex ideas and aspects of things to the perspectives of people in reciprocal interactions. They insist on everything staying the same. Communication remains rigid and often even in those who have developed language this is usually concrete and literal and can be highly repetitive.

The Asperger group is notorious for going on and on about these fascinations, unable to shift out of them or to learn how to read the signs of others' boredom – from the normal non-verbal eye shifts through to more obvious yawns, picking up all their belongings and looking obviously at their watch through to clearing the entire room of people – every time.

Self-esteem or simply self

Repetitive self-talk is an important feature for very young children in play, their social work, which seems to help them absorb and consolidate information, which gradually becomes internalised as part of thought processing and increasingly abstract.

Many children on the autistic and ADHD spectrum need to be taught this instinctive skill. Some older children and adolescents talk 'out loud' to themselves, which can sometimes concern parents, but it is a normal process for the younger child just kicking in a bit late. After a phase of talking things through, out loud, as a guide, the child should shift to thoughts which guide action without needing to talk out loud.

The parents of one of our tapestry kids told me that they would hear him often guiding himself through chores and tasks. Occasionally this would extend to talking out loud to make believe friends. His parents told me how they heard him in his room, 'talking to himself in an American accent as if he had a roomful of friends'. This child (one of many) told me that talking to himself 'helped me understand things better'.

The skills of *reflection* are poor on the ASD continuum and in many on the ADHD continuum who overlap. Having failed to develop an awareness of the 'other', this in turn is not woven into their own sense of self. This affects more than social engagement.

Children with these problems seem to have a problem getting on with their work without a person hanging over them permanently. Researchers have found that when they placed a mirror near to an ADHD child, his work performance went up. Like the self-talk, the regulating quality of incorporating the 'other' into our world, like a monitoring process, seems valuable. In a school situation, a guide, consistently presenting a rule using appropriate language within a structured environment, helps keep the neurotransmission system on track.

Achieving engagement takes many forms over a life's course. The more verbal Asperger group is renowned for blurting out inappropriate comments, some of them enjoying a certain notoriety as they realise that their comments 'shock' or make people laugh. The normal methods of making connections usually do not work. One young man with Asperger syndrome would talk endlessly about the Thames Basin when he was only 5 years old. He told me that he was 'hopeless' with jokes and would watch how other students at school would 'hold the floor', which he could never do. He bought a 'book full of tacky jokes' and recalled them 'word for word' to make friends. He said that even then after he had told the joke the others would say – 'What???'

An interesting study also showed that people with Asperger syndrome are less suggestible than their normally developing peers. This is not a surprise as they do not assimilate shared ideas. In an experiment in which misinformation was provided to a group, the normally developing individuals clearly seeing the duplicity, the Asperger group exposed the duplicity and found themselves isolated while the rest went along with it. Such problems, which can include an acute awareness of injustice and strong desire to do something about it, do set aside the Asperger individual from others who prefer to fit in with the prevailing modus operandum. Conversely, Asperger individuals can fall foul of manipulation easily as they fail to see it and are seen as a soft touch. In a transparent attempt to please or to be accepted they can walk into many life traps set by 'normal' people!

Many obviously ADHD children, who may well have a tic disorder, have social communication problems and will often make peculiar involuntary high frequency squawks over and over again, most often when in groups of people, like some primitive attempt to interact. Our tapestry kid Graham has always done this. At first this behaviour is reinforced as other children laugh but over time this can lead to the child being excluded from games, others thinking he is 'weird', especially if they fall into the group of children who are fixed on 'imitation' without incorporation and can pull faces to match the sounds! Like a centrifugal force, this child can find himself hurled increasingly outside of the world in which he has no choice but to live. This makes the child's behaviours worse.

One 9-year-old child I assessed had already been diagnosed with ADHD and it was clear that he also had an autistic continuum disorder with a possible facial agnosia. He was monotonic, had clear semantic-pragmatic problems, could not put together a puzzle of a face, nor recognise it, and was increasingly playing with gangs of boys whose contorted facial expressions accompanied with ripe language shocked his neurotransmission system into action and he had no difficulty understanding their meanings.

One young man I assessed had spent his life confused about the features of his world. He came from a normal home but was unable to understand it. He mentioned his perceptions of a team game, an activity which he avoided as a child thereby reducing his chances of engaging with others and which led to bullying. 'I've looked and I've looked but I just can't work out what's going on.'

One highly intelligent young man with Asperger syndrome and obvious dyspraxia became deeply depressed by his inability to make friends, to play sports and to read and write properly. He was also taunted constantly which culminated in a suicide attempt, fortunately unsuccessful.

The fundamental problems deciphering the social cues and clues and the consequent inability to engage with others appropriately easily leads to social isolation:

> He wants to play but just doesn't know what to do. The others get fed up with him and make fun of him.

In time, the young person will want to find a girlfriend or boyfriend and it is likely that significant problems will present themselves. Either the person will be overly friendly, inappropriate in their friendliness, or withdrawn, invariably misreading the situation and unable to understand the feelings of the other person.

One young man with Asperger syndrome and ADHD was over the moon with excitement when a group of young women befriended him at college. He spent many hours at night working out how he should manage this piece of good fortune. His desolation was palpable when they had to make it very clear that their friendship was purely platonic. They had felt safe with him as he gave out no demanding sexual cues and he was interesting and funny in his unusual way of acting, thinking about the world and blurting things out which others thought but didn't say. But a young Asperger man still feels the pull of testosterone and is too young to appreciate what the friendship of those young women could offer him. He is also unlikely to recognise when he is being manipulated by those who see his unusual naive nature, possibly brilliant ideas and impulsive generosity in many cases, and decide to take advantage.

Another young man with Asperger syndrome and very severe dyslexia had been asked out one afternoon by a female student of the same age. He was so anxious that he was rendered speechless when he accompanied her. He waited until he knew she was not home the next day and left a message on her answer-phone saying he did not want to see her again as 'it was pointless.'

The mother of another male Asperger adolescent told me: 'He's always had problems with relationships. He would call girls "lady" and could never remember their faces'.

Flex was 25 years old when I assessed him. He had never had a girlfriend and had very poor eye-contacting skills. In his worst nightmares he 'couldn't imagine holding a girl'. He said: 'I can only get to talk to a girl two out of ten times – and when I do it all goes wrong'.

Pattern and colour

Many autistic adults can now inform us about their perceptions of a fragmented world. They talk about patterns and our assessments and observations reveal obsessive behaviours relating to patterns, colours and textures. One young Asperger student discussed how he saw the fractals between the branches when he looked out at trees.

A highly intelligent woman with autism was so introverted and gauche that counsellors over many years thought she had been sexually abused, and had put her through a great deal of suffering while seeking a 'disclosure'. She had studied Hebrew at university simply because she loved the pattern of the letters.

Another charming and passionate young ADHD American woman with Asperger syndrome, who adores *Star Trek* and who sent me a wonderful card with 'Data' on it, was always clumsy as a child, unable to cope with the rhythm and patterning of dance or gymnastics. She decided to take up the challenge as an adult of beating this problem after a degree in Russian and a lot of complications in relationships. She took up flamenco dancing, learning every detail of the pattern of the dance. She would have been magnificent.

Donna Williams (1998) talks of her own relationship with a complex visually fragmented world and has found that the use of appropriate coloured lenses has removed the distortions. Helen Irlen speaks of another autistic woman whose visual distortions were removed after wearing her lenses (personal communication). The woman said she could now drive but the world was 'boring'.

I have assessed many children with autism and with executive dysfunctions following head injuries of varying levels of severity. Each time I have found that they have perceptual distortions and these are removed by colour. For some people volatility is reduced. Does our perception of colour link with the brain processes which are also linked with social and emotional regulation and communication? Like the chameleon, humans do react to colour, and certain wavelengths, translated into perception of particular colours, engender certain emotions within us, like certain tones and rhythms within music. Common parlance talks of 'risky red', 'red flag to a bull', 'calming blue', 'green with envy', 'feeling blue'. One autistic adult could be stopped from a rage only by showing him red – mis-wiring here!

Links have been found with these distortions, removed by colour, and the magno and parvocellular structures behind the eyes which regulate perception of depth and pattern. The reticular activating system is also implicated (Robinson 1998) which links our perceptions of the world and our social development (Trevarthen 1998). Irlen (1983) found a range of difficulties associated with perceptual distortions which could be removed by colour, with the main focus initially concerned with the use of colour to remove distortions in reading for dyslexic students (Irlen 1991). Helen Irlen has pioneered the use of coloured lenses, each prescribed for the individual person, throughout the world. Increasingly links with other difficulties have been found including headaches, migraine and eyestrain.

It is likely that the medications which focus on the neurotransmission system, the application of colour, meditation and visualisation and intensive behavioural interventions to maximise the motivational system, are all involved in changes to brain function through the neurotransmission system which restores balance, improves perceptions and interactions with the world.

The sister of one of our tapestry kids developed a compulsive self-harming habit – despite a happy and comfortable home and a good job. She also had an eating disorder and was very overweight. In turn this made her very depressed and against going out, although she wanted to. Three weeks after putting on her new Irlen lenses she had lost 28 lb without trying. When she first wore them she said it was 'like the most wonderful massage, bathing my eyes'.

Observing others using Applied Behavioural Analysis (ABA: Lovaas and Leaf 1981; McEachin, Smith and Lovaas 1993) methods with pre-school autistic children, I have now seen the fascination with pattern and intense repetitive behaviour rise and fall dependent on the level of intervention. Interest in people emerged as the repetitive behaviour subsided in a number of cases and this fits with the typical development of the disorder in many cases. Some children had 'lost' acquired communicative skills at 18 months and parents saw that other skills were not built upon: 'He's just not learned anything at all in the last few months like other children. He just seems to have stopped.' Repetitive behaviours increased from this point.

Details of this particular approach will be briefly mentioned in Chapter 9 on Interventions, but for the purposes of this chapter on communication there are certain elements of the intensive use of the behavioural method within autism which I find quite fascinating.

The highly detailed body of research into ADHD and executive functions has looked in detail at the motivational system within the non-autistic group. The University of California Los Angeles (UCLA) project (Swanson 1988) found value in the intensive use of the same principles of behaviour modification. Barkley (1997), who was involved with Swanson in his work, states that we need to be creative to help the ADHD child externalise 'the internalised forms of information you desire the person with ADHD to be guided by (stimuli, events, rules, images, sounds etc.)'. This applies to autism. Barkley makes the point that even if we externalise these internalised forms of information – through timers, visual timetables, for instance – we still need to find a way of *motivating* the 'internally generated sources of motivation' linked with this information. We need to find salient stimuli and frequent rewards.

Trevarthen eloquently explains the biological mechanism which seems to be failing within the brains of children with autism, and the motivational system (driven by neurotransmission circuitry as it weaves in and out of perceptual, memory and emotion circuits) is explored (Trevarthen 1998).

Left to their own devices young autistic children, increasingly not motivated appropriately to engage with others, will become more and more angry
when we intrude. As they sink into a world of pattern and colour and detail, the
world of people becomes less and less relevant. But, if we can intrude with
novelty, with detail, with interactive processes, intensively, creatively, using
motivators, musical, colourful and visual stimuli, we may mimic the processes
of early engagement in which the same processes take place imperceptibly.

New creative and non-aversive forms of interpretation of basic Applied
Behavioural Analysis (ABA) methods aim to focus upon tiny targets which are
repeated over and over again in various forms to consolidate information. The
methods are also of a long duration, intense and daily but have been shown to
make a difference at some level, to even the most severely affected children
with no language.

Furthermore, the need for motivators through the use of ABA are also
proven at a less intensive level with the ADHD child, but Barkley also makes
the point that artificial forms of motivation must be 'maintained over long
periods of time or the gains in performance they initially induce will not be sustained' (Barkley 1997).

Therefore, research in both autism and ADHD recognises the fundamental
problems related to the internal motivation to initiate and sustain goal directed
behaviour, the need for methods such as ABA 'at the point of performance'
which, in relation to autism, needs to be early and in the home, if possible,
where the first communications develop. The quite clear need for consistency
between those working with the child exists alongside the need for long-term
intensive support.

A musical interlude

Music reflects the rhythms and tempo within basic normal development and
triggers emotion. Musicality within infant-mother communication is well
recognised in the literature (Papousek and Papousek 1981; Trevarthen 1979),
'mother and infant both adjusting the timing, emotional form and energy of
their expression to obtain intersynchrony, harmonious transitions and
complementarity of feelings between them in an emotional partnership or
"confluence"' (Trevarthen 1993, p.57).

Truly simple instinctive processes are woven into people interaction in
order to engender and sustain relationships, and I risk being misunderstood but
would like to use music to elaborate on this point.

I have sought permission to use the lyrics from a song by Tony Wine and Carole Bayer-Sager, most notably sung by Phil Collins, in order to illustrate engagement through the weaving together of the tapestry of rhythm, emotion and touch–talk–gaze basic interwoven modalities.

The night before I discussed this and referred to the song at a conference in Birmingham UK (Promoting Parenting Skills; Springboard to Success September 1998) I read a newspaper article about a paper (Dowker, Hermelin and Pring 1998) presented that very same week in Cardiff, in which the work of the savant poet Kate was discussed. I was struck by the asymmetry between 'Groovy Kind of Love' and Kate's poem and will briefly compare them.

Basic modalities are used to engage in rhythmic interchanges in order to develop shared meanings and to make each other happy. Many love songs draw simple but powerful images which can be superimposed on the tapestry image of normal infant interaction with the carer. For the infant who simply cannot engage in such a way the world can be isolated and confusing. The lyrics of 'Groovy Kind of Love' reflect quite simply some of the fundamental features which make up interactions which achieve engagement, cementing human relationships and lifting the human spirit.

Weaving the power of these lyrics with music seems to me a reflection of how the brain works to achieve such forms of engagement. The various sensory processes occur in rhythmic patterns, like the beat of the heart – a modern love symbol.

Groovy Kind of Love

When I'm feeling blue
All I have to do
Is take a look at you
Then I'm not so blue
When you're close to me
I can feel your heartbeat
I can hear you breathing in my ear
Wouldn't you agree
Baby You and Me Got a Groovy Kind of Love
When I'm in your arms
Nothing seems to matter
My whole world can shatter
I don't care

Wouldn't you agree
Baby You and Me Got a Groovy Kind of Love

(Tony Wine and Carole Bayer-Sager 1965)

In these lyrics we find the colour blue representing sadness, changing through looking at (the gaze effect); touching/holding/feeling; and hearing natural rhythms – breathing, the heartbeat. When held, touched, worries drift away; 'nothing seems to matter', there is agreement, synchrony and reciprocity.

As humans we have the power to think in abstract ways and are primed to relate instinctively to others through complex brain patterning involving multiple interwoven neurological processes linked with our senses – including touching, seeing, hearing and talking through a rhythmic process, like music – and the ability to interrelate in synchrony to these human musical forms.

Development involves interwoven operations. How can music or the lilt of the human voice trigger emotion, the gentle touch soothe the senses or the powerful gaze of the new mother draw the child into the social world if the brain cannot perceive it?

If these latter mechanisms fail appropriate powers of abstraction about people and in turn about self cannot develop – failure to incorporate the 'other' into our experiences in positive and reciprocal ways leads humans on to socially isolated and, in some cases, socially destructive paths. We have these two powers of emotion and cognition so that we can coexist, trust each other, feel empathy and be successful in societies. The rhythmic interweave of emotions and thought is crucial to an individual's development and to prevent social isolation and destruction.

Most autistic people cannot weave these connections into the dance of life. Isolated and sad, unable to trust, alone and forever picking up the pieces that wouldn't thread together.

Remarkable Kate (Dowker, Hermelin and Pring 1998) refers to herself as a 'puzzled jigsaw'. Kate writes (no music):

> *I was contradicting my own patterns very intelligently*
> *till society hit me*
> *I knew my own patterns to create much leisure, pleasure, safety,*
> *till society whacked me*

(Dowker, Hermelin and Pring 1998)

We have always felt that people with autism should be given the opportunity to engage in this behaviour 'to create much leisure, pleasure, safety' especially as they protest so terribly when 'society whacks them', have so little and can expect to spend their entire lives dependent on others. There is a greater optimism that certain forms of support can create change, to help them reweave these patterns so that engagement with others emerges, especially as some adults with autism can share their childhood experiences with others and can tell others what helped/helps them.

For very young children there are now new opportunities to enable some to *emerge* from this lonely state.

The autistic person's relationship with detail and pattern is remarkable because all their intelligence is used to manipulate it and remain safe within it. The work of adults with autism and Asperger syndrome has helped us enormously to understand these conditions; Temple Grandin, for instance, recognised the importance of touch but couldn't tolerate it, so she built her own 'touch machine' (Grandin 1992). The savant poet found by Dowker, Hermelin and Pring (1998) can now add to this knowledge.

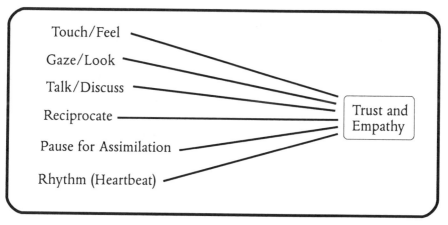

The poem
By Kate

I put out my hand but your hand avoids my hand
I cannot get close to kiss you
I open my mouth to say I love you
But your mouth is closed to me
Silent silence between us
Did it end when I was not looking?

This poem contrasts well with 'Groovy Kind of Love' in terms of how engagement occurs or fails to occur/how it is sustained and the emotional effects.

In the latter, the looking and holding, the feel and sound of the heart beat serve to reduce the 'blueness', the loneliness, Kate's terrible, palpable silence, to breathe life into their contact, their engagement. The holding means the world can shatter and all will still be well.

For Kate, there is no 'touch'– 'I put out my hand but your hand avoids my hand'; no 'gaze' – 'did it end when I was not looking?' And no 'talk' – 'your mouth is closed to me – silent silence between us'. Unable to interweave these processes instinctively, her world has shattered into the patterns she must 'contradict' to keep her mind alive, herself a 'puzzled jigsaw'.

There is no 'talk' – the 'silent silences'. No music.

Revealingly, Dowker, Hermelin and Pring (1998) find that Kate referred more often to aspects of self-analysis than a comparison poet and 'made less use of rhyme and alliteration'. Temple Grandin speaks of her inability to understand rhythm (quoted in Attwood 1998) and of her tactile defensiveness. She made herself a 'squeeze machine' as she knew this 'holding' process was important but could not bear to be touched or held by another person.

Problems with understanding self, with rhythm and temporality, tactile defensiveness and auditory sensitivities are threaded through Asperger tapestries and many ADHD tapestries.

Some forms of meditation involve mechanisms which include a focus on auditory processing and use the squeeze machine principle. Those who have used it have found themselves more able to engage with people afterwards. The person lies on a 'specially undulating couch which moulds itself to every contour of your body'. Speakers are wired up to the chest. The specialist says that the principle is to 'fascinate the sensory system, in particular the ears. The melange of sounds includes the heartbeat'. He also feels that 'it works' because 'it is not made up' and it is 'an adaptation of spiritual technology practised by sages'. A deep sense of relaxation is achieved and the writer said, 'your thoughts become clear…it turns down the chatter in your mind.' Revealingly, he finds this method is useful for 'people who suffer from anxiety, an inability to express themselves, difficulties in relating to people in general, or their partners' (Lorna 1999, p.34).

For many with Asperger syndrome and ADHD, their lives are spent on trying to work out their own minds and motivations, constantly engaged in what others see as egocentric and self-indulgent behaviour.

Given what we know about the development of communication, we may reasonably speculate that problems with rhythm and temporality may interfere with the development of self in relation to their impact on various sensory, emotional and cognitive processes, to their understanding of others and in turn our relationships. Just telling other people about the often deep feelings they experience can be impossible, making the 'normal' person think they don't care and pushing them further and further away.

It is therefore not at all surprising that attempts to engage in self-analysis form the features of the private poetry of the sad and lonely Kate with Asperger syndrome as she spends her life 'contradicting her patterns' but never manages to weave them into the tapestry of the social self. Her obsession becomes her 'self' – there's no one else.

For many males with severe communication disorders, rage and anger define them. If the limbic brain acts alone, other structures shut down which relate to cognitive processes; a person is unable to reason properly or to read social clues and cues.

Take the example of Casey, the furious and wildly active boy who had a wonderful grasp of complex words and a fascination for human mechanical processes but was confused amongst people, threatened by eye-to-eye contact and instantly distressed when he had to reason – in his distress a simple word could trigger fury. The process of reasoning did not connect with the emotional system. When Casey tried to reason, the flood of emotion drowned it all, like a tidal wave crashing down the canyon of his mind, glancing the rocks of human imagination, memories, perceptions of others' responses, unable to attach, unable to connect or get a hold to listen or understand, finally coming to rest exhausted and desperate, rationality glinting through the clouds above, reflecting a hint of the recall of his actions.

Like the wreck of the *Titanic*, treasures of the mind drown, the music drowning with them. He needed to be held once he came back to earth in order to recover – rocking calmed him, his fascinations and obsessions the only stable rocks he could hold onto, his potential a shipwreck sunk in the fathoms of his mind.

Emotions, rhythms, perceptions and abstractions, communication woven in a synchronous tapestry of reciprocity culminates in the most beautiful and dramatic musical event – being a reciprocal being in the real world – this social world.

We now have new ways of exploring the deep, of raising shipwrecks and of recovering treasure – we can restart the music to reweave the tapestry.

Tapestry kid

Jamie

Reason for referral

Jamie (aged 8) was referred for a psychological assessment, given a diagnosis of Asperger Syndrome and a dispute between the LEA and the family with regard to future schooling. The purpose of this assessment is to ascertain Jamie's needs from an independent specialist perspective. I have had access to a comprehensive file of information, which clearly describes a child with classic Asperger syndrome, allergic features and poor perceptual motor skills.

Family history

Jamie's father is a naive, literal and poorly co-ordinated man who has had many jobs, having had to leave when he became so 'paranoid' that he lost trust in people, unable to understand their thinking to anticipate their plans and intentions or to decipher their emotions. He was easy going but felt that others were 'getting at him' and chose to avoid them. He also avoided reading and writing.

Developmental history

Jamie was born at full term by the use of forceps following a normal pregnancy and long labour. Nurses often 'lost' his heartbeat. He did not cry. The midwife referred to him as one who had 'been here before'.

Jamie needed to be tube fed as he had a poor sucking reflex. He also slept excessively and was given hospital tests for his excessive sleeping. He went on to be a very passive infant who did not respond appropriately to his environment and to his own internal needs.

Protodeclarative and protoimperative pointing did not occur and Jamie was tactile defensive (could not tolerate touch). He began to use single words at 12 months, which did not translate into more complex language forms. He was 5 or 6 years of age before he could easily construct sentences and even then his speech was not clear with distortion of vowels. He can still slur his words.

Walking skills were slightly delayed with Jamie walking at 16 months. He went on to be exceptionally clumsy; he 'often falls over nothing'. He frequently fell on his head and has been taken to hospital on three or four occasions with apparent concussion after a fall. At the age of 3 years he lost consciousness while at playschool, hitting his head on a wooden floor.

In terms of play, Jamie did not engage in symbolic play or indeed any form of play. He copied adults and did what they asked him to do. Jamie did not show any interest in other children, and continues to have problems in this respect. He likes to be involved with people but on his own terms, usually involving telling them what to do or, lately, trying to 'sell' them one of his business ideas.

Jamie had ENT problems as a pre-schooler and illnesses developed in relation to these problems and in relation to change. He now reacts to change with agitation and occasional illness.

There is a history of poor attention, lack of concentration and distractibility with Jamie's mind 'usually on overdrive'. He has no temporal judgement, has become obsessed about making money but 'will happily give money away'. Jamie has a number of sensitivities and motor stereotypies. He will react variously to light, sound and too many people. His eyes often water in bright lights and he will become angry and confused if uncertain about people and their intentions.

Comments used to describe Jamie include 'very endearing', 'a genius', 'eccentric', 'little old man' and 'been here before'. He learns in a rigid manner in incremental leaps and has a number of obsessive behaviours. Currently his special interest is 'business' with Jamie taking every opportunity to set one up and make money. His mother said this all started with a relative offering to pay him if he had a bath and there has been no looking back! He used to fail to see 'the point of things but now the point is - money'. He goes to the extent of including bar codes and of setting up contracts which people have to sign. He wrote out a strike notice on one occasion and 'permanently fired' his mother from her particular role in his elaborate plan. Despite this obsessive interest, his written presentation is very poor given his motor problems. Jamie is particularly interested in numbers, but they must be even; he says 'odd numbers are crap' and shares this view with his teacher!

Jamie can become aggressive through confusion and frustration and will always put blame for his own behaviour onto others. He will take words very literally and can become angry if he has misconstrued meaning, which is frequent. His mother has known him to 'cough and cough with anxiety'.

He is a child who does not have the internal cues to tell him if he is hungry or thirsty, cold or hot. He has problems judging where he has pain, rarely informing his mother if he is in pain. After being bullied at school he is unable to explain the bruises or cuts. Whilst Jamie is capable of clearly explaining things in theory he cannot easily translate this knowledge into action. His mother reports that he is getting worse socially, finds school increasingly irrelevant and she fears he will end up a social outcast.

Professional involvement

Over the years Jamie has seen a number of professionals who have focused on specific aspects of his functioning. He has been described as dyspraxic, which is a frequently found feature among those with Asperger syndrome; poor motor function actually forms one of the criteria for this condition in the Gillberg and Gillberg (1989) list. A sole focus on dyspraxia fails to treat the more fundamentally important social communication problems pivotal to the condition.

Speech and language therapists focused on his expressive language and he was discharged once his expressive language improved, with no support provided for his social communication. Recently he has been seen again with the conclusion that he 'presented with speech and language skills within the average range for his age' and, within a one-to-one, he was able to maintain and shift topic. It was noted that he was easily distracted which led to errors. In a larger group we can expect this to be a greater problem. Although his use of spoken language was not seen as a cause for concern it was recommended that various forms of support would benefit Jamie.

The consultant paediatrician recognised that the cluster of problems experienced by Jamie fitted into the autistic spectrum and he was diagnosed as having Asperger syndrome.

Educational psychology became involved with Jamie in 1994 with his most recent comprehensive assessment occurring in June 1997. His patchy profile was mentioned, his good reading alongside poorer comprehension of what was read and his social impairments. Psychological assessment using the Wechsler Scales revealed considerable between-scales discrepancy and discrepancies within his verbal profile. Various recommendations were made which included 'Access to a broad and balanced curriculum...he will need a curriculum which primarily focuses on his complex needs' as identified within the report. 'Structured programmes, adult support to provide encouragement in social communication and modelling in a one-to-one situation plus an individual programme planned by an advisory teacher related to the development of his communication skills.'

Test results
Wechsler Intelligence Scale for Children (3rd Edn UK) (WISC)

Average Range = 8–12 with 10 being average and with a range from 1 to 19
Symbol Search Scaled Score = 7
Age = Below 8 years 2 months

British Ability Scales (BAS II)
INTELLIGENCE SCALE

	Score	Percentile
Immediate Verbal Recall	38	12th
Immediate Spatial Recall	30	2nd
Delayed Verbal Recall	39	14th
Delayed Spatial Recall	31	3rd

CORE SCALE

	Score	Percentile	Age equivalent
Word definitions	60	84th	12 yrs 3 mths
Pattern Construction	38	12th	7 yrs 7 mths
Matrices	52	58th	11 yrs 3 mths
Verbal similarities	66	95th	14 yrs 3 mths

DIAGNOSTIC SCALE

	Score	Percentile	Age equivalent
Quantitative reasoning	39	14th	8 yrs 8 mths
Speed of information processing	31	4th	6 yrs 4 mths
Recall of digits forwards	53	62nd	11 yrs 9 mths
Recognition of pictures	36	8th	5 yrs 10 mths
Recall of digits backwards	41	18th	10 yrs 9 mths

ACHIEVEMENT SCALE

	Percentile	Age
Number skills	12th	8 yrs 9 mths
Spelling	53rd	10 yrs 3 mths
Word reading	66th	10 yrs 9 mths

Discussion

Jamie is a little boy with clear Asperger syndrome with co-morbid ADD (without hyperactivity) and Irlen Syndrome. He could also be said to fit the criteria for DAMP syndrome (Gillberg and Hellgren 1996) as the criteria involve motor perceptual problems and attentional deficits and it is noted that many show signs of Asperger Syndrome.

Current knowledge informs us that both the Asperger group and the ADHD group have executive dysfunctions and that the pre-frontal cortex is implicated. The pre-frontal cortices have a much more central and pervasive role in human cognition than is usually recognised (Pennington and Ozonoff 1996).

In 1819 Burdach called the frontal lobes 'the special workshop of the thinking process' (Rylander 1939). Skills such as planning, problem solving, set shifting, time and working memory are linked with this processor. People with Asperger syndrome, including Jamie, have considerable problems in these areas, often over-focusing on particular activities and unable to shift. Motivational, perceptual and memory skills are also linked and need the central executive to engage in meaningful activity. Other parts of the brain are felt to be implicated with regard to social communication in this group but the important point about reference to executive dysfunction is that it prevents the individual from manifesting what is regarded as their potential from IQ and attainment tests.

From my assessment we can see a similar profile to that found by the local psychologist. I used the British Ability Scales II (BAS II) for validity, as the local psychologist had used the Wechsler Scales within the past year. I was involved in the standardisation research for the BAS and find its structure very useful. Looking at the results we can see that the core scale is split into Verbal, Nonverbal and Spatial. As expected Jamie was significantly better on the verbal items, scoring very high percentile scores for Word Definitions and Verbal Similarities. By comparison his spatial skills were particularly poor with Jamie achieving a percentile score of 12 and an age equivalent of 7 years 7 months when tested at 10 years 3 months. His Quantitative Reasoning, involving a motoric component, was also poor and at odds with his score for mental arithmetic with the local psychologist. Clearly when motor tasks are introduced Jamie has extremely significant problems.

On various tests within the diagnostic scale, Jamie manifested severe problems in Verbal and Spatial recall of pictures and a related very poor score for Recognition of Pictures in which his functioning was at the 5 year 10 month level. He was also very poor on the Speed of Information Processing subtest with a functional age of 6 years 4 months. His best score in this scale related to the rote task of recall of numbers forwards. His performance was much worse when he had to recall them backwards. (The Wechsler Digit Span undertaken by the local psychologist adds together both Forwards and Backwards recall and we lose the detail.) I would expect that Jamie was better on the Forwards rote task and poorer on the Backwards test, tapping working memory skills.

Jamie's achievements were broadly as expected. He is much worse at written arithmetic than mental arithmetic, as tested locally.

When I walked into the waiting area to collect Jamie, I observed him to engage in arm flapping. He came in for the assessment and immediately began to behave as if he were the one assessing me! He proudly showed me a number of business items, setting each one down and describing them rapidly, following this with – 'and they are just £29.50 per set'. He was actually quite persuasive, but I declined the offer and we got on with the assessment.

He persevered with the long test and in a novel one-to-one situation he still has motivation. He was clear about which things he could not do, for instance Pattern Construction (similar to Block Design). He said: 'This is impossible for me.'

I was impressed by Jamie's skills in important areas such as Similarities and Word Definitions. Unfortunately, many people with Asperger syndrome present with a similar promising profile but have such crippling problems related to the executive dysfunctions, social impairments and motor skills that they easily lose motivation to succeed, especially in written work, and become increasingly obsessed by the rigid, one-track verbal interests, often boring or irritating to others, producing less and less work.

As we can see the skills required to produce work which would match Jamie's verbal abilities are very poorly developed. To make judgements therefore about his needs on the basis of these high scores would be failing Jamie. As Howlin has written:

> Although often described as a 'mild' variant of autism, the symptoms of Asperger syndrome are, in many cases, just as pervasive and as devastating as those of less able children. However, because of their relatively high cognitive ability, and their apparently competent use of language, this group of children is often least well served or understood. In fact, many have extensive linguistic and comprehension difficulties (especially involving abstract or complex concepts); their understanding of the more subtle aspects of social interaction is often profoundly limited, and their obsessional interests and behaviours also prove a barrier to social integration. However, only a minority receives any specialist provision. Most have to cope in mainstream with little or no help. The children's good vocabulary, and their well-developed obsessional interests, frequently give the impression that they are capable of far higher levels of achievement than is actually the case. Others' expectations of their social and academic potential tend to be unrealistically high, and when these expectations are not met the children are viewed as negative, unco-operative, unmotivated, or rude and manipulative. Seemingly so close to 'normality' there is constant pressure for them to 'fit in' in ways that would never be demanded of a less able autistic child. This can lead to enormous pressure, resulting in extreme levels of anxiety and stress, which in turn further impede social and educational progress. Because of their very uneven profile of skills and deficits, these children may require even more highly specialised help than those with global learning difficulties. (Howlin 1998b, p.317)

Conclusions and recommendations

Jamie's mother and grandmother are both fully aware of the peaks of Jamie's performance and they are also aware that he has never met his potential and is unlikely to do so. They want to see Jamie in a structured environment in which communication is central to the applied curriculum and sewn into it. They recognise his need for small classes, a predictable day and one-to-one support from specialist teachers. In their local search they have found a school for children with moderate learning difficulties, and certainly many of Jamie's skills fall into this category.

Ideally Jamie needs to attend a specialist school for children with autistic continuum disorders and the other children need to have a similar high level of functioning. Knowledge about Asperger syndrome amongst the staff is imperative.

Programmes such as the Social Use of Language Programme are very helpful for groups of children with social communication problems, currently not addressed at all within school. The flexible use of the TEACCH procedures will also help Jamie and he needs to learn about himself and others through photographs and video.

Given Jamie's considerable motor problems he urgently needs to become proficient on a laptop computer and to have this available to him throughout his schooling. Jamie's eyes actually watered when engaging in the Irlen screen and I would therefore recommend that he has a full diagnostic test with a view to glasses being prescribed.

I look forward to hearing about the progress of this very interesting little boy.

Tapestry kid

 # Phillipa

Reason for referral

Phillipa (aged 9) was referred for an independent psychological assessment to ascertain her needs and to establish whether these are being met, given the introduction of the Code of Practice which led to the cessation of Phillipa's Statement of Special Educational Needs. (SEN).

Developmental history

Phillipa was born following a normal pregnancy and delivery. She was reported to be a happy infant who didn't need much sleep. She was a baby who didn't like to suck and wouldn't breast-feed. By 4 months she was fed by spoon. She didn't like to lie in a prone position and didn't crawl. Her parents cannot recall Phillipa being particularly interested in sharing her attention with others, preferring to engage with the world around her in a more insular way. They reported that she loved to look at things, but on her own terms.

Once walking Phillipa was extremely active, and the parents recalled how Phillipa would normally be pushing a pushchair whilst others would be asleep within them. Sleeping has always been a problem, and this continues. She will go to bed at night but just cannot go off to sleep.

Motor difficulties were in evidence from the earliest days and Phillipa has had treatment from that stage to date from the physiotherapy department in the local hospital. In her play as a young child she had a tendency to line up dollies, and would imitate events which had occurred around her rather than develop her own imaginative play. She engaged in a number of repetitive routines, insisting on wearing a red hat having been told that she looked like Fireman Sam in it, whom she watched and read about constantly. She also carried a plastic bottle around with her everywhere. She has always had a tendency to be interested in particular television programmes and to want to watch these repetitively.

Phillipa has never showed a particular interest in building constructions and generally is not keen on games, becoming bored quickly. She has never engaged in symbolic play. Phillipa will tend to flit from one activity to another rather than to focus on one thing.

In terms of Phillipa's relationships with same-age peers, this has always been a problem. Parents report that her behaviour tends to be inappropriate, and she would want to be involved but behaves in a socially clumsy manner which causes other children to isolate her. Essentially she has problems with the fundamental skills of interaction. Whilst she can pick up on some cues this is not intuitive and other children recognise social awkwardness.

When Phillipa attended playschool she would remain isolated inside the Wendy House. She is not a competitive child and, given her poor motor skills, doesn't have the opportunity to engage with peers, even within a sporting situation.

Professional involvement

Phillipa attended for physiotherapy, the purpose of this being to improve her motor organisation and motor planning skills. Her parents have tried to engage Phillipa in other groups held for children with dyslexic and dyspraxic problems. Within small groups of, say, three children, Phillipa has enjoyed herself, but has still needed one-to-one attention. When the support is removed she is reported to be quite lost.

The physiotherapists have noted tactile defensiveness and immature sensory motor development. It is noted that she would benefit from sensory integrative therapy. Phillipa's poor ability to make eye contact was also referred to, as was her difficulty in coping within the playground, where she was reported to be apprehensive.

Many recommendations were made in order to improve the variety of problems previously reported by the physiotherapists. In addition, during 1992 Phillipa was seen by the occupational therapy service which assisted and advised the family on activities which would help Phillipa. Reports by the occupational therapist in February 1995, which were set within a care plan, referred to Phillipa's problems in terms of concentration throughout a whole session, while engaging in table-top activities. It was also reported that Phillipa was still fidgeting but that motor organisation had improved. Bilateral integration and fine motor skills were still problematic, as were sensory perceptual functions. Phillipa's support from the occupational therapist continues during monthly sessions. She is also attending weekly gym sessions and she engages in two half-hour swimming lessons per week.

From January to July 1991 Phillipa attended a nursery school during the afternoons, and during this time began her first physiotherapy treatment. In September 1991 she began at school. The statementing procedures began during the same month. In late 1991 Phillipa attended for speech therapy and was discharged after two or three sessions. Phillipa presented with immediate problems fitting into the nursery routine alongside her peers. These problems were picked up immediately by the staff.

She was seen by a psychologist, who noted in a later report, as part of the advice for the Statement, that she lacked concentration and was impulsive, and that she played alongside other children rather than interactively, tending to be over-enthusiastic in her attempts to play, i.e. giving "inappropriately strong hugs". She also noted awkward gross body movements.

During the first two weeks of starting school Phillipa went home for her lunch and attended only for half-days. Tests then began to ascertain her problems. The local educational psychologist advised that she was statemented. Her parents reported that Phillipa couldn't cope with the children and the noise. Apparently there were 32 children in a class. Her parents felt that Phillipa was a very lonely child who cried for two years at school, and then suddenly stopped. She is now behind her peers and becoming increasingly isolated.

Phillipa's Statement came into play in September 1992, with Phillipa having been given some welfare assistance time for five mornings per week since May 1992. During the summer of this year she also attended family therapy. Phillipa's Statement referred to her problems with regard to making progress within school, and it was stated that her needs were very complex, needing further investigation. The LEA explained that Phillipa found school life "very confusing and threatening", and listed many goals which were to be aimed for under the auspices of the Education Act 1981.

The medium-term goals essentially related to improving Phillipa's ability to interact socially, alongside independence in self-help skills, improvement in understanding instructions and concentration skills, and an improvement in her physical skills. The LEA also noted that the longer term goal was for the authority to understand more clearly Phillipa's needs in order to develop plans "to ensure Phillipa receives appropriate educational provision". In order to meet the medium-term goals the LEA outlined the need for a special support assistant on five mornings a week integrated within the whole school approach, alongside the need for the involvement of a co-ordinator and an educational psychologist, an occupational therapist and physiotherapist. The LEA then clearly set out a plan involving meetings to ensure appropriate evaluation of its objectives.

The rapid recognition of Phillipa's considerable problems and the early provision of a Statement, which seemed thorough and appropriate at that stage, unfortunately didn't lead to dramatic changes in Phillipa's behaviours, or improvements in terms of her difficulties.

The psychologist reported early on that whilst occasionally there would seem to be improvement for Phillipa, she would easily be unsettled when routines changed. Her distress was noted on a number of occasions, and in particular during a physical education lesson in the hall, where she was noted to be extremely upset, unable to follow the instructions or the children. The psychologist reported that she felt Phillipa was easily distressed by a range of situations in the classroom and outside, and that she seemed to find being within a group of children threatening and confusing. Her repetitive questioning was also referred to, as was her immature language and her fidgety nature.

During formal testing Phillipa was found to have ability within the normal range, using the Wechsler Pre-school and Primary Scale of Intelligence, although the psychologist did feel that her scores could well be an underestimate.

The psychologist stated quite clearly that Phillipa would benefit from:

> being within a small structured class setting with a high staffing ratio so that she can begin to develop self-organisation, social skills, attention span, within a controlled setting. Alternatively, to enable her to function appropriately within the classroom she would need to have additional welfare support, preferably full time, to keep her on task, to help her

develop independence in dressing and to develop awareness of and interaction with her peers.

Unfortunately, with the introduction of the Code of Practice as previously mentioned, the five half-days a week of welfare assistance time finished last summer, and the LEA concluded that under the terms of the Code of Practice her needs should in future be met by a mainstream school in line with the school's SEN policy. The LEA therefore intended to cease Phillipa's Statement of SEN. From that point the LEA then expected the school to make appropriate provision for her using delegated funding. This decision was made following Phillipa's annual review in February 1994. Within this review Phillipa was reported to have additional special educational needs because of bullying; the need to develop further independence and social skills; and a need for more emphasis on academic achievement.

The review reported that Phillipa had made reasonable progress. A number of strategies were outlined in Phillipa's individual education plan.

A report by the educational psychologist around that time commented on Phillipa's difficulties in communication, socialisation and making sense of her environment, her problems coping with changes in routine and place leading to confusion and distress, although the psychologist reports that she is gradually becoming more adaptable. She reports that Phillipa plays alone, appearing to enter a fantasy world, which often includes odd gestures, spinning and hand flapping. Facial grimaces were also referred to, with Phillipa keeping her mouth open when listening to stories. Despite the cessation of the Statement the psychologist felt that in the future consideration may well need to be given to a special school for youngsters with difficulties in socialisation and communication.

Phillipa's parents have written to the LEA to request a Statement of SEN in order to move their child into an environment which they believe will meet her needs more appropriately. Despite the intensive support she has received since being very young from the health authority, and in terms of additional support systems, such as the swimming club, the exercise class run by a dyslexia support group, the family therapy, plus additional English tuition, none of these focused therapies has enabled Phillipa to fit any better and to be significantly less anxious within a large class in a large school, pointing to the need for a change in the educational context.

Her parents comment in a letter to the LEA that:

> although during the period of the Statement and for six months thereafter Phillipa seemed to be making some progress in coping in the classroom, it now appears that the presence of the welfare assis-

tant did, in fact, only mask her difficulties. These have now come back to the fore in many ways.

The parents go on to comment that they have noticed that Phillipa wants friends but is rebuffed at school because of her lack of social ability and her difficulty in processing information. They comment: 'This processing difficulty also leads her to perform well below her true academic potential.'

The family are increasingly concerned about Phillipa's attitude towards school. They feel that she is getting to the stage where she doesn't want to go, and when she is ill she doesn't want to go back. A phobia seems to be setting in and on one occasion she was physically sick on returning to school. The development of peer relationships is just not happening and Phillipa always ends up isolated. The family, in their continuing and unrelenting attempts to help their child in whatever way necessary, moved her into a playgroup during the summer, but Phillipa didn't want to return and came back each time saying that she didn't like it.

For some weeks now Phillipa has been attending a Saturday school. They assessed her in December 1995 and found her to be a bright and articulate child who was friendly and co-operative, but who fidgeted, fiddled with her fingers in her mouth, and wasn't able to listen, think or follow instructions easily. They noted that she was very easily confused, giving up before she started to think, became very anxious and worried, asked repetitive questions following instructions, which had been reported by the psychologist, for example 'What do you have to do? What do you mean? What shall I do?' and these repetitions occur almost in a whisper. They also noted that her behaviour was inappropriate and immature, and that her tone of voice seemed too loud and not controlled. She also had a tendency to interrupt, an inability to notice what the rest of the class were doing (this was clearly demonstrated in the description of the observation by the psychologist in the PE lesson), poor eye contacting, poor ability to relate to others, etc. They felt that she had specific learning difficulties as there was a very wide gap between her verbal and written skills, and referred to the dyspraxic symptoms, which of course had been recognised since she was very small. The centre referred to the possibility that she may have an attention deficit disorder, which had been suggested by the physiotherapist, and there was a query that she may have a problem allied to Asperger syndrome, and a semantic-pragmatic language disorder.

The parents have noticed that within the highly structured setting of this centre Phillipa is better able to concentrate and take advantage of what is on offer. There is also provision for very specifically targeted social skills training and support for parents.

Test results

Asperger syndrome

Phillipa presents, and always has presented, with problems within the triad of impairments, the triad being imagination, communication and interaction. She is also typical of the Asperger group in relation to clumsiness, prosodic problems, difficulties picking up cues and clues, odd tone of voice, repetitive behaviours, odd facial gesturing and odd posture. Difficulties with change, early tendencies to want things her way and to engage with the environment in an isolated manner, signs of extreme distress at seemingly trivial changes and events.

DSM IV-R criteria

Phillipa meets all the criteria for inattentive ADHD and six of the criteria for hyperactivity and impulsivity.

Wechsler Intelligence Scale for Children (3rd Edn UK) (WISC)

VERBAL SCALE

	Score
Information	11
Similarities	19
Arithmetic	8
Vocabulary	13
Comprehension	17
(Digit Span)	8

PERFORMANCE SCALE

	Score
Picture Completion	9
Coding	8
Picture Arrangement	4
Block Design	8
Object Assembly	6
(Symbol Search)	8

IQ AND INDEX SCORES

	Score	Percentile
Verbal IQ	122	93rd
Performance IQ	78	7th
Verbal Comprehension Index	128	97th
Perceptual Organisation Index	79	8th
Freedom from Distractibility Index	88	21st
Processing Speed Index	88	21st

Wechsler Objective Reading Dimensions (WORD)
WISC III UK SCALED SCORE

	Score	Percentile	Age Equivalent
Basic Reading	97	42nd	8 yrs 3 mths 9
Spelling	92	30th	7 yrs 6 mths 8

Discussion

Given Phillipa's increasing maturity we are now much more able to ascertain her strengths and weaknesses. In fact, Phillipa presents with a quite remarkably discrepant intellectual profile. She has a very clear performance problem which has hindered her throughout. These poorer developed skills will have largely defined Phillipa when she was much younger, and not surprisingly tended to give the suggestion that she was a child with moderate learning difficulties, and indeed her score in this area falls within that range.

However, on the verbal side Phillipa has verbal comprehension skills which are into the gifted range. As we can see her Verbal Comprehension index score, which removes some of the lower scores pertaining to working memory in the verbal scale, is exceptionally high at the ninety-seventh percentile.

An example of Phillipa's paradoxical presentation of her intellect is well depicted in the response to the Similarities subtest. As we can see Phillipa did exceptionally well in this fundamentally important aspect of intelligence. She was well able, without moving into any tangential thought, to tell me the overriding concepts which linked various ideas, thus when presented with the words 'temperature' and 'length', Phillipa was clear that these were both measurements, and that 'a painting' and 'a statue' were both art forms. However, once Phillipa had completed this and I said to her 'You are clever', she responded by looking very puzzled and asking 'Why?'

Despite Phillipa's brilliance in terms of straightforward abstract reasoning, when presented with a sequence of pictures in a jumbled order depicting a variety of scenes, mostly social involving people, she had tremendous problems. As we can see the score of Picture Arrangement, described by some as an executive function and one which I find many children with Asperger syndrome and ADHD have difficulties with, was the lowest in Phillipa's total profile and vastly discrepant to the score she achieved in Similarities. It was clear that Phillipa knew what to do in this sequencing task, and she tried very hard to understand what was going on and to use the clues that existed within the pictures. She also used self-talk procedures, which were referred to by the previous psychologist. Despite Phillipa's ability to describe the pictures clearly and slowly, she nevertheless missed out some essential details which were necessary to make sense of the stories. Children who have problems in this area frequently have difficulties within the social arena. Unable to pick up on cues and clues around them, they misinterpret and misconstrue circumstances as frequently as others misinterpret the cues and clues which they give out, or fail to, as the case may be. During this exercise Phillipa also asked very inappropriate questions. Throughout the assessment she was keen for me to see a variety of very interesting books which absorbed her interest.

Phillipa's relationship with the rest of the world was interestingly disjointed and very typical of a person with Asperger syndrome. When we engaged in the puzzles in the Object Assembly test, the first one being that of a girl, Phillipa said to me 'Can you tell me this girl's name?' As we can see from the scores Phillipa did poorly in this test also, in fact failing three of the five items.

She told me about playing a game before I arrived and that she had made up a particular and rather off-beat scenario, which I found quite fascinating. Essentially, every time a girl said 'thirteen' her eyes went orange. Phillipa also told me that she could imagine with her fingers when we were involved in Mental Arithmetic, also problematic for Phillipa compared with scores in other areas on the verbal side. She also told me that she had worked out why it was that nine came after six, and that it was because the nine had to roll round more than the six before it looked like the figure it was supposed to be. She was very excited by this 'discovery', and I found this to be a very interesting line of thought.

Phillipa was extremely quiet when completing the Block Design, unlike throughout the other tests when she had been quite active and talkative. She showed clear problems in terms of problem-solving skills and didn't turn over the bricks, the outcome being that many of the features were put together by accident. It was also significant that Phillipa had immediate problems once the lines were removed from the pictures on the template, providing a clear visual stimuli as a guide for her.

Phillipa's father discussed with me the vastly increasing gap between Phillipa's social skills and those of her peers, and the difference in the maturity levels, which are clear to see. From the history, observations of Phillipa, and assessment, there is no doubt that she is a child who presents with a combination of well-recognised features of both attention deficit disorder and Asperger syndrome. The dyspraxia and the semantic pragmatic difficulties are recognised within these groups, although given that both are spectrum disorders the level of severity varies from quite extreme to mild forms dissipated amongst the normal population. There is an interesting overlap of symptomatology with the attention deficit disordered and the Asperger syndrome group. These difficulties interfere with a child's ability to read others' behaviours, and also to fit in through their own motor and language skills with their same age peers. This group of children are also far more likely to feel highly anxious and sensitive to lots of noise around them and also with a vast amount of fragmented stimuli, which they cannot understand or make sense of.

It is therefore not surprising that it is precisely during the sessions when circumstances are not structured, i.e. lunchtimes, playtimes, or during lessons where the very specific skills which are so problematic are actually targeted, such as PE, when these children are under the most strain.

Increasingly, despite fine brush strokes of support which have been admirably applied to Phillipa since she was very young, it is the total environment which is alien to the child. While it is imperative that she learns to function alongside her peers, this cannot be done by dropping her in at the deep end, which is what has occurred. It is not at all uncommon for children such as Phillipa to be given the support but to remain within mainstream classes in large schools, and to seem to cope during the early years and then deteriorate badly as they become increasingly isolated and under pressure.

Phillipa will be isolated not only by her clearly evident social difficulties, and this includes non-verbal skills as well, all of which make up the fabric of social mediational skills, but also by her verbal giftedness, unusual thought processing and styles of play. It has been demonstrated that when Phillipa is placed within smaller groups, with a very clear structure and provision to develop her social interactional skills, many of the odd behaviours and phobic responses actually reduce.

Conclusions and recommendations

Phillipa is a child who presents with Asperger syndrome and an attention deficit disorder, meeting the criteria for both. Sewn within this are clear dyspraxic and semantic-pragmatic problems which have been recognised, and certainly in terms of the motor difficulties Phillipa has received a considerable amount of support from the health authority. Despite a good start by the local LEA, the early recognition of her difficulties, and provision of a Statement, which was admirable, it is unfortunate that she was not considered to have severe enough problems to continue with her Statement of SEN. I am of the opinion that she should not be taught within a mainstream school. The trial has occurred and failed. Whilst Phillipa is still reasonably self-confident, and before she begins to perceive and be concerned about the vast differences between herself and her peers, she ought to be transferred to a school which will more appropriately meet her needs.

My feeling is that in the longer term Phillipa will need the kind of provision referred to by the local psychologist a number of years ago, and that is a specialist environment which caters for children with the kinds of difficulties Phillipa is experiencing. The problem at this time is that, despite our increasing understanding and recognition of children with these social communication problems and associated dyslexia, dyspraxia, semantic-pragmatic disorders, etc., the schools are simply not available. Therefore, one has to seek out a best fit, and it may be that some of the establishments catering for gifted, clumsy, dyslexic pupils will provide the curriculum, the ethos and the attitudes needed to see Phillipa through.

I admire her parents for continuing their ongoing quest for the right kind of educational environment for their clearly very talented daughter, and believe that once in the right place she will have a great deal to offer. Unfortunately, if this does not happen and Phillipa is faced with the daily pressures of large classes and an increasingly demanding academic timetable, alongside little input in order to improve her communicative skills, she is likely to develop increasingly odd behaviours as she becomes more anxious. We need to recognise that intuitively Phillipa does not have the social skills of the peers around her. With the additional attention deficit disorder in evidence from the earliest months of life with Phillipa's overactivity, she will be greatly hindered, confusing internal and external stimuli. Phillipa's expressive social dysfunction and distractible behaviour will never be understood in a mainstream environment, and as such she is also increasingly likely to be a target for bullying, which is yet another reason to ensure that she is provided with a placement within which she will be protected as well as understood and supported.

Phillipa will need to be taught specific social skills regularly, and it would be useful for any school system to set up a social programme, in which issues relating to eye contacting, listening, taking turns, etc., are component parts.

Phillipa will also need to be taught through structured learning, which is a psychoeducational behavioural approach providing instruction in prosocial skills, and is concerned with:

- modelling

- role playing
- performance feedback
- transfer of learning.

The skills are broken down into constituent parts and examples of people performing the steps are shown to the child. They are given the opportunity to rehearse and then receive feedback from others.

Alongside the specific work tackling pragmatic and social difficulties, it will be important to extend the work specifically into the development of self-esteem; Ladd (1981) found that training in conversational skills improved social standing with peers. I believe that this is an important feature which needs to be added to any package for Phillipa. Sewn into the sessions would need to be support in order to help Phillipa with the appropriate use of affect, including body language. I would recommend that the book *Self-esteem Enhancement with Children and Adolescents* (Pope, McHale and Craighead 1988) is used, and that the social learning model is applied. The structured learning approach is also well described by McGinnis *et al.* (1984).

Finally, I discussed briefly the possible benefits of medication for Phillipa to improve her impulsivity and distractibility, and recommend that the family visits a suitable practitioner who can discuss this treatment as a possible way forward.

Chapter Six

Failing systems

Sadly, this chapter is not positive. It details how systems can sometimes fail and how things can go wrong. The issues are obviously not addressed to those who work unstintingly at providing excellent system support for children, working respectfully with their families.

Step inside my shoes

Our practitioner systems need to be more flexible: we need to see all perspectives and incorporate them into our plan with the child as the pivot. Creative systems and early intervention have a better chance of making a real difference and real honest dialogue with families, involving really listening to them.

The long-term financial saving within each community is likely to be significant. This needs to be understood as it has been the desperately escalating and hysterical need to restrict spending to meet targets and work 'to budget' through stringent imposed policies on education and health authorities which has led to our current knife-edge position.

In most geographical areas spending has actually increased in the managerial ranks to manage the professionals, reduce spending and in turn limit the support for children. An intriguing tangled effect has been the metamorphosis of some professionals into money managers, decreasing the very limited pool of trained sole professionals as their essential focused duty to each child makes seismic shifts while claiming to be able to see both sides.

The social experiment *has* led to a better ability of professionals to see the contents of the public purse and step inside the shoes of managers, but I wait to be convinced that this has operated the other way round. Indeed, rather than assimilating an understanding of the child's difficulties, there would appear to have been an escalation of various tactics to eliminate the opposition – the parents.

These include, for instance, in the UK, a rising number of parents accused of causing or exaggerating their children's problems and an increase in parental complaints about children's needs not being met, resulting in appeals. In turn more money has been spent in LEAs to buy in legal support to fight these complaints. Evidence from UK budgets of some local authorities reveals that spending in this area of the authority protecting itself from the children has dramatically increased, outstripping spending on special needs itself.

A spin-off effect has been the sharing of a great deal of knowledge within a legal framework for each case which in turn has led to some responsible authorities making important changes for the good of all of the children.

System stumbling blocks

These include some general issues for all types of special needs and more specific ones relating to ADHD and autistic spectrum disorders.

- Over the years we have tended to overuse the wait-and-see policy, designed in more respectful times to help reduce parental unfounded anxieties, reassure them that their child was fine and in some cases there can be improvement over time with no intervention. Unfortunately, given the very limited nature of our resources many more whose problems have not improved have found themselves left. Years can pass as a child gets worse.

- Strict research criteria are used by practitioners, who need to be more flexible in school systems. This limits allocation of support and it can result in grossly limited and restricted perceptions and opinions in school systems – where it is crucially important that a child is understood and supported. Research criteria designed to remove all the co-morbid conditions in the sample – which is impossible anyway – are then inappropriately applied to practical situations in school.

- Given the limited opportunity for assessment and diagnosis within the education system, many are referred to specialists within teaching hospitals whose contract is to engage in research based work, write papers and meet their department's deadlines. Some have no brief to help children clinically. Families are frequently unaware of this issue.

- A child can be on a waiting list of 18 months to 2 years before he or she is even seen for the first appointment. In some areas the waiting lists have been closed.

- Initial referral may be inappropriate, leading to wasted time and resources and leaving the family no further forward.

- Using the strict criteria for inclusion in research groups, some hospitals may fail to recognise a child on the wider spectrum as limited questions are asked and tests undertaken. There is a guiding paragraph in DSM-IV which is invariably not mentioned and which refers to clinical judgement being paramount in diagnosis. When some researchers, looking for causes, have found an overlap of underlying dysfunction, they have concluded that the behaviour in question is therefore not a cardinal underlying feature of their particular condition as it is shared by others, and then abandon that thinking to pursue the search for the cardinal feature. However, the overlap represents what is really going on in human minds and this needs to be recognised as well as recognition of the cardinal descriptive features. An over-focus on the detail can result in missing the whole picture, just as autistic children seem to do (Frith and Happé (1994).

- Researchers and clinicians working exclusively in one or other field often fail to recognise the other condition as co-morbid; instead it will be more likely regarded as a differential diagnosis.

- The interwoven features which are common to many disorders can lead to professional confusion.

- Many health professionals work in specialist areas and this can lead to children receiving a single diagnosis or none at all and to later confusion if other professionals disagree with the original diagnosis or if the child has changed over time.

- There has been a difference of perception of similar disorders in different parts of the world. This has led to the use of different terminology for certain clusters, which are very similar.

- Even if a diagnosis has been provided, many parents can find their child left out in the cold through differences of opinion or through funding authorities – education and social services – being unwilling to accept the specialist's opinion, even in some cases thwarting and sabotaging their attempts to support the child.

- For many, the label of ADHD is regarded as 'naughtiness' and 'an American condition', while the perception of Asperger syndrome, as an autistic spectrum disorder, is often regarded as 'just' a behavioural problem; or there is the expectation that a child should conform to Kanner's (1943) description of extreme autism and appear 'mute and aloof', or the condition as a form of autism will be dismissed.

- Within the world of education management, there can be a projected cynicism which denies any behavioural condition in a child – other than describing it as just that – a behavioural problem – or mockingly referring to the condition as the latest fad. The culture in the UK has not been towards early intervention and support for families but many areas have proven strengths at blaming families while standing at a distance to watch them fail. This is improving with government commitment to the family and the broad-brush support which has been put in place. There is increasing evidence that the early intervention message is finally being heard. This needs to be fully extended by dynamic policy and resources directed at fine-brush professional methods at the early stages.

- Old habits die hard within systems and the culture of family blame has been very strong. Many professionals feel threatened by new ideas which may cast doubt on the value of their own, given that advanced thinking demands empirical and evidence-based practice not only in relation to hypothesised causes of problems but also in relation to the effectiveness of the suggested recommendations for positive change. We have a very poor track record for making obvious differences to our children with developmental disorders, which at the least requires us to reconsider the doctrines which we have held so close in the past.

- In this transition period there are the inevitable fights when systems gang together to shoot messengers, denigrating professionals who disagree. Such cynicism has nothing to offer to help the child, and energies would be better directed at working positively together toward new discoveries.

- Many education professionals are restricted in the individual work they can undertake and overwhelmed by responsibilities for thousands of children in a given geographical area. Inevitably the single child assessment model has to be woven into a wider systems approach. It can be easily worked out that a school could wait years for one cohort of children with special needs to be individually seen by their designated psychologist – and this is not the fault of the psychologist. Taking a simple example: let us say a school of 400 children has just a 5 per cent group of children with special needs; this results in 20 children having to be assessed. If just half a day is allocated to an assessment on each child this adds up to 10 days each year actually face to face with the child. A school of such a size may be allocated one in-school day each half-term lasting six weeks – six days a year. You need to add more days for each child for writing the report, consultations, phone calls, meetings etc. The psychologist could have a total patch of about 10,000 children in mainstream and also other specialist duties to special schools. Additionally, multi-professional involvement, development of new systems and ongoing professional development have to be fitted in with all the administration. There are still only 24 hours in a day, 7 days in a week. If resources can be found for increasing numbers of managers and legal advisers to local authorities, then it can be found for psychologists to help more children and improve professional systems.

- Education professionals are discouraged from making diagnoses or from referring out for such diagnoses.

- Cultural differences and differences in status and resources available to different professionals have also driven circumstances.

- It has to be possible that some professionals do not diagnose autism or ADHD because of their limited knowledge and possibly limited resources.

- While a considerable amount of research has been undertaken on ADHD in universities and hospitals in the USA, Australia and Scandinavia, in Britain until very recently such work has been limited to looking at hyperkinesis, occurring in only about 1 per cent of the population. This led to at least 4 per cent of children falling through the net, who would have met the wider ADHD profile and who could have been supported.

- Diagnoses of autism have been as elusive as social engagement among the children who are severely impaired. Uncertainty led to a failure to recognise the fundamental problems of poor reciprocity. It may be decided that a differential diagnosis is most appropriate, for instance, that something else explains the problem better, such as a conduct disorder. While this may be correct, there is an increasing recognition that maybe the something else coexists with an underlying developmental disorder rather than being the cause of it.

- Local authorities can put pressure on schools to sabotage assessment processes by refusing to complete questionnaires as part of the comprehensive assessment for ADHD or by deliberately down-scoring a child who has a strong recorded history of problems. It is likely that there are unwritten policies in some authorities not to assist in ADHD multi-professional assessment. A head teacher involved with one of our tapestry kids refused to complete questionnaires on the child and wrote positive but erroneous reports about the child. The parents and other parents were all aware that he was constantly in trouble for his hyperactive and sometimes unintentionally harmful behaviour and some parents were threatening to sue the school as their child had been hurt by him. Clearly aware of unwritten authority policy not to recognise ADHD, the head teacher wrote behind the scenes about his dreadful problems, which she denied existed to parents, begging for extra help. In another area, a newly appointed class teacher was asked by a mother if she could complete a questionnaire from the paediatrician to help him decide whether the child had significant problems warranting a medical trial. The teacher was only too happy to oblige. She was very concerned about the child and had felt that he fitted the ADHD criteria herself. There was no lack of evidence from other sources that he was highly hyperactive in school but the LEA had consistently denied there were any problems and told the mother that she could not appeal to a tribunal for special educational needs as it could find 'no evidence' of any difficulties after a 'thorough investigation'. Rather than refuse to assess formally, as this gave the mother the right to appeal to the tribunal, the LEA deferred its decision. The teacher completed the form honestly and the paediatrician confirmed the ADHD diagnosis. When the head teacher found out, she was furious and wrote a hurried letter to the LEA explaining that this questionnaire had 'not been sanctioned' by her and that the teacher had been well intentioned but misguided. By that time the child was proving to be a good responder to medication and his behaviours dramatically improved. When the case arrived at the tribunal some months later, the legal adviser for the local authority attempted to prevent the appeal going ahead, saying that the mother had no right to appeal as the LEA had merely 'deferred', not refused a formal assessment, and therefore the tribunal was unlawful in allowing it. Such a tactic could ensure that the child stayed on a deferred list until he left school at 16, denying him and his mother their right of appeal. The tribunal underway, the head teacher totally accepted that he *had been* hyperactive – although this had previously been vigorously denied. The LEA had not shifted its position and continued to argue that he did not need a formal assessment – because his hyperactivity was now no longer a problem thanks to the medication! Heads we win, tails you lose.

- Assessments limited to brief interviews, half-hour observations in schools or the sole use of questionnaires alone with no neuropsychological testing or attainment assessment, can lead to too little information to make a serious diagnosis; instead no evidence of the condition is put forward, which, in these circumstances, would not be a lie.

- There is no formal recognition of ADHD and autism together despite practitioners' recognition of the overlap; using current criteria, if one exists the other cannot. Hence there is confusion at the diagnostic stage and the end result of no diagnosis at all for many children.

- A culture of blame has developed; this has had an influence on social policy with parents, and particularly mothers, blamed for the problem. In the worst-case scenarios double-jeopardy tactics are brought in through the use of Munchausen syndrome by proxy to prevent support and totally stop complaints. Once a mother has been blamed, the professionals responsible for the blame, who place the children into care, will *never* be open to recognising the child's problem as this would be tantamount to admitting they were wrong in the first place. This is likely to have led to thousands of children in care with unrecognised ADHD and autistic spectrum disorders. These children, further damaged by the stress of being removed from their families, do not succeed in the educational system and go on to be highly vulnerable, easily manipulated and at high risk of later offending behaviour.

Special education and special excuses

Despite the exciting breakthroughs in many areas of intervention and real evidence of improvements, our cynicism has reached such a peak that the world of special education can appear to be like a criminal high court, with its adversarial and punitive approach fitting well with our attitudes towards children and their families during the 1980s and 1990s. All evidence can be twisted to suit, 'truth' consigned to the perceived plausibility of the witness. Black becomes white. What we see can be turned on its head, not least because different specialists and different professionals with varied roles are involved and each considers their perspective to be the most salient one and will fear losing face and possibly their job if they are 'proved' wrong. Vested interests and financial considerations are also sewn into this suffocating tapestry of competition and cynicism.

Below are some examples of excuses made not to provide support in the first place for our very special children:

- 'We do not accept the evidence' – of comprehensive independent testing when no testing had been done locally for seven years.

- 'These children are perfectly normal' – paediatrician about brain-damaged twins born at 27 weeks.

- 'We don't do any of that anymore – we can't afford it.'

- 'We only accept the evidence of our own psychologist because she knows how much money we have to spend on special needs children.'

- 'There's no point getting a private assessment – we will not take any notice of it.'

- First move: 'We must listen to our health advisers' – LEA when the speech and language therapist said no support was necessary.

- About turn: 'If Health advises support it is their responsibility to provide it, not our responsibility' – LEA when the health adviser said speech and language therapy was necessary.

- 'It's nothing to do with us – his problems are home related.'

- 'Don't send loads of letters out to other professionals when you have seen a child' – principal psychologist advising a team in a local authority: 'Just send one to the Director – you will have done your job.'

Even if one group of professionals uses an intervention which helps the problem, others can still dismiss its relevance. The following are real examples of statements made about children's needs:

- He would have improved anyway.
- All children benefit from the kind of support on offer and so it doesn't 'prove' anything.
- The parents liked the professional and so 'allowed' their child to improve.
- If they had been given the chance (or a bit longer) with their methods the same result would have emerged – after nine years, the child out of control.
- The mother is abusive and seeks out interventions for attention. If the intervention works it is because she has 'got what she wants'.
- A 'halo' effect is in operation in which parents *think* the child has improved because they have invested time, energy and maybe money into the procedure.
- The original diagnosis was wrong: 'I have gone back to the specialist to get them to change their diagnosis – it's a very difficult thing to do, to get these specialists to change their minds.' This statement was made after a child made significant progress on Lovaas treatment.

The different roles of those likely to be involved with a family of a child with a developmental disorder can lead to the child being batted around like a ball in a game.

Untangling the system

A tangled system, an over-focus on set guidelines, limited resources and the powerful influence of sometimes skewed reasoning and illogical modus operandi on the part of non-professional or quasi-professionals in local affairs, spanning health, education and social work, assures that the status quo remains in place. This has contributed to a stifling of professional development for decades, which can only harm children. There are numerous arguments which can quite reasonably be applied if one over-focuses on either the detail or the apparent whole. Perceptions and labelling of disorders and interventions vary considerably depending on where a person lives in the world and within a country; the magical movable feast of excuses and justification is infinitesimal, *always* resulting in the same outcome – 'I'm right. You're wrong' – instead of moving toward shared meanings.

Difficulties have arisen with the acceptance of specialist diagnoses at local level when children with developmental disorders, especially autism, change as they develop. First, children will always change – in real life people do; indeed Wing (1996) has referred to the way in which children with autistic spectrum disorders can shift along the spectrum in different contexts and over time. Second, our interventions must surely seek to create change and we are increasingly recognising that considerable change can be brought about if the child and family are supported by intensive methods undertaken at an early stage. It is then highly likely for the disorder to change in its presentation and indeed, this should be an aim of intervention. It occurs to me that staged diagnostic statements are perfectly reasonable, would fit with ongoing evaluation programmes and help us to chart the progress of such disorders more efficiently.

The metaphor of the tapestry *allows* us to incorporate change once the nature of the child's problems is understood, leading to a reweaving of the tapestry. Within this positive model one would expect diagnoses to change over time and for practical purposes staged diagnostic statements can be made, reflecting our better system skills of monitoring and evaluating change and the exciting evidence that we can create positive change through early interventions. In the past our interventions were piecemeal and poorly evaluated; brick-wall diagnoses were the norm.

Guidelines are being developed in the UK to help professionals set up dedicated teams which mirror some well-researched multi-professional models from the USA, and to understand the complex issues. In some areas excellent teams are in place. A number of forward-thinking practitioners and researchers are recognising that there is something essentially pointless about ignoring the overwhelming evidence of the tapestry nature of these disorders, reflecting our understanding of the tapestry nature of the way in which our brains operate and people interact. Some practitioners are understandably wary of introducing conditions which are not their speciality into a diagnosis, and others stick rigidly to vested interests, which stifle creative problem solving.

Families can become desperate to find out what is wrong and how to intervene to help their child. Instead they all too often have found themselves caught up in an inexorably slow process of diagnosis and in some case intrusive surveillance. We have all been at the receiving end of angry parents who are desperate about their children, need to blame someone and make complaints given increasing recognition of child and parental rights. Managing to cope professionally under this stress while also being able to see the parent's point of view and positively apply support is one of the most challenging aspects of this work.

Overall, the system is just advancing but there have been highly significant increases in early emerging developmental disorders and this fact is undeniable. Governments must accept this reality and look at how this has happened, what we need to do about the children with the problems, and methods of prevention.

The most important central threads must be our integrity, well-founded self-confidence and personal responsibility to others – the triple features that all humans are primed to aim towards. With this as the pivot, a certain openness and mutual respect can prevail between various professionals and managers and between professionals and families.

As guidelines are developed, applied and research professionals need to work together to improve understanding and address the child's problems. Using the tapestry could be encouraged for families to help them understand the issues. If each local area assigned parental support duties to a dedicated person, they could link with increasing local support and provide a small, specialised library as part of their existing leaflet and booklet support for other illnesses. Parents are then in an excellent position to help other parents in a quasi-professional role, and with elements of professional backing without taking over. With the greater understanding of parents, through their own education in the area of concern plus the addition of general support from the government parenting initiative, and specific support from self help groups dedicated to the particular problem area, such as ADHD/autism/Tourette syndrome, professionals can focus on the most complex cases.

It is in the nature of the interweave of the international knowledge of different professionals and specialists – practitioners, researchers and parents – and of different causal, presentation and intervention models where the future focus needs to lie. Positive, empowering facilitative approaches are the only way forward.

For some years disparate groups of professionals involved with children, their development and their various needs have worked to their own agendas. Energies have been expended in arguing strongly against the diagnoses and methods of others and for those responsible for paying, arguments have been levelled at most methods! Parents and children have been at the centre of this maelstrom of confusion. Gradually, many countries are emerging from this stultifying period and professionals are beginning to look at the ideas of others, recognise their value and move toward shared meanings.

Weaving a tapestry of professional perspectives mirrors the complex developmental perspective-taking process in the young infant, which shifts from the processing of the unseen order of universal complexity into separate but multiple 'threads' to more efficient abstract processing of understanding each other's contributions and in turn enriching our own. Positive elements of the separate views of professionals and parents need to be respected, and woven together to help the children as we shift to a new exciting era.

Chapter Seven

Tangled tapestries

He was like ten naughty boys all rolled up in one.

(Mother of Flex)

Complex tapestry cases challenge us all. The child with such problems may have clusters of faulty genes or congenital problems which in turn make them susceptible to over-reacting negatively to environmental agents, allergens and interventions which may have no effect on other people, resulting in a triggering of other difficulties. It is also likely that certain problems will be set off at particular points in time through the life span, according to a predetermined developmental blueprint.

Infants who are born very prematurely, before the last layers of the brain – the frontal lobes – are laid down in utero, are more likely to present with developmental problems relating to the functions of the frontal lobes. Attentional problems and difficulties with social awareness within this group have long been recognised clinically in such populations and recently these observations have been confirmed in research (Sykes *et al.* 1997).

Difficulties with basic rhythmic functions are also frequently reported in the histories of such children, such as breathing, feeding, sleeping and eliminating. Research in the USA (Biederman *et al.* 1991, 1993, 1996) has clearly demonstrated the 80 per cent incidence of co-morbidity in populations of children who meet ADHD criteria, and informs us that some children can have a number of additional disorders (see Chapter 4).

For most people with a presenting ADHD tapestry, many other problems coexist and the more they have at an early age combined with the severity of each disorder, the worse the prognosis.

Important issues are:

1. the severity of the problem

2. the nature of the problem

3. the timing of its emergence.

Potential for serious tapestry disorders obviously increases as the risk factors increase and the nature of the behaviour of, say, the highly hyperactive child can easily lead on to accidents and head injuries (see Chapter 4). There is a higher incidence within the ADHD group in particular and a deterioration in language, and behaviour which includes volatility and impulsivity can emerge.

Tangled tapestry kids often have the 'gut brain' problems discussed in Chapter 3. They are therefore much more likely to be allergic, adding to their problems and leading to a greater propensity for reactions to medications etc.

If a child with a significant ADHD also has a social communication problem and dyslexia, there is not one area in which they can succeed unless a relative or a mentor can find what they can do well and encourage them, while attempting to understand and seek support for their difficulties.

Most families know very little about such fundamental potential for problems in their unborn or new infant, as western culture has avoided the issue. As a consequence, many parents have found themselves struggling at home with difficulties but naively expecting that normal parenting was all that was needed. The failure of the child to respond to that could lead on to greater problems without recognition and appropriate interventions.

Parents are usually highly intuitive about their children and know if something is not quite right. If they survive the first couple of years, hoping that the child will 'grow out of it' according to advice, they can often be devastated if the child goes on to develop highly challenging problems. In tangled histories it is not unusual to hear of sleeping, breathing and eating problems of the infant and toddler which exhaust and scare the family, replaced by language and/or motor problems, extreme hyperactivity, social communication difficulties and high risk behaviour leading to head injuries.

These cases are challenging for many reasons.

- Certain single 'threads' may be extremely resistant to change, resulting in entrenched behaviours.

- The child may have multiple problems at a biochemical level which affect multiple areas of functioning.

- The fundamental difficulties may have led to a compounding of problems over time increasing the severity of presentation.

- Early problems create later problems, confusing issues.

- Failure to detect early problems/put appropriate support in place will obviously exacerbate all of the above.

Many children inherit risk factors for later developing disorders. In the most difficult cases whole families present with the problems which have led on to failure in life, made worse by addictive features commonly threaded through these disorders and the knock-on effect of frustration, through failure to achieve life's goals and associated stress. In turn these problems make child rearing very difficult. Support for the families who suffer in this way must be positive, focused and intensive (see Chapter 9 on interventions).

Even in the majority of families who do have positive support, children with tangled inherited and obstetric tapestries, or just the latter, can find themselves faced with enormous problems, which seem inexplicable. Without appropriate intervention the child can be rapidly set on an ill-fated trajectory. Unable to engage or learn from the earliest days of life, the extreme cases can soon add severe learning difficulties to the list. They will fail to move forward as their developmental tapestry prevents them from appropriately focusing on salient information and this in turn cannot be consolidated. Early processing does not shift into memory and then move forward to cognition. Many young autistic children seem to remain stuck in what they learned before repetitive behaviour became the sole activity, but failed to emerge as normal behaviour, the child moving further and further away from perceiving people as relevant.

A young girl who had been highly hyperactive, non-verbal, repetitive and unable to learn at age 4, but showing skills appropriate to that of a 3-year-old, was still at that level when seen aged 14. By then she was big, strong and frequently aggressive. Because she could play 'making tea' with plastic cups at age 4 it was felt that she was not autistic and she existed for 11 years in a no man's land. She was obviously autistic and always had been.

One child, a premature infant, typical of many, quite clearly failed to link appropriately with people as an infant and toddler. He had various allergies to foods. Objects and parts of objects excited him the most. Local professionals, seeing his ability to make eye contact, apparently normal speech, an ability to sustain attention on certain things and a caring family, were unable to recognise his problems. Once in school he could not be contained. His hyperactivity, inability to consolidate learning and inability to relate to others resulted in referral to a special school for children with learning difficulties.

Another child could not share attention with others as an infant, although he could make his needs known. He walked before he could talk and when he talked he made up his own words, known as neologisms. He was highly overactive and his school felt certain that he had a hyperactivity disorder and was dyslexic. He was seen by a psychologist and ultimately sent to a specialist hospital for consideration of hyperactivity disorder, but did not meet the strict criteria. As he failed to consolidate his learning appropriately over time his IQ levels dropped and he was not given support for dyslexia as he was no longer felt to meet that particular criterion, and was regarded as a maladjusted boy with global learning difficulties. Ultimately he was placed in a school for maladjusted children where he was bullied and manipulated. He soon learned to imitate the behaviour of the other boys. When I saw him he had not had a psychological assessment for seven years and had begun offending.

Tapestry children have a number of coexisting problems or co-morbidities. Clearly the nature of the *combination* – the nature of the weave – and the *severity* will determine how the child presents and should help us weave matching tapestries of support.

Professionals, clinical and research, are at the cutting edge of these issues, recognising first that people are more complex than a single diagnosis. Although a main presenting feature may be obvious, recognition of other overlapping features help us to understand the specific tapestry better. This has led to a recognition that a person may meet many diagnostic criteria while others may not appear to do so given some of the anomalies in current practice.

Concern about the use of multiple diagnoses and the over-medicalisation of the presenting features of a child could lead to practitioner professionals becoming overly strict in their use of categorical systems or interpretations of experimental research, which leads vast numbers of children without support and very vulnerable.

The use of dimensional systems exemplified through the metaphor of the tapestry and inherent in the tenets of Chaos Theory will allow us to describe a child's tapestry more clearly. If parents are also allowed to be involved in recognising features in their child as part of their unique tapestry, as opposed to defining the child in cold medical terms, and also recognising what they need to do to help, serious psychopathological outcomes and tangled tapestries could be avoided.

As professionals learn to use such methods and share findings with each other across traditional boundaries pertaining to different departments, to researchers vs clinicians etc., we will be more likely to establish the threads of common pathways, understand the effects of sudden events which totally alter the presenting tapestry, and explain why a particular presenting interweave leads to different outcomes in different contexts, i.e. home, school, laboratory.

Closer focus on these variations in individual children, combined with the ability to learn from research in different but overlapping fields of research and clinical practice, then leads us, for instance, to recognise how even a different word, the accent of the examiner or expression can totally alter meaning for a particular child and in turn affect emotional responses and other reactions.

Potential for serious tapestry disorders obviously increases as the risk factors or threads increase, and in some of the most difficult cases a child may present with hyperactivity, impulsivity, poor ability to judge consequences of actions and poor social communication alongside fascinations and obsessions at a very early age. The latter are particularly worrying if these relate to dangerous objects or activities such as knives and fire, or if the child is becoming very anxious and aggressive.

Complex ADHD or Asperger cases challenge us all. The most challenging are those in which the overactivity and sleep problems of the infant exhaust the family and whose later hyperactivity is so extreme that the family is in fear for their child's safety. These cases are challenging either because certain single threads are exceptionally severe and extremely resistant to change, or because the child has many different problems that have led to a compounding of difficulties over time. Over time such children are much more likely to fail in school, at home and in their social lives.

Certain rules of thumb need to be applied in these cases:

- early recognition and assessment
- early and intensive intervention of various types with behavioural models interwoven
- trained facilitators in every school
- dynamic and effective multidisciplinary action plans
- positive no-blame support for struggling families
- close monitoring of effectiveness of plans over time
- small class sizes – large classes and groups with complex fragmented stimuli only add to perceptual and cognitive confusion in such cases
- positive parent and professional attitudes.

Irlen syndrome

In the last few years I have been fascinated to find that many children with ADHD, autism, closed head injuries (CHI) and combinations also experience what is known as Irlen syndrome, after Helen Irlen, who has pioneered the use of coloured lenses for this problem throughout the world since the early 1980s. While the condition and the remedy have been mainly associated with dyslexia, from my work I have seen a high incidence of significant difficulties within the tapestry kids; this is found by Helen Irlen (personal discussion) and has been confirmed by others (Barbolini *et al.* 1998).

Many of these children see distortions in the wider environment as well as on the page, a number see colour in black and white and find that a particular colour removes the distortions they see. Understanding the nature of this disorder and the results from research around the world, it seemed obvious that a blow to the head could knock systems out of synch. What was fascinating was that *colour* could remove the problems – but only while wearing lenses or looking through an acetate sheet. Thinking back to our musical interlude section in Chapter 5, we talked about the wavelengths which make up colour perception. If cells related to perception are knocked out by a blow, and research suggests that the magno and parvocellular systems behind the retina, linked with the cingulate gyrus, are implicated in this perceptual problem, it is perhaps not a surprise that the warped perceptions need some help to perceive the world again, and the appropriate colour will help to balance that particular regulatory system.

I now always ask about blows to the head as well as convulsions and problems such as meningitis, in the information-gathering stage of assessment and automatically include an Irlen screen in my battery of tests, especially as immediate support can be provided.

If a young child, just learning to read, inherits or acquires this problem, we will observe his reluctance to read. One Asperger adolescent felt physically sick just looking at print, which I assumed was an emotional reaction to his dyslexia. However, with a coloured overlay this no longer happened.

A very young autistic girl, with no functional speech but the odd word, looked at one of the designs as part of the Irlen screen and sort of flicked her finger against the box design, saying 'orange'. Her lovely parents told her not to be silly – there was no orange on the page! But a number of children do see colours and Helen Irlen calls them her 'rainbow' children. They see parts of the prism of colour which makes up white. When I placed an overlay on the page for this autistic girl she said 'gone'. Whatever the mechanism, it is quite a remarkable experience to watch both the children and their parents when they see such results.

Usually children do not talk about these problems. They will struggle and eventually may just avoid reading. From discussions with children I have found that they might not understand their difficulty with reading, which might actually give them a headache, and they will just become angry and refuse to read, angry at anyone who tries to help. Others assume everyone sees the same 'distortions' and somehow manage to read – they will not realise that they are actual distortions. In some extreme cases the child or adolescent is scared, thinking they are having hallucinations.

Phonological problems

Many children experience phonological problems, which link with language and auditory processing. A child with an early language problem will invariably go on to present with later literacy problems, with the phonological system implicated. Even though there may be signs of hyperlexia, the child showing apparently good skills in the mechanics of reading, closer analysis will reveal considerable problems with the understanding of what is read or, more accurately, memorised. Some children may be struggling to read phonologically and this problem could be compounded by perceptual confusions and distortions.

Environmental damage

For the children whose difficulties have been caused or exacerbated by effects of a vaccine or the side-effects of other drugs or agents in the environment which warp the immunological process, their entire system will be pervaded and subsequently compromised, with gut problems, including diarrhoea or constipation, allergies, asthma and eczema, ADHD problems and social communication difficulties. If parents are blamed this adds to the trauma for the children. In the worst case scenario the children are removed from innocent families and inevitably their problems get worse, not better.

Developmental co-ordination disorder

Many children with ADHD also experience motor difficulties which are recognised as developmental co-ordination disorders or dyspraxia. In certain cases children can suffer from one of the dystonias. Research into dystonias finds an interweave with early speech problems related to the use of voice, spasms including writer's cramp and eyelid tics. In infants there are also links with torticollis and with the function of the diaphragm, in turn linked with gastro-oesophegeal reflux and elimination problems.

Gillberg uses the term DAMP (disorders of attention, motor and perceptual skills) for a group of children with attention deficits and motor problems and finds that a number present with 'features of Asperger syndrome' (Ehlers and Gillberg 1993). Over time, problems with written work, dysgraphia, if not dyslexia, and mental arithmetic problems usually also add to the difficulties suffered by such children. The very common presenting cluster of attention, perceptuo-motor and auditory/language/social communication problems implicates shared neurodevelopmental pathways.

Tourette syndrome

Comings and Comings (1993) consider that there is such an overlap of ADHD and Tourette syndrome as to be one and the same. More recent research shows that there is indeed an overlap. In 20 studies involving more than 2000 people, the average rate of co-morbidity was 52 per cent. Spencer *et al.* (1998) comment: 'Little doubt remains that ADHD is highly prevalent in patients with Tourette syndrome and often represents the main clinical concern and the principal source of dysfunction and disability' (p.1041). Higher rates of co-morbid learning disorders are found in this population.

This further confirms my observations that in all of these disorders we can find ADHD symptomatology, given that we define this term as relating to the functioning of the dopaminergic system linked in part with the shared executive problems.

Often this syndrome, either as a tic disorder or in the full Tourette form, will emerge around the age of 7 or 8. A child may develop odd little vocal mannerisms or facial twitches. Some people learn to disguise the odd mannerism which demands to be expressed – the hair flick, the symmetrical movements to balance up. In severe cases the 'bark' or the whole body movements cannot be suppressed or disguised. One young man had friends in school who were able to help him suppress his shoulder shrug in the classroom. As soon as he was out of class his shoulder 'went into overdrive' as the suppressed tics demanded expression.

Within Asperger syndrome many people also have tics alongside other obsessive traits. Over time they may try to incorporate what they must do into habits and rituals which can turn into obsessive compulsive disorders as the person validates their expression by developing superstitions. 'If I don't catch the ball 50 times – perfectly – someone will die,' said one young girl. Counting in threes or fours is one, precise 'dotting' of words in spelling tests another. Some children develop numerous complex rituals which conform to their pattern and this can be exhausting.

Family reactions

Many families are driven to breaking point with their children's problems, which impact on the whole family. Some caring and honest parents openly admit that they have tried everything to make their child conform and that this has included a lot of nagging, shouting and screaming at and sometimes hitting them. Children with severe behavioural problems can drive parents and siblings to total distraction. Older siblings can leave home prematurely and younger ones can suffer physical harm. Even some parents, especially mothers, can be the target for adolescents with tangled tapestries. I have met many mysogynist adolescent Asperger males who have resorted to violence toward their mother. This can be rapidly compounded by understandable physical punishments being meted out.

Over time many have realised that the child is not able to make the connection between the hitting and their behaviour and admit that 'it never worked'. These punitive reactions to difficult behaviour are often *blamed* for it. Most have no desire to hit their children at all and feel demeaned by their actions, recognising that they emerged out of desperation and sheer frustration. Some fathers have told me that once they have become educated about the real nature of their child's problems and also the dangers of hitting, quite apart from the morality, they have been able to put methods into place which are positive and far more successful. The brave and honest father of one of our tapestry kids said: 'I never realised – but I was making things worse!'

Constant negative nagging, confrontations and screaming sessions can whip the tapestry kid up into even more of a frenzy – but if families do not know what to do, and the system does not do its bit for these children who need *more* than normal parenting, the system cannot blame them.

We can reweave this tangled tapestry through understanding and support, using positive, intensive, non-confrontational interventions from professionals to parents and in turn from parents to children. The introduction of the coach or facilitator into the daily lives of families and teachers is crucial. It requires major input from governments.

From my experience, most parents have become exhausted through long hard struggles with their children made worse by also having to struggle with the authorities. One would expect that with early recognition and self-help using support groups, considerable numbers of children would not need intensive support later.

Alerts

Parents of premature infants and other infants at risk of developmental problems must be provided with facilitator support as soon as the child is born. If a child presents with speech and language problems, hyperactivity and/or obsessional and rigid ritualistic behaviour or obvious motor impairment in the first three years of life, the child must be provided with family, educational and medical support.

If a child suffers from a head injury, especially if he or she has already had medical or developmental problems before, during or after birth, a tapestry of support must also be provided by family, educational and medical systems.

Children who start fires, have fascinations with weapons, sit glued to the TV for hours on end and watch videos repetitively need very early – before the age of 4 – professional assessment and support before their obsessional and potentially addictive pattern of behaviours escalates. If other problems include hurting others, the situation is very serious and must be taken seriously by the local system, the child prioritised for fast-track intensive support.

It is also most important that we do not panic or become overly anxious as the child will be aware of this state, but for too long we have expected children to grow out of it. It is now abundantly clear that they do not, especially in severe tangled tapestry cases. With greater awareness we can approach even serious conditions with knowledge and increasingly realistic expectations that we can improve the problem.

Chapter Eight

Creating the tapestry

'Something's not quite right'

(Mother of autistic child)

Most parents of tapestry kids have a suspicion that 'something's not quite right' at some point when their child is young. This feeling will vary in accordance with the extent and severity of the problem and other factors interweave such as cultural and family differences, tolerance and awareness levels. In some cases professionals find themselves trying to convince parents that support is necessary, with the family disinclined to accept any difficulties, partly through defensiveness and fear in many cases. In my experience it is largely the other way round, parents concerned and keen to get help, disputes normally related to the description of the difficulties, the suggested cause which can affect the nature of the intervention, and the suggested support.

Merging perspectives and emerging images

Weaving and reweaving tapestries requires planning. The end result is a product of your plan. No plan, or a poor plan, problems with the canvas, the threads or the weaving process can all result in a very poor representation of the original idea. Even when all the separate components are intact, the emerging picture will not be immediately obvious. Hard, intensive and repetitive work over time, according to a pre-set plan on multiple tiny details which are all the same – only the colours and their changing hue differentiating the threads – will ultimately result in a rich tapestry depicting a story as planned. As multiple perspectives merge, the image very gradually emerges. This illustrates how the child's mind works toward its goals and it should help if you keep this in mind when planning how you will manage the support for your child.

The practical tapestry

Two-dimensional tables begin the process of understanding your child. Try not to be hidebound by your own understanding of a particular disorder, which may be based on a variety of forms of information, which could include misinformation. Using the blank tapestries and the lists, compile the various threads which make up your child's tapestry. Using a time-line and a family tree you will need to chart the nature of relatives' problems and this will help you to decide how much you will need to do during the early weeks, months and years.

Drawing up visual tables to represent parts of the tapestry of interwoven problems and solutions may help some people to understand these concepts in a practical manner. This will involve drawing up strengths tapestries, problems tapestries, tables in which scores can be placed from assessments, intervention tapestries and tapestries which chart progress over time. Lists of traits need to be drawn up, with each trait forming a thread which can be judged according to severity in various settings. Children with ADHD and ASD may exhibit certain behaviours in every setting, and the nature of the behaviour and the severity need to be recognised. Certain behaviours may exist only in particular contexts.

Threads of particular traits such as hyperactivity are judged according to relative severity. A useful 1–30 scale of measurement can be created. The severity of the problem will be scored along this thread. Other threads pertaining to strengths can also be given a score or rating and the tapestry drawn out to help families visually understand the problems. As greater understanding is achieved, interweaving threads of environmental effects and the interwoven effects of the tapestries of other family members can also be included. It is also important to consider creating a time-line, which allows us to look at when certain events or behaviours emerged and how these accumulate and interweave over time.

Understanding the interwoven nature of developmental processes is a crucial issue. The following factors need to be considered:

- the nature of problems

- the number of problems

- the timing – when the problem first emerged

- the context – where the problem reveals itself most obviously and why it appears less obviously in other contexts

- the severity of the difficulties.

Thinking about children's development in this rich and respectful way should help us to understand when faced with an apparent confusion of different diagnoses with the child apparently not ideally fitting any one diagnostic category or another. By weaving tapestries we can better understand the problems; by reweaving them we can alter the developing story.

It is essential that parents know what to look out for at the outset and can put methods into action and contact broad-brush support early. The speed with which children with severe presentations of developmental disorders can deteriorate is much more rapid than the speed of system support. Inevitably many professionals will feel concerned that parents are imagining that their children have loads of different syndromes and will encourage them to forget it all and leave the child without anything. Most parents do not want to highlight their child's problems and would prefer to be talking to schools about their child's success. They usually know if their child has a problem: leaving it for years may mean that the problem emerges later when it may be too late and when the family may find themselves blamed for being over-concerned to start with, when in fact they were right but no one would listen.

Our understanding of autism through the past century must be understood in this modern context, in which more complex forms of autistic behaviour have been observed in the 1990s in association with gut disorders and allergies, pointing to problems with the auto-immune system.

A child may therefore have developed a tapestry of autistic/ADHD disorders in a number of ways, but research and clinical observation throughout the century shows that this is mainly through genetic propensity – through the family. Viral infection has always been recognised as one of the culprits linked with such disorders, but the autistic/ADHD group which increased dramatically in the 1990s is increasingly looking as though it is made up of children who are vulnerable to vaccine given in multiple form at the crucial stage of brain development, as the images of the social awareness tapestry emerge.

For the parents of the child with an autistic spectrum disorder, or the wakeful, overactive, constantly crying, possibly highly allergic baby, no amount of instinctive relating seems to make any difference. This can so easily cause mothers to become depressed as the threads of their communication web fail to weave with their precious child's tapestry and the instinctive responding built into a mother of a new infant is not responded to. If a mother does become postnatally depressed she will be less able to intrude intensively into her child's world and may find herself blamed for the problem when observers just see the depression, which is like blaming the sun for not being visible in a solar eclipse – unusual circumstances eclipse and interfere with the expected order of things.

Our understanding of the genetic nature of autism and ADHD-type disorders will ensure that some parents may suffer from similar difficulties, and the recognised co-morbidity of such disorders with anxiety and depression further compromises interactions. A wider perspective enables us to incorporate such circumstances and realise that our current models are limited. Greater understanding for families and professionals leads on to *respect* for each other, another crucial thread.

The metaphor of the tapestry can be used practically to understand the individual child better and to aid assessments. Tapestries of presenting difficulties can be unthreaded in order to understand the parts, and these can be separated into traditional areas pertaining to a professional's focus of work and then woven together. However, what is important in the notion of the tapestry is that we understand that all perspectives are needed to work together, just as in normal social development. It is the weave which matters most. Tapestries of strengths and positive interventions are crucial to reweave the tapestry. Multi-modal intervention tapestries spring from such multi- modal perceptions.

Drawing the grid

The first task is to draw a grid as shown for each tapestry, but add extra squares on the vertical axis as you need them. The horizontal axis is for severity ratings (or high–moderate–low ratings) and you will be simply drawing a line across the grid corresponding to the problem area.

Precise percentile or standard or T-score ratings from assessments such as the Conners or psychological scales should be set into a separate table to be interwoven.

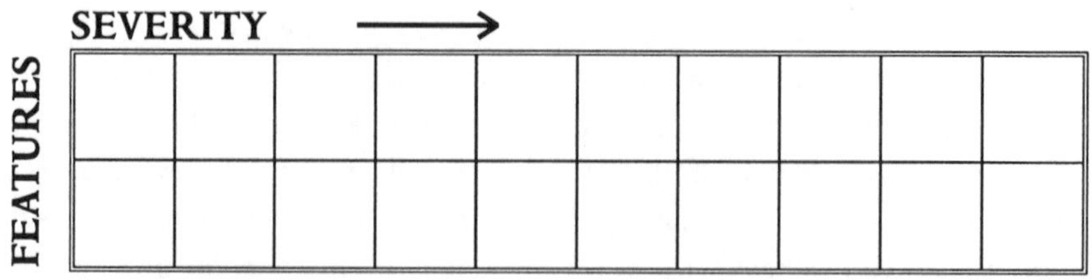

SEVERITY ⟶

(FEATURES — vertical axis label)

Features

You will be writing in different *features* along the vertical axis which may present risks. Examples are hyperactivity; getting the wrong end of the stick/misconstruing what you say; how others interpret what they do; clumsiness; rigid routines; obsessional and repetitive behaviour; rages; whether a child remembers information and the type of information; whether the child can engage in dual/multi-tasking; the nature of the child's speech and so on.

Severity

The severity level at which you judge the problem needs to be inserted on your horizontal scale. In a number of cases, each problem may not be severe but it will be the cluster of difficulties which is important.

Choose which seems the most appropriate for you. Some people prefer a mild-moderate-severe scale while others prefer one which allows for finer detail of judgement. Some prefer a 1–10 scale while others would feel happier with a 1–30. It is entirely up to you.

To get going

First think of how you would describe your child in one short sentence – these are the first impressions that can be helpful but can also mislead those who know little about the child. Phrases like 'little professor', 'off the wall' or 'off the planet' give a snapshot view.

Next, focus precisely on any problems in the following areas and just draw the severity of three threads – the core tapestry – from your first subjective thoughts.

- communication skills – listening/eye
  contacting/turn-taking/babble/language

- motor perceptual skills – crawling/walking/balance/co-ordination/tactile responses/motor planning/imitation
- attentional skills – concentration/focus/sticking to a task/organising/joint attending.

Add two more – don't ponder – go on your first thought:

- sensitivities
- rigid, repetitive behaviour.

Look closely at these. You will find yourself considering whether the child is the same in all tasks or all situations or with all people. This relates to what is called the communicative context. You'll need to make up a few tapestries for the same basic skills for different contexts. Cross-context similarities will help you to understand inflexible behaviours. These could be attention to task while doing Lego, puzzles, lining up toys or looking at video and TV, for instance, compared with attention to people who are giving instructions, both of which may be the same in lots of settings. Typically, the young child will over-focus on the former, and those who do not engage with blocks and Lego type activity may well have motor difficulties. On the other hand, attention when people are speaking or rules have to be followed will be much less well developed. Some children will drift off into a daydream in the middle of any activity.

Context tapestries

This can be as simple or complex as you can deal with. The context refers a variety of threads which create a richness for the child's tapestry. In talking with parents they can give incredible insights into why their child behaved in a certain way in certain tasks, in a certain situation, with a certain person, under certain conditions. It is this detail which will add richness to both the understanding of the problem and the potential for success of the intervention plan.

Include the place such as home or school or Grandpa's house. You can detail the features within these places.

Include the child's mood, which will regulate how he or she communicates and receives information. Mood will also be in part determined by how the child interprets the nuts and bolts of the social milieu within which he or she exists. The nature and amount of language used by those trying to communicate are important details. For instance, many teachers and parents (and some psychologists!) talk too much and often do not realise that the child is picking up only on certain aspects of the language used, or may be picking up on novel associations which they would not have dreamt of without truly *knowing* the child. Or they may be focusing on the emotional behaviour of the other person, and how that makes them feel, or the expression on their face, or even what they are wearing. Combine language confusion with anxiety when confronted, confused and embarrassed and it is not surprising that many children with such problems do not listen to most of what is said to them.

If your child is very young, one table will suffice. If he or she is older, especially if a teenager, you will need to do a table for pre-school, 5–11 and then beyond. That way you will be able to see at a glance how your child has changed.

Not every child with many high-risk factors will develop the problems discussed in this book, and if you are completing this on a very young child, the interventions and references are intended to provide you with information to help yourself as early as possible. Professional intervention is not always desirable and if the family can put support in place and use particular strategies early, later potential difficulties can be offset or at least reduced.

If your child is older and problems have already arisen, you will be in a better position to understand and to seek out support. You will need to create a current tapestry and also one which shows how your young child developed. These early behaviours are very important as they indicate the nature of the early tapestry. The early development of many older children with difficulties is often not taken into account: this is vital information to understand how tapestries have been woven. I know that psychologists and psychiatrists working with adults who have knowledge of child and adolescent development are greatly helped in their formulations when faced with complex adult problems.

Most parents understand why they have to give a full history of development if we are trying to understand later problems. However, on a few occasions I have found that parents query why I have a section in my developmental questionnaire about their child's baby and toddlerhood when he is a strapping six-footer. Many leave out questions pertaining to the younger child, or write 'N/A'. Some write 'N/A!' Some will question my competence and ask whether I have given them the right questionnaire; on one questionnaire a parent wrote: 'These questions are TOTALLY inappropriate for a 17-year-old's behaviour. This is completely and utterly irrelevant to understanding him.'

Examples of some tapestry threads

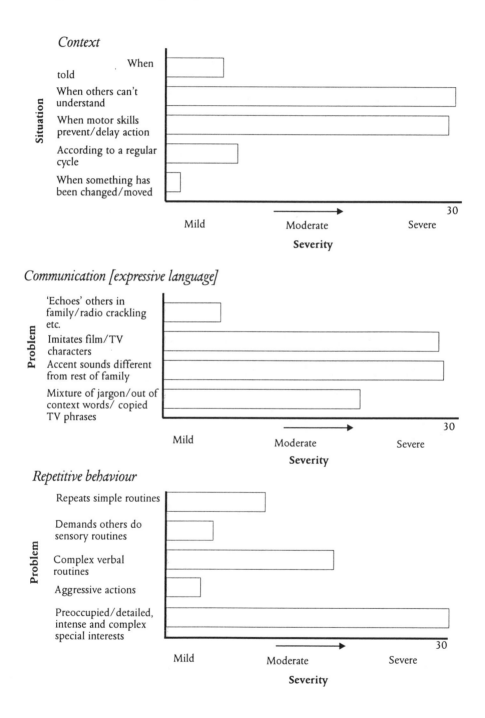

Context

Situation

- When told
- When others can't understand
- When motor skills prevent/delay action
- According to a regular cycle
- When something has been changed/moved

Mild   Moderate   Severe   30

Severity

Communication [expressive language]

Problem

- 'Echoes' others in family/radio crackling etc.
- Imitates film/TV characters
- Accent sounds different from rest of family
- Mixture of jargon/out of context words/ copied TV phrases

Mild   Moderate   Severe   30

Severity

Repetitive behaviour

Problem

- Repeats simple routines
- Demands others do sensory routines
- Complex verbal routines
- Aggressive actions
- Preoccupied/detailed, intense and complex special interests

Mild   Moderate   Severe   30

Severity

Repetitive routines and unusual forms of imitation

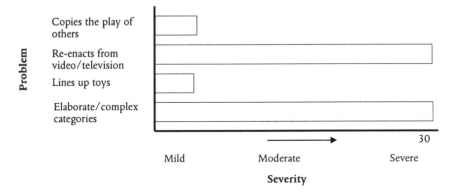

Motor perception

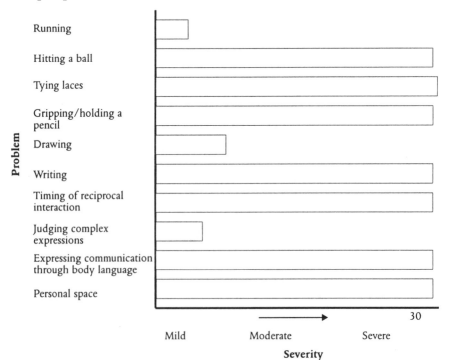

Getting more complicated

Each child's tapestry is woven onto a potentially fixed base – inherited features and acquired pre- and peri-natal problems – and sewn onto these bases are the threads of illnesses, viral infections, etc. There is a much higher rate of such difficulties among children with these developmental disorders, especially if there is a family history. The timing of acquisition and presentation of these various features are other important threads, as is the severity of the problem and the number and nature of coexisting disorders.

For the problems/risk tapestry the following need to be considered:

- family history
- pre-natal, birth and developmental history
- presenting features
- severity
- timing of onset of problems
- age of child
- gender
- intellectual and neurological profile (if you know – find out if not).

Family history

At a support group for families a few years ago, a young woman poignantly told how she had blamed her mother for years for her early childhood hyperactivity, school failure, trouble in developing relationships and later drug problems, all difficulties experienced by her father and a paternal cousin. She had been given years of counselling in which she was encouraged to continue to blame her mother although no one could actually explain the mechanisms by which her mother had caused such problems. The idea of abuse was played around with but the woman had no memories of such events. In fact, many of her childhood memories were positive and she described her mother in a very normal and balanced way. As time passed and her life problems did not abate, she came to believe that somehow, through no clear mechanism, her mother must have imposed such a negative effect on her during her childhood that she would never recover. She refused to have anything to do with her mother any more.

It took the emergence of similar early childhood behaviour in her son but in none of her other children for the woman to start the long and painful process of self and family awareness. Her counsellor tried to convince her that she must have been unwittingly re-enacting and imposing her own unrecalled experiences at the hands of her mother – who also did not recall them – on her son. She found this a bit far fetched and went for the more obvious – her son had inherited what she had inherited from her father's side of the family. She was told that her son suffered from a hyperactivity disorder with obsessive behaviours and social communication problems. After thorough investigation of ADHD and tic disorders she realised that a number of people in the wider family had similar difficulties, variously managed. The struggle she suffered with her son as she tried to change his difficult behaviour mirrored that of her own mother's experience with her, who she thought had caused her problems. Complex and intensive but successful management of her son and positive group support for her and her mother was enough to allow this family to reconstitute. She wept for the lost years and the wrongful blame of her mother.

As parents we need to look at our family histories – whether we like it or not! There will have been secrets and lies, excuses and denials of problems in certain family members and maybe exaggeration in other cases. This is normal, especially as none of us like to admit that there may be a problem with our child, especially over the past century. The terrible fear of the stigma of anything to do with the mind strongly affected most parents throughout the twentieth century and those in the older generation can still hold the same fears. This is no surprise. As long as systems continue to blame families parents will disguise children's problems.

One of the worst examples known to me of the effects of pretending children do not have the difficulties they clearly display relates to a great-grandmother who was so afraid of everyone knowing that her daughter was mentally ill – she had been in and out of psychiatric hospital since a teenager – that she hid evidence of her daughter's abuse of her own daughter and her grandchildren. She let the system blame her granddaughter for events caused by her own daughter, who in turn lost all her children. If society had allowed for a greater openness early in her daughter's childhood when she was very hyperactive, she may never have developed the later mental illness, or it may have been less damaging to her and less contagious amongst the entire family, which was completely destroyed. If there had been more openness and honesty about her mental illness as an adult and more honesty in the system, her granddaughter would not have been blamed and she would not have lost her great-grandchildren.

This is an extreme case but illustrates some of the problems of denying difficulties when we try to find out about our wider families. I ask families to think about hyperactive behaviour, social problems, learning difficulties, speech and language development, motor development and tics in relatives within the wider family. In many Asperger cases there is evidence of eccentricity, rigidity, poor money, time and deadline management, temper control, job and family problems. The ADHD family history may include a similar list, with less evidence of eccentricity or specialist interests. Creating such a tapestry can be very interesting, especially as one explores how resilience and novel factors have helped people to cope.

Finding such difficulties within the wider family does not automatically mean that you or your children will have the same difficulties. But it could point to a genetic vulnerability, especially if there are numerous severe cases, as there is strong evidence of the heritability of these disorders.

Always remember, the tapestry is part of the wider tapestry of normality. Many people have similar difficulties and are not affected by them. As the saying goes – 'If it ain't broke – don't fix it'. My experience, and the purpose of writing this book, is that there are very many people who *are* badly affected by these problems and the compounding factors. Recognising them and the resilience factors early reduces the potential for later damage.

So, in the family history tapestry, consider how severe the problems are in your relatives and score it. It is quite acceptable that this scoring system is subjective, because it reflects how much importance you place on certain behaviours occurring.

Presenting features

The second step involves charting the features, which is best achieved by chatting with the family about the pregnancy and birth and the baby's early months of development. Modern technology means that there may be video recordings of young children to examine, which is very helpful, alongside photographs and memories.

There are a number of risk factors compounding inherited traits which need to be taken into account; these include complications during the pregnancy, smoking, diet, drinking and drugs, prematurity and exposure to viruses. The extent of any prematurity and the birth weight of the infant are also important. Furthermore, brain haemorrhages and other complications which may affect the appropriate amount of oxygen reaching the infant will add to the risk factors, as will obstetric complications.

The first few weeks are really important for babies to learn about people, and if they have illnesses or problems sleeping and eating they miss all the fun. If a child has suffered with allergies, problems with body regulation such as sleeping, homeostatic control and feeding, these at the very least prevent the child from having fun with people. There may be ear infections and the child may be feeling pain which he or she cannot explain. Make notes in the tapestry if any of these things are happening.

Many parents of children with later recognised ADHD and/or autism notice signs of overactivity and excessive crying in their infant, or they are very placid, but this is not always evident. Make a note if this was a feature. Some infants avoid being held and seem unable to make eye contact.

Infants should engage in play each day but some may sleep a lot and not seem at all interested. Make a note of whether your child seemed to look properly at you and if your child would look in the direction you were looking and where you were pointing.

Later in the first year the child should begin to use babble to communicate with you and should point to things of interest as well as to things he or she wants, as well as sharing interest with you. Once into the second year pretend play should be observed – for instance drinking pretend tea, making pretend cakes, turning a cardboard box into a vehicle.

In a piece of research in the UK psychologists looked at which salient factors in the first 18 months of life predicted autism later (Baron-Cohen *et al.* 1996). They screened 16 000 18-month-old children. If a child consistently failed to engage in three particular skills he or she had an 83.3 per cent chance of being diagnosed with autism in later testing. The three factors were:

- gaze monitoring: following the gaze of another person when they look at and point at an object
- pretend play: pretending one thing is another in play
- protodeclarative pointing: pointing out something so that another person will share your attention and look at it.

From this research a screening tool for health visitors and family doctors was devised (see Table 8.1).

Table 8.1 CHAT – Checklist for Autism in Toddlers – A Screening Tool

The following test can be used by a paediatrician or family doctor during the 18-month development check-up. The CHAT should not be used as a diagnostic instrument, but can alert primary health professionals to the need for an expert referral.

Yes	No	1. During the appointment, has the child made eye contact with you?
Yes	No	*2. Get the child's attention, then point across the room at an interesting object and say, 'Oh look! There's a [name of toy]!' Watch the child's face. Does the child look across to see what you are pointing at? (a)
Yes	No	*3. Get the child's attention, then give child a miniature toy cup and teapot and say, 'Can you make a cup of tea?' (Substitute toy pitcher and glass and say 'Can you poor a glass of juice?' Does the child pretend to pour out tea (juice) drink it, etc. (b)
Yes	No	*4. Say to the child, 'Where's the light?', or 'show me the light.'(c) Does the child point with his/her index finger at the light?
Yes	No	5. Can the child build a tower of bricks (blocks)? (If so how many?) (Number of bricks….)

* indicates critical questions that are most indicative of autistic characteristics.

(a) To record Yes on this item, ensure the child has not simply looked at your hand, but has actually looked at the object you are pointing at.

(b) If you can elicit an example of pretending in some other game, score a Yes on this item.

(c) Repeat this with, 'Where's the teddy bear?'. or some other unreachable object if child does not understand the word 'light'. To record on this item , the child must have looked up at your face around the time of pointing.

The British Journal of Psychiatry, 1996, vol. 168. pp. 158–163
The British Journal of Psychiatry, 1992, vol. 161, pp. 839–843

Some children who can do all the things in the Checklist for Autism in Toddlers (CHAT) in the first 18 months and who have begun to speak sometimes lose these skills at 18 months. Within that group are those who may have reacted to vaccines. The Baron-Cohen *et al.* (1996) study may have included children whose failure to undertake such tasks related to vaccine or it may not. What is important is that the study highlighted certain features *very early* in a child's life which strongly predicted a later diagnosis of autism and which in the past have simply been suspected. Many children *appear* to be developing normally but a consistent lack of these three features, and quite probably others more subtle, indicate that they are not and their absence is linked to problems at later stages of language and social development. Evidence of such difficulties may also indicate susceptibilities to developing such problems given particular triggers. For some, this could be a vaccine. If the child has allergies or medical problems, it would be wise to consider all the issues around vaccination. Many children in this category will not shift from single words to sentences and there will be no evidence of any vaccine damage or other viral infections.

False negatives, saying a child does not have a problem when he or she later clearly does, do occur and certain children who could engage in pretend play – for instance Jack, one of our two little brothers in Chapter 1 – later develop elaborate games which become obsessive and do not involve people. The early evidence of pretend play does not preclude a child from falling onto the autistic spectrum, but this survey showed that the most robust cluster for later diagnosed autism was the motor skill of pointing in shared attention, sharing gaze direction and then being able to pretend.

False positives, saying a child is autistic who then proves not to be, can also occur. This is why it is important to introduce the various ideas mentioned later and in other books at the early stages if a child is having trouble engaging appropriately. Many children with highly active behaviour who fall into the hyperactive group may also fail to develop such skills.

In severe cases of autism it has been suggested that if we miss the developmental windows of time during which our children should develop certain skills, it may be too late to make a significant difference. It is this realisation that if significant change is at all possible in severely autistic non-verbal children, intensive interventions must be trialled before the age of 4 years. This does not indicate that any intensive support later will not make a difference to the majority of tapestry children, as the efforts to intervene must never stop, but in severe cases in which children are extremely obsessive with no language, hyperactive and lacking imitative skills, very early, very intensive support appears to be absolutely crucial.

Note the progress of your child's motor development. Many children with hyperactivity, whether on the autistic continuum or not, rapidly move into trouble at very early stages, requiring very close supervision. Most infants do not need to be watched as closely as this group who can cause damage to things, themselves or others in the blink of an eye.

Reading through the tapestry kids case studies you will occasionally see reference to bad falls. Dependent on severity and vulnerability of the child, executive dysfunctions can follow from a head injury and the child may begin to exhibit behaviour similar to the inherited ADHD group and the inherited autism group. If they are already on those spectra such events will add to the problems and increase the tangled tapestry. Research confirms this clinical impression (Gerring et al. 1998). One child I assessed fell from a very high seat in a circus. He fractured his skull and subsequent to this time he presented with less language ability, poor social awareness and ADHD behaviour. The examples are numerous and obviously prevention is the key, but very difficult to do.

Some children have a terrible habit of smashing their heads against hard floors and walls. This will not help matters but it is likely that these children have neurological problems which cause them to engage in such behaviour. Bashing their own heads will only tangle their tapestry. Perhaps there ought to be more hard hats for toddlers.

Other difficulties might relate to sensory skills including the proprioceptive and kinaesthetic skills, sensory sensitivities and so on. Some children on the autistic spectrum have enormous problems with patterns of movements, even with copying a teacher or other children with very basic modelled actions such as touching the nose with right and left hands, hands on heads, hopping, striding etc. Music helps and close observation of the conditions required to help the child to do such skills obviously helps to create the intervention tapestries.

Loss of skills

You may find that you can draw simple tapestries which show absolutely normal behaviour and development for your child in the first year, although there may be subtle features (as above) which indicate some vulnerabilities which need to be tackled. Others will have no problems at all.

In your medical first year tapestry you will need to include allergies such as asthma and eczema and reactions to milk and other dairy products.

Your reason for thinking about weaving tapestries will be because your child has acquired a disorder later. Some children on the autistic spectrum lose skills in the second year at around 18 months after appearing to develop normally. They may stick on using one word and not move forward to developing more complex language. They may start to be aggressive and avoid people. They also seem to increase repetitive behaviours at the same time. These can include a variety of repetitive behaviours such as shaking the same toy in the same way over and over, examining objects through the corner of their eyes, picking up and examining tiny things or showing a fascination for certain colours or shiny materials. Routines may become more rigid with the child desperately distressed if anything is changed or if items of fascination are moved.

It might be noticed that a child will watch a particular television programme or video over and over and become furious if pulled away from it.

Look out for daydreaming, highly active behaviour or odd mannerisms. Make a note of the way your child uses language. It is useful to know whether children speak on time – using single words around 1 year; whether their speech is clear; whether they make up their own words. Can they follow rules? Do they appear to understand instructions? Do they seem to misconstrue what others mean through their language or action? Do they have problems picking up on the social cues and clues in their social environment? Do they have problems demonstrating what they mean through facial expressions and body language? Can they understand the consequences of their own actions? Do they take risks?

The histories of all young children with autistic continuum disorders and many young children with ADHD refer to difficulties at varying levels of severity with relationships. Previous chapters and the tapestry kids case studies will give you ideas about the kinds of problems which can present during the pre-school years. Some children will seem to want to engage with others but will sit at the periphery of the group, unsure what to do, while others will avoid children at all costs.

Some bright Asperger children may show an early disdain for children, finding their ways of playing childish or pointless, or they may try to control the play of children, insisting that they play according to particular rules designed by them or that they engage in particular activities. Telling and understanding jokes can be a problem, as we have seen.

The more severely Kanner-type autistic child may literally walk over other children as if they haven't seen them or remain locked into stereotypic behaviours oblivious to the others. Even amongst this group one can detect a fleeting glance at people or the child will move toward adults and maybe look at them very closely and then move away again. One child was attracted by the herringbone pattern on my suit and kept returning to look closely at the pattern again and again. In between she looked at the patterns on leaves and tried the feel of soil from the school garden in her mouth.

As we move along the reciprocity thread we find children who insist on controlling games and irritate the other children to the point that they reject them. One of our tapestry kids has now taken to demanding that everyone jumps on the bouncy castle for exactly ten jumps.

So many of the combined group cannot work out the point of games unless they are in charge and tend to prefer sports in which they can participate alone, if they like any at all.

For those with motor problems, making friends can be particularly difficult. Some may want to play but their poor co-ordination and poor motor planning may let them down. They might have problems catching and throwing balls, difficulties riding a bike. They will not be asked to be in teams. One adolescent was asked to be goalie, as this was all he could do. Unfortunately his team was so good the ball hardly ever got past their defence in his direction. So he took to leaning on the goal-post and reading his book. The one time the ball came his way he was oblivious to it landing in the net – until the team screamed at him.

Many ADHD children with no obvious autistic features will thoroughly enjoy games and the rules of games – more than when they are required to engage in conversation, when communication problems will affect their social use of language. Games provide structure and rules which they like and need, they can get away with using little language and the rough and tumble helps them.

By comparison parents of the combined group or the Asperger group find that it is during playtime or unstructured times that their children have the greatest problems – and the teachers can have the greatest problems with them! For those with the most severe problems, walking round in circles might be their activity. Others will stare at walls and pipes. One of our tapestry kids, Lorelei, said 'Well, the wall needs a friend too' (see Chapter 3).

The children who present with many of the above features, including some obsessions, may develop dangerous fascinations. In some cases these can relate to objects and in others to activities or both. As early as 3 years of age some children can begin to show a fascination for knives, matches and/or lighters. If these interests are combined with hyperactive risky behaviour and poor social awareness perhaps showing aggression toward others, urgent professional action is needed. This is particularly important if the tapestry includes conduct disorder and the child undertakes anti-social acts such as stealing, lighting fires, hurting people or animals. The combination of such behaviour and ADHD makes this group very much at risk of later poor outcome and possible serious offending. As angry and increasingly bitter outsiders, their obsessions become bound up with attacking those they blame for his isolation. The more danger-ous the obsession, the more aggressive and isolated and the more damaging the potential outcome. Drawing up severity tapestries for such behaviours will give an immediate image of the serious concerns.

Many children may respond well to the institutional structure and the rules of school and may be able to learn and make friends, showing no apparent problems at all, despite an early history of problems. As long as everyone is truthful about children they should rapidly build on their success. Some schools and local authority psychology services have an excellent reputation for providing the appropriate environmental factors. Regular contact with school should ensure even greater success.

For many children with a number of early difficulties the school environ-ment can be very challenging. They cannot filter out noise, some saying 'make the noise go out of my head' (see Jack's tapestry in Chapter 1) and the complex fragmentation of stimuli which they have to process, including lots of children, may be intolerable. In large classes of 30 or more children it may prove impossi-ble for the teacher to give the time required to the child and for the child to cope with the fragmented world which they cannot process. Trying to process more than one task or information from more than one sensory channel can be enormously difficult.

Others may cope with the children and the school but not the work. For many parents this is the point at which the children who they managed to hold together at pre-school fall apart as they fail. Motor problems may lead them to be highly reluctant to write. Understanding time and where they are supposed to be and when may confuse. Dyslexia, possibly caused by or made worse by Irlen syndrome, especially if they have had some form of head trauma during a hyperactive childhood, may be the last straw. It may actually be the first disorder seen by others, but in children with these developmental disorders it forms a further highly damaging compounding effect. Expectations and demands to function in the abstract and independently increase, while the obvious structure, support, practical and visual aids are removed.

From a number of children I have seen, each blow, whether literally or metaphorically speaking, seems to have a cumulative effect. Such a blow could be described as an unexpected event which could dramatically change the future for the child. Our clinical awareness of this potential should lead to rapid action.

First school may be able to contain children without a tangled tapestry but containment will not have prepared them for the shock of the shift to secondary school, with larger school buildings, many changes of teachers, lots of new rules, instructions, timetables, teachers' names, and homework assignments to remember.

Invariably the ADHD children who make it this far in mainstream without support will have trouble meeting deadlines, trouble getting to class on time or at all, trouble concentrating in class and trouble with planning and organisation of their work. They may be struggling socially but hiding this and finding this particularly difficult during puberty. Many adolescents with tapestry disorders confess to not having a clue what others mean through gesture, facial expression and/or their conversations. They may make attempts to conform, even extending to engaging in undesirable activities to make an impact, or they may become depressed and isolated in their own world, over-focused on their particular interest. Others may find themselves bullied and/or manipulated by peers, who rapidly see their vulnerability. Motor problems can be embarrassing and highly frustrating. To have to repeat the same actions over and over again in simple everyday activity because of clumsiness can lead to dramatic rages. I had toothmarks on one of my puzzle pieces for some time to remind me of the child who was so angry that he could not fit the pieces together that he bit hard into the piece to make it work.

The early years give many clues as to later developing behavioural and learning problems which may or may not emerge. Remember, if you are developing the tapestry in order to prevent later difficulties, there may be no need at all to find professional support. Where you are on the time-line will determine how you use this idea.

Threads of presenting features, for instance hyperactivity, and the potential environmental impact of particular behaviours and of behaviours on others' reactions are then added. The extent or lack of various types of support within the environment also form threads in the tapestry, which enhance or restrict the child's potential. This includes how children are taught, methods and delivery of instruction, how we support children at home, how we interact with them, our methods of discipline and so on. One adolescent boy with Asperger syndrome had made a highly detailed model of Postman Pat. His teacher, who could not understand his difficulties and became highly frustrated with him every day, dramatically threw the model into the dustbin in front of all the children. This was not a helpful intervention!

The context within which a child functions must be taken into account. It is failure to recognise this issue which can often lead to a total lack of understanding of the individual person. For instance, if a child functions in a certain manner in a clinic or school-based context we may dismiss parental descriptions which do not seem to match.

However, it is now very clear that children operating in real-life situations, as opposed to, say, the clinic, function very differently. Once the structure and rule-governed nature of the clinic and school fall away – so does the learned behaviour. Home is not an institution and parents are not professionals to their children, nor should they be expected to be. Children with autism have well-recognised problems with generalising skills from one context to another. Years of practitioner insight has shown that even if they can tell you exactly how they should interact or behave in the teaching session, it does not follow that they will shift their learning to other contexts.

Many children are held in pressure-cooker mode all day in the institution of the early junior school, only to explode on return home. For years I have seen local authorities blame parents and say it is a home issue as the problems occurred outside school, to save money on interventions in school. This fragmenting of children does not adequately match with how human behaviour works and certainly does not help us toward better understanding and cheaper methods of improvement.

Weaving tapestries allows us to look at the detail of the unique individual's responses to apparently well-designed interventions. Taking population outcomes and expecting the individual to conform does not always work out. The unique weaving of the individual tapestry using the self-similar threads is the only way forward.

The tangled effect of interweaving problems over time cannot be ignored. If we find out about a child's pre-school problems when he or she is 15 years old and proceed to put in support that was more appropriate at pre-school, our intervention is weak, limited and quite possibly a waste of time and money. Our attitude to the truly difficult business of reweaving the tapestry is hopelessly naive. We need to look at how the tapestry has been woven as time has passed and apply an appropriate tapestry of support.

Other factors which need to be taken into account also alter the weave of the tapestry. Girls, for instance, are less likely to develop such disorders. Boys outdo them by four to one. If they do, they may be more adaptable or their problems may go unnoticed, and this may apply to the statistics. Invariably it is the boy with troublesome behaviour who is most likely to be noticed over a daydreaming girl. However, in relation to depression and anxiety disorders, the girls outdo the boys.

Within ADHD research, it is likely to be the more difficult behaviour of the boys that leads them to the clinics which do the research. There is a strong body of evidence that many girls present with ADD behaviour – without the hyperactivity which brings in the support – and that odd or addictive behaviours are just attributed to the child being neurotic or over-anxious. Abuse will be suspected in some cases and it is right that this should be explored if there is evidence apart from the ADD behaviour. If the latter is all that is in evidence, a specialist assessment is necessary.

Many girls with early ADD, daydreaming and subtle communication problems will fail in school but are unlikely to be recognised. If they begin to self-harm, develop eating disorders or try to self-medicate using illegal drugs, perhaps sinking into criminal activity, the assumption may be that they have been abused all their lives. This may be a feature in the tapestry but it does not explain everything in every case. Without appropriate recognition of the problem, abuse continues.

The level of intellectual ability will also affect the tapestry and determine interventions and placements. For the highly intelligent but deeply anxious male or female with Asperger or ADHD they can be overwhelmed by the details which their minds try to process. This includes trying to understand people and their natural competitiveness and deviousness, and relationships can end in great sadness. A tendency to take on too much work or try to manage too much information can result in all activity and no action – but a lot of intense frustration and more crippling anxiety as deadlines are missed and people let down. One adolescent described her life as one of total exhaustion which I suggested was like climbing a perpendicular mountain – with no ledges to pause for a break.

Parenting skills

In discussing weaving a child's tapestry I start from the basic premise that families have good broad-brush parenting skills. Other books can be consulted for parenting programmes which outline ideal and essential features of good parenting. There are also excellent books for improving the motivational problems of normally developing children. Children with developmental disorders push parents to their limits and once problems are recognised, an over-reaction to the hyperactive child can be understood, as well as its potential for tangling the tapestry.

Understanding these effects has led to the development of multi-modal plans which include parenting of children with problems, as part of the basic tapestry. In my experience, families have been able to access a considerable amount of information, have educated themselves and made changes if necessary in their reactions and management of their children. Despite this input, children with these disorders can wear down not just parents but whole teams of professionals! The truth is quite simple: tapestry kids are HARD WORK! Hence the need for well-planned and well-informed tapestries of intervention. Behavioural programmes, which incorporate well-recognised methods to improve motivation and learning, also know that the involvement of families in this work is essential.

Knowing this, it is enormously helpful for families to make up tapestries. You will find that each child's tapestry is unique. For instance, one may involve severe hyperactivity, minor motor problems and moderate social confusion. Another child might present with no hyperactivity, but significant motor problems and severe social confusion. Sleep, eating and toileting issues also need to be taken into account alongside evidence of allergies, infections, loss of oxygen prior to or at birth and any brain injuries through prematurity, for instance, prematurity itself, head injuries through accidents, effects of vaccine and so on.

One would expect variation in different contexts as the child interweaves with multiple stimuli. Other threads such as ability level, presence or absence of learning difficulties (LD) and the presence or absence of many other features, events and life circumstances can be added to the tapestries.

Assessments

Scores from standardised scales such as the Conners and the Vineland can be used as additional threads, the whole process ideally completed by families and professionals working together. Families should ask professionals for results of testing and this information needs to be added to the tapestry. IQ as a general score is not precise enough. Parents need to ask for specific information about a child's profile of neuropsychological functioning, level of ability in verbal and performance skills and, within those, ability to sequence, memory skills, visual and auditory skills, ability to define words and ability to abstract both verbally and non-verbally. Functioning with the speech therapist will help to refine the tapestry: speech and language tapestry could be drawn up to help with monitoring of progress over time. The same could apply to any other areas of difficulty in which there is specialist involvement and targeted aims and objectives.

Strengths tapestries

Once you have worked out your first impressions and your tapestry focusing on the basic problems, you may have shifted to a much more complex position. Whether you did or not, create a second tapestry which uses a scale from high to low to include all the good points and the factors which help. These can include, for instance, measures of how helpful relaxation or certain music is for your child.

Consider the contexts – people, activity, setting, how people act and speak, language used and so on – in which your child functions *best*. These are very important considerations for when interventions are put in place.

Factors to look out for

The following is a list of common ADHD or autism factors taken from various criteria with some additional features which I find helpful:

- prematurity
- difficult pregnancy, especially if evidence of the child suffering
- smoking, drug taking and excessive drinking during pregnancy
- born late for dates
- traumatic birth
- breathing problems at birth or during first year
- highly restless infant and/or toddler
- physically impulsive
- verbally impulsive

- can't listen
- doesn't seem to understand instructions
- makes silly noises
- never stops talking
- talks about one topic of interest and bores others
- fascinated by edges, angles and details of things like leaves and shiny objects
- fascinated and obsessed by complicated games, ideas, machinery or diagrams
- interrupts
- blurts out
- pedantic speech or accent different from peer group or family
- emotional
- aggressive
- violent to animals
- violent to people
- steals from family
- steals outside home
- fascinated by fire
- starts fires
- swears
- odd body jerks or swearing or movements
- difficulties playing or engaging with peers
- wants to take over in games with peers
- wants to remain alone away from peers
- has no friends
- odd body posture or odd way of standing, walking or running
- overweight
- insatiable drinking or eating habit
- resistant to change

- sensitive to sound, light or people
- fascination with the smell, taste or feel of things
- odd facial grimaces
- inappropriate facial expressions
- inappropriate emotional response for events
- poor judgement of others' body language, emotion, facial expression or reaction
- says or does inappropriate things outside the home
- poor understanding of jokes or certain types of jokes
- problems cracking jokes – timing wrong or forgets a crucial part of the joke or blurts it out before the punchline
- paces the room
- talks to him or herself
- fiddles with special objects
- loses things
- room a total mess
- poor at organising own daily routine
- easily distracted
- forgetful
- daydreamer
- can't finish written work
- reading problems
- spelling problems
- writing problems
- mental arithmetic problems
- can't engage in multi-modal tasks like listening, pausing and talking in conversations
- misses parts of information given to him or her through not registering (orienting) at the start
- misses parts of information given to him or her through impulsively darting off or shutting off before you've finished

- can't learn from punishments or lectures
- soon tires of reward systems
- needs novel information
- obsessive and ritualistic about activities, toys or other objects
- obsessive and ritualistic about routines to do with the self
- problems catching and throwing
- problems kicking a ball
- late learning to ride a bike
- late learning to tie shoelaces
- can't coordinate actions
- can't imitate gestures, actions and postures
- late learning to speak
- does not speak
- spoke single words then lost ability at 18 months
- put words together in unusual ways or makes up his or her own
- rambles
- suffered a head injury
- suffered loss of oxygen
- allergies
- gastrointestinal problems now
- gastrointestinal problems as a baby
- sleep difficulties as a baby
- sleep difficulties now
- excessive crying as a baby
- very placid as a baby
- no pointing to items of interest as a baby (before 12 months)
- no looking in same direction as you as a baby
- no shared pointing to items of interest
- difficulty gazing appropriately as a baby (looks too long, doesn't look at all, doesn't gaze monitor)

- difficulty gazing (as above) now
- problems picking up on social cues and clues leading to arguments and relationship problems
- can't work out consequences of own actions
- problems understanding time
- always late
- poor sense of direction
- repetitive behaviours
- imitates others too precisely
- odd sounding voice
- copies chunks of sounds from radio or television
- acts out exact scenes from TV shows or own videos
- obsessed by TV
- non-animated face when speaking and poor regulation of body posture and gesture to regulate social interaction
- does or says exactly what you do or say but a little later
- rages.

You will see that the above list relates to various checklists for different disorders. You may find that your tapestry child meets many of the criteria. The severity of the problem and the way your child responds to your own interventions will decide for you whether further action with professionals is necessary.

Teasing out tangled tapestries

Parents and children may feel highly confused and frustrated when juggling with a number of significant problems – and maybe this is what they feel when considering the tapestry! By drawing up separate tables and setting out the separate threads, the whole tapestry can be defined and analysed and interventions better applied when the whole tapestry is put back together. Nevertheless, it is important to recognise that even this complexity only represents a fraction of reality. Be prepared for the unexpected!

Summary

Tapestry 1: Problems

Choose the main areas of concern or include features from the areas of communication, attention and perceptual motor development. Don't try to put all the threads from the above list into one table! Remember, this is just a rule of thumb, an idea to help those who prefer it, to be able to explore ideas and represent their concerns and chart progress visually. Score the severity according to a scale of your own choice. You can focus in on a few threads and be more detailed about their nature once you gain more awareness and move toward interventions.

Tapestry 2: Strengths

In these tapestries we draw the resilience factors to be used to help reweave the tapestry. Each and every person born has wonderful features. These can so easily be lost if serious problems prevail and take over. Make sure these are sewn into this positive tapestry. This tapestry could also hold the things which soothe or calm the child or these features could be in a separate 'Things that Help' tapestry. Find out what type of music really calms the child. Experiment with music and colours and poems and songs.

Tapestry 3: Context

A full understanding of behaviour cannot proceed without including the context. You might want to use this tapestry when focusing on particular events or problem behaviours to start family or staff discussions about how the child responds in different situations, settings, with different people etc. and why that may be. Work out if the child mainly learns/learnt visually or if he or she also seemed to respond well to language and would speak back without problems.

What to do next

From your tapestry and an examination of the diagnostic tables in Appendix 1, you will have a reasonable picture of where your child might fit. The more severe scores you fill in (get another family member or a friend who knows your child to do the same and compare) and the younger the child, the more important it is that you take your tapestries to professionals. On the other hand, if you have been to professionals to no avail, try once more with your information and then contact a support and/or advice group from those listed in Appendix 2.

If your child's problems are not particularly severe you might want to look at home behaviour programmes, read more books on the problems, try out some of the games which can be bought from educational suppliers (see Appendix 2) and/or discuss modifications with local health and education professionals.

If there are concerns about your child's difficulties in school, good nurseries and schools will welcome your involvement, as you know your child best. Working together will help your child to function normally if he or she can.

Serious difficulties require early and intensive professional involvement. Parents are the advocates for their child and must ensure that they do all they can to help and ensure that health and education departments are supporting the child. In most countries there are laws in place which provide for children with special needs. These are constantly being modified, but you will be able to access the Code of Practice for your country and area. There are also support groups who are available to help if local systems are unwilling. As you move forward to developing intervention plans, actions need to be included in the tapestry and outcomes closely monitored and evaluated.

You should choose to define clearly the areas of difficulty. Dependent on the nature and severity of your child's problems this could involve you in a variety of *forms* of intervention but certain *principles* will be common to all (see Chapter 9 on interventions).

A time tapestry can be added to chart progress over time with the child participating in this process. Monitoring and evaluation of progress are utterly crucial.

You can colour code separate tapestry threads and experiment with bright colours and even coloured paper – your child will love it and you might too! If you feel really artistic and adventurous you could try using see-through plastic and indelible coloured inks for the tapestry relating to behaviour which can be changed. One could be completed each week and superimposed over the previous week's chart to reveal change visually. Comparing behaviour in different contexts should also inspire discussion and action. Put some mini (attainable) targets in there so the child can see what he or she is aiming for and when he or she gets there.

The next stage involves how this information, including professional multidisciplinary assessments, is mapped onto intervention tapestries.

Chapter Nine

Interventions

'He didn't come with a manual'

(Mother of an Asperger adolescent)

The normally developing child poses only the normally expected difficulties for any home, school or social system. Parents who experience difficulties with the normal range of typical growing-up problems now have a rich variety of interventions, books and videos which they can access.

The children about whom this book is written have neurodevelopmental problems leading to special educational needs, and special health needs in some cases. They can be perplexing, exhausting and frustrating as well as delightful, unique and enigmatic. The behaviours and processes of learning that we take for granted in normal development do not operate effectively. Instinctive responding and normal interventions do not work effectively, and in some cases not at all, at home or school.

Furthermore, over decades of increasing our understanding of conditions, many interventions we would have expected to have worked have not done so. A survey undertaken by Jordan, Jones and Murray (1998) at the University of Birmingham details interventions and issues around research into interventions for children with autism, and this work and approach will not be repeated here.

I will continue my theme of discussing my observations, interwoven with others in relation to various features, processes and methods which seem to fit with the notion of the tapestry (the interweave) of behaviours, impairments and methods.

We need a special manual of special knowledge about how these special children adapt and learn. In the severe autistic cases this starts at the point of finding people behaviour salient enough even to engage with.

Soaking up normality

Children on the autistic spectrum with no help provided could be placed into nurseries and schools with the expectation that they will just soak up the social milieu. This does not happen for most in the moderate to severe group. Imitation, when it does occur, can be very wooden, or a child may imitate only the screaming, the odd behaviours or bad language of others. Generally they will remain in their own world, 'contradicting their patterns' as the savant poet Kate writes, engaging in complex play on a myriad of themes from the TV, radio or video.

For some children, almost as a form of self-talk, they re-enact their day experience in complex streams of language, sometimes a direct copy of what they have heard during the day. Naive professionals can misinterpret these monologues and in some cases children are put through extraordinarily stressful inquisitions or counselling in which they are asked about their experiences and do not understand what is being asked of them. Great stress can be caused by such interventions, which start from the erroneous premise that the child has an emotional problem and make a million out of adding 2 and 2 together when they hear some of their jargon.

Communication

First, professionals and parents need to look at the complete tapestry and at the nuts and bolts of communication, moving along the *thread of communication development* and seeing where a child might fit, considering the following:

- Children with severe problems fail to master even the basic nonverbal processes discussed in Chapter 5. These must be focused upon in intensive programmes which recognise the context and the interweave of executive dysfunction, including auditory and visual processing.

- As we shift along we find children who have mastered the basics but have problems with posture, with facial expression and gesture to convey meaning, and also misconstrue the meaning of others' expressions and gestures, largely instinctive.

- Some children who give out all the wrong messages and do not appear 'normal' in their nonverbal skills actually can understand what others mean in their interwoven nonverbal and verbal behaviour.

- Some children have normal expressions but misconstrue the meaning of others' expressions.

- Skills of turn-taking can be taught, but appear wooden in isolation if they do not emerge within a tapestry in which other threads (including those above), and the developmental nature of many of them, are not understood or addressed. The use of various rhythmic and harmonic interventions can be used to improve these reciprocal skills.

- Skills relating to language and the way we inform the partner in interaction can also be broken down very precisely. Our children can present with considerable problems, from actually generating language at all through to appearing to be very verbal but often hiding difficulties.

- The decoding of language can be enormously difficult for some children who give an impression of normal ability. For some the difficulties relate to an inability to unravel the threads of complex nonverbal expressions within which the actual *words* are embedded. For others central auditory processing interferes with their decoding of such stimuli. Others have problems in all areas.

- Vast numbers of children appear normal but when they begin to speak, problems are obvious in terms of their tone, accent, pitch, the emphasis on the wrong part of the sentence and so on. Not all children present with all of these difficulties and not in all contexts. Unusual language use such as reversing pronouns or suddenly repeating chunks imitated from favourite videos can appear when children are uncertain and anxious, but also when noticing an association in the environment with those favourite videos or plays, or engaging in a typical form of play whenever they are alone or in a certain situation.

Transfer of learning

Our moderate to severe children do not easily shift or generalise anything which they may manage to learn from one context to another. Context means not just whether the child is in a clinic, a home or a school, although this must be taken into account, especially if there are stark contrasts between environments. The child may function very differently with different people and analysis of this issue is important. I have seen children's cues missed by staff too busy with a class of children to teach, not engaged with the child in a small group or not exuberant and fast enough to inspire and motivate the child who finds communication with people lacks salience. Dewart and Summers (1988), combining the important psychologist and speech therapist skills, developed a helpful profile which suggests an interview format for children that breaks down skills into communicative intentions, responses, interaction and conversation and the contextual variation linked with time, place, person and topic.

Salience

A child's motivational system needs to find something salient, or intrinsically motivating, to grab the child's attention. In children with severe ADHD and autism, their attention will shift onto inappropriate detail and activity or there will rarely be any focus. For the autistic child, even people and the way they try to interact are not salient. To create this salience remains an enigmatic problem but involves novelty, humour, unusual associations, visual and kinaesthetic experiences and materials sewn into the tools and method of delivery. Medications may be implicated and in some cases breakthrough may not occur.

Motor activity

The subtle processes of motor perception, planning and praxis or action can be seriously compromised in the tapestry children. Even basic forms of motor imitation, such as gesture and facial expression – which is fundamental in engagement – can be exceptionally difficult for the child.

Intervening to prevent the problems

Interventions pertaining to perceived *cause* take us to new discoveries in science and technology. Recognition of faulty genes, faulty processes, cells and even the point in time when this happened is within sight now. Damage to neural structures before birth, at birth and through environmental effects such as toxins and vaccines can cause damage to vulnerable children and this will be increasingly obvious. This can then lead to preventive measures for the vulnerable, and exciting findings of the possibilities of cell regeneration after brain damage may lead to even obvious damage being repaired.

Essential processes

Given the existence of problems and before such interventions can be put in place, we need to explore the early normal behaviours which appear to translate into important skills; the interwoven importance of pause and rhythm to create balance and assimilation of information, and the need for repetition and intensity – as in the early months of life, in the taken-for-granted instinctive responding of the normally developing infant. The extent of the repetition and the intensity will depend on the severity of the problem.

Weaving these threads together takes us to known efficacious methods for many – but not all – in large studies and then to interventions which seek to enhance these findings by incorporating the essential processes and also the skills of professionals working interactively with each other.

> The aim is to superimpose processes on the child which operate in normal development.

However, given the severity of their problem, and as we all now know, this is not a simple issue. Gaining eye contact, having a cuddle, structuring a day, giving speech and occupational therapy every so often, does not reach in to the parts we must reach. In part this relates to the delay in getting support. Early intervention really does mean 'early' – in the first years of life, and parental involvement really means parents being trained to intrude positively into their child's impaired functioning in the first communicative environment – in the home with mother and father.

While this chapter will concentrate on the early years, the intention is to explore the processes thoroughly. Older and less severely impaired children can be helped in the same way – if the hypothesis is correct – and are likely to need watered-down versions.

From this shared base, the unique child tapestry will provide us with clues about unique child needs which can be mapped onto the basics. These will also be affected by ability level, age and gender.

Interweaving tapestries to start the process of change

The thread running through this book has been the interweave at different levels of explanation. Normal engagement and learning include the processing of various sensory modalities which interweave in multi-modal fashion, action in one modality often subtly improving functioning in another. Pausing between activities helps assimilation and becomes part of the balanced and rhythmic process of learning. For many children discussed in this book, these processes do not interweave as they should and some cases basic processing is not efficient. Glitches in the child's development can rapidly tangle and compound with lack of understanding and poor provision.

Certain glitches in brain processes cross descriptive diagnostic categories and children with different disorders share similar problems at various levels. This is not an attempt to say that all disorders are the same, but to say that there are shared underlying processes which will change hue depending on the individual in dynamic interaction with the environment, and this will be rapid over time. These need to be explored especially to help us understand how to intervene and when. A tiny change in the early months could ensure that two very similar individuals with similar processing problems emerge as quite different at school. Knowing their similarities as well as their differences is key.

Understanding what works in different groups for similar problems helps us to create richer intervention tapestries with a higher chance of them succeeding.

A focus on children with severe forms of disorders can help us not only to understand the tapestry but also to realise that if certain principles are effective in these groups, they should be applicable to less severe forms given flexibility in the system.

Controversies will always rage about what is deemed successful and whether procedures are appropriate or ethical; this is healthy, provided there is dialogue and a sharing of perspectives which leads to greater overall awareness. Constant negative criticism and assumptions that there is only one way are unhelpful.

Sensory processing

Psychologists have always been fascinated by basic human functioning. Early laboratory experimentation involved exploration of the central and peripheral nervous system, including the general and fine tactile pathways and pathways linked to pain and temperature control. The basic cutaneous senses, tactile sensitivity and adaptations and thresholds of touch were all explored as far back as 1846 by Weber.

Studies of audition (Hubel 1959) have found that if attention was directed to a source of sound, cells in the auditory cortex responded, showing that attentional variables modified the magnitude of nervous system responses to auditory and other stimuli. Rhythm and harmony are created in the auditory system through various beats, the perception of them and adaptation to them. Audible harmonics seem to be related to the sound levels of the eddying movements of the fluid in the inner ear. Many ASD and ADHD children suffer from inner ear problems which would interfere with balance and affect harmonics. These inner ear problems may also implicate allergic reactions.

Experiments on colour vision recognised that the experience of colour was emotionally charged.

Taste and olfaction, perception, information processing, motivation, orientation, learning and memory, language and motor development and why it is so difficult transferring learning from one context to another are all areas of intense interest.

Impairments within all these areas have all been noted in the ADHD and autistic population and in earlier chapters we have discussed the essential interweave of impairments linked to sensory, motor and attentional skills.

If autism and ADHD can be placed along a continuum of severity of impairments in relation to such basic skills and the neurotransmission system driving them, as we move along the thread from normality we can move along the thread toward Asperger syndrome and autism. The imbalance of over-focus and no focus alters as we shift. So we can find the stereotypical ADHD child who cannot focus at all on anything as a very young child – although a closer look will find addictive qualities. The stereotypical autistic child is exceptionally addicted to his or her obsessional routines and fascinations and cannot focus at all on everything else; in particular, this over-focus on environmental detail prevents engagement with people, as such features become increasingly salient.

Methods which focus on the senses, the integration of the senses, therapies relating to separate skills and methods which aim to reduce the over-focus and improve the lack of focus, have all been put into place with reported success for some children, but resounding failure for most over the decades. We know about this failure because we have seen the behavioural outcomes for children with autism, Asperger syndrome and ADHD.

Research has been limited and actually very poor in terms of interventions for autism in particular, but even when there are reports of success, the interpretation of research outcome remains difficult as we are dealing with complex tapestry dynamic systems which do not easily fit into limited black and white linear models.

Given this, I consider my professional perspective as useful as any other and hope it contributes as it weaves positively into the perspectives of others. I also believe that we must start with the individual child, and it is the grounded data of observations of many hundreds of individual children and adults which has led to the emergence of my perceptions.

From 1970 when I first visited a unit for children with autism, the variation of the group as well as its essential similarity has stuck in my mind.

There have been certain constants which remain largely unchallenged. One is that the prognosis is exceptionally poor if a child meets the Kanner criteria for autism, the first impression of 'off the planet', reaching the far end of the severity scale for disengagement with people, with hyperactivity a common feature in the pre-school years. These children tend not to develop language, to be unreachable, which is a devastating experience and prevents others from attempts to engage as the efforts meet brick walls. As the gap widens, odd stereotypes such as hand flapping, jumping up and down, twisting hand movements and looking out of the corner of the eye, inspecting detail close up, can occur. As this group looks so normal, these behaviours could be misinterpreted as a sign of great intelligence, of giftedness and unusual interest in finding out how things work. While this may be the case, the problem is that there is largely no shift from looking at all this detail to sharing the findings with others! Locked into such activity, aggression could follow and came to be expected in many whenever adults intruded into the increasingly distant world. Terrible screaming tantrums often followed which served as very good aversive stimuli to prevent further attempts! It was expected that these children would become increasingly difficult to manage as they grew bigger, especially as the fundamental lack of engagement with people prevented the mediating development and use of language to guide, explain and structure.

Instead of using the skills of repetition to learn language and other interpersonal skills, the initial failure to find salience in people led to repetitive imitation of odd sounds picked up from sources other than people. These could include the sound of a crackly radio, animals, robot-like sounds or snatches from repeatedly watched films or TV programmes. These could be accompanied by a myriad of repetitive actions that the child turned into his or her own game and re-enacted at various points in time.

Another constant related to children who did *not* meet the high severity score for 'off the planet' and disengagement with people, but who were so highly hyperactive and 'off the wall', it was similarly impossible to limit that behaviour. Over time, and despite language emerging, what we now recognise as semantic pragmatic types of disorders were also in evidence and the children had sequencing problems, poor reciprocal skills, difficulties understanding and following rules, sustaining attention and consolidating learning. They also had problems orienting to a learning situation, tended toward concrete thinking, understood a lot less than the impression they gave, were unable to understand or retain understanding of consequences or to accept blame. Normal rules and sanctions hit stony ground.

Understanding the Asperger group – as the consultant psychologist involved in setting up the very first residential school for this condition in the world – has allowed me to recognise more fully the interwoven similar features between the two 'outlying' groups of ADHD and autism as well as the emergence of differences which are the stereotypical defining variables. As Wing (1996) has reported, this group could start out as more obviously Kanner autistic as pre-school children, then shift into the Asperger presentation later. *All* of these children have language problems of the semantic pragmatic type and *some* of them have more obvious language impairments earlier in life. Many within this group demonstrate obvious motor impairments and all have motor difficulties at some level, even if this has to be ascertained by assessment. The types of difficulties are usually linked with the sensory skills related to proprioception, tactile and vestibular skills and to inappropriate (as opposed to none at all) eye-contacting skills and inappropriate (rather than none at all) contacts with people. In fact because this group very much wants to engage or to control, this is often seen as a reason to dismiss the idea of an autistic spectrum problem.

These more subtle (but just as devastating to development) features are also shared by the autistic and the ADHD group at varying levels of severity, but the extreme nature of the off-the-planet or off-the-wall behaviour disguises them.

Interventions understandably first try to reduce the behaviours that prevent us starting with the children. This will range from just *breaking through* the mental fugue for the Kanner group to *grappling* with the misconstructions and confusions of the Asperger group to just *stopping* the impulsive actions of the ADHD group. If we think about it, we have to do all these things with all these groups at one time or another and all the children need help to focus on what is salient before they do anything else.

The obvious impairments in motor, language and attentional skills would indicate the involvement of certain professionals, but without managing the non-compliance in its various guises, such work could not begin.

If a child was behaviourally non-compliant and had no language, there would be little point in bringing in the speech or occupational therapist who would not even be able to engage with the child to start with. Once this layer was removed, and focused work shifted the child into a more compliant position in which he or she had begun to use language but then displayed obvious semantic pragmatic problems, the therapist could then not only work with the child, but also focus in on the precise area of need.

In extreme cases, the tapestries can become so quickly tangled by extreme behavioural problems that it is impossible to tease out separate threads for action. In the past there has been great emphasis and enormous effort on methods to control and reduce problem behaviour, just to *start* the learning process. It was never expected that children would significantly change their hue.

Although this has occasionally happened, the evidence for this is at single case level – and this is good enough for me. If a single case responds well to musical integration therapy to engage with people, then this is a positive approach for that child. If a child responds to a casein- and gluten-free diet by massive reduction in temper tantrums and bowel problems, then it works for him. Unfortunately, parents can be so completely confused by all the possibilities that they do not know where to start: this is where the basic tapestry helps. From this and professional support or even support groups, parents are better placed to understand the problems and then attempt to match these with interventions. This is, of course, easier said than done.

Many of the therapies that we would expect to have an effect have not done so. This in part relates to a false assumption that one problem explains all. Therefore, if children are provided with therapy for their most obvious presenting problem, perhaps over many years, a lack of discernible progress can relate to the fact that the other interwoven threads – albeit less obvious – have not been taken into account and a robust tapestry of intervention put into place.

Increasingly this is being recognised and in all the types of support listed below, forward-thinking therapists and other workers find threads of other disorders which they realise need attention if their work is to have an impact. Consequently, the occupational therapists will have to make sure they get the attention of the child before they can start work on motor activities and will know that poor communication will prevent the child from following their instructions. In some cases obvious visual and auditory perceptual problems will interfere with rhythmic functioning. Addressing posture and imitation of others' movements maps onto the work of language therapists and psychologists who are interested in communication skills.

Language therapists will have to focus on various attentional skills relating to auditory and visual perception to orient the child and reduce sensitivity to features that should not take top place for saliency. They will need to work on all the gestural and postural behaviours which make up communication alongside expressions and watching out for eye movements to facilitate understanding of what other people mean, as well as improving the child's own demonstration of what he or she means. For many of these children, it is difficult to interpret their meaning from all the non-verbal cues normally given. Instead there may be none at all or they may be quite inappropriate. The wider population may grossly misinterpret what people with these conditions actually mean, instead putting their own spin on it that could be totally wrong.

In *Being There* (1979), the last film that Peter Sellers worked on, he plays the part of a man with very little understanding of the world, who spends his days gardening for his carer, imitating actions of others and watching TV, imitating actions off the TV. Once his carer dies he is all alone in the world but he wears his deceased carer's very expensive clothes and looks very respectable. Those around him misconstrue all of his actions. They impute meaning into his actions and interpret them variously as it suits their own position. One character loved his company as he thought the echo of his own comments and then long silences were indicative of profound and absolute agreement, which in turn made him feel rather proud of himself. He failed to recognise the many subtle imitations of gesture but these served to bond this character to Peter Sellers. Due to serendipity and the misconstructions of others, this lucky man found himself next in line to be President of the United States.

Now, most of our children are not so fortunate. What is more likely to happen is that they could become highly agitated at not being understood, or retreat more and more into their own world, angry at any intervention. Other high ability children may become utterly furious at other people's misinterpretations and fundamental misunderstanding of who they are and what they mean.

In the latter group of children, usually found within the Asperger and the ADHD group, are a smaller group who are non-conformist, failing to develop shared meanings with others over many years. This group can often develop very rigid views of the world and have a very intense sense of justice. Life is a great struggle, but some of these individuals prevent everyone else from making drastic errors of judgement through misplaced loyalties and social influence. In one interesting experiment by Bowler and Worley (1994), a group of adults with Asperger syndrome were brought into experiments on social influence. A stooge was put into the groups and also into the control group of non-Asperger individuals. They had to solve a problem. The stooge set out to influence the group by offering rather obvious wrong information. The non-Asperger individuals tended to go along with the duplicity and agreed with each other that black was white – effectively. Most of the Asperger individuals did not conform to the duplicity and seemed unable to detect the deception. There was a lot more laughing and coughing in the non-Asperger group when the confederate gave his 'wrong' answers, as they clearly sensed the duplicity but still went along with it. The Asperger group did not attempt to communicate and made no comments during the experiments.

Later it was shown that the Asperger individuals were less likely to conform to such duplicity and seemed unable to sense the duplicity. Lacking the mediational skills to interpret the myriad of social cues and clues and often giving out the wrong ones themselves, individuals with this type of Asperger syndrome are very easily misunderstood and very easily manipulated.

You might consider that they were clearly not manipulated in this experiment and you would be right. In this experiment what they missed was the deception and duplicitous behaviour of others. They did not comply in a situation when others probably would. This combination results in rigid and inflexible black and white opinions, sometimes absolutely right, responded to with high emotion and no balance or flexibility. At the same time such a person could also be drawn into the sphere of duplicitous others who see the naivety and opportunity to gain from them.

Interventions dealing with such problems are also not the domain of just one type of professional and the problems have not emerged from just one type of impairment. A focus on each thread to the exclusion of others in part explains why methods have failed to work. The whole tapestry, in all its contexts, interweaves and each thread interweaves with other contexts such as who the child is with, where the child is and so on. Problems with transfer of learning are well recognised in children with autism and ADHD who have proved to be successful in optimal conditions. Furthermore, as we are dealing with rapidly developing dynamic systems, they can weave a tangled tapestry very quickly – so early intervention becomes essential. This is all the more important given what we know about changes at cellular level after the first few years of life. Additionally, given the speed of processing which could be faulty, and its repetitive nature, our forms of delivery must be fast and repetitive – the more so as we move along the severity thread.

Parents want to know what works, but what works for one child may not work for another. Research using large studies can help guide us generally, but the unique child guides us specifically, the fine-tuning depends on the individual tapestry and on the changing tapestry as time passes and interventions are carefully monitored and evaluated. With a closer look at the individuals, professionals are more able to recognise clusters of children more likely to respond to certain types of intervention.

This may sound bleak, but we have moved on from the days when nothing seemed to work at all for extreme groups, and knowing what works for the extreme groups informs our thinking for the less severe. Painstaking work by many people in various fields has enabled us to start the process of unravelling entrenched problems, in order to reweave the tapestry.

We know that there are general principles, processes and methods that we can keep in our sewing kit to start this process. I will briefly discuss these, then move onto why even these seem to have failed for some children – and to methods which address style of delivery, intensity, early intervention, transfer of learning, the importance of looking at the individual child and the fine-tuning.

The end result (for now) is that we have general threads at our fingertips which we know can be applied to all; our baseline child tapestry will lead to additional methods and through constant monitoring we can fine-tune programmes or change the colours of our intervention to weave more precisely the unique child tapestry.

General threads

- reciprocal interpersonal action and communication
- sensory and rhythmic motor action and planning
- learning theories

Reciprocal interpersonal action and communication

Our understanding of interpersonal issues demands that we recognise the importance of the interweave of making sure of eye contact, of gently touching, holding or at the very least becoming very close, gesture and vocalising. These actions must be interspersed with pauses at various levels to allow the child to look away to assimilate (this is normal) and to weave in other essential activities which facilitate learning and engagement. This could be exercise, relaxation, feeding, music and play.

If we focus in on the most severe group – the Kanner autistic children – it is the child's inability to attach any relevance or find any salience in engagement with people, which makes first steps so very frustrating and difficult. Our efforts are not rewarded and can easily subside as hope drains away.

Chapter 5 on the threads of social engagement touched on some of the processes which are impaired, including eye contact, joint attention and expressive vocal and physical reactions. Attempts to train children in these processes – i.e. to make eye contact, to take turns – have also met with limited success in the past. It became a very wooden trained feature in those who responded and it was easy to see who had been trained in these methods. For instance, some children would hold back from leaping impulsively but failed to do what the *pausing* was designed to do – they did not *listen* or *assimilate.*

Some children could be trained to make eye contact but they over-stared and did not do what the eye contacting was designed to do – they did not engage with the other and did not read or monitor their expressions and emotions.

The challenge continues to be not only how to get the child to use these processes, but also how to ensure that the right image emerges from the detail – the engaging reciprocal person.

For years we have looked at bad behaviour as the wall we have to break down, and interventions have focused on methods to reduce such behaviours. With an increasingly more refined way of looking at children's difficulties, we have moved to a position within which it is recognised that a crucial problem relates to communication. Once this improves and the child begins to learn, difficult behaviour can abate. This communication is wide angled. It incorporates the myriad of actions, expressions and gestures, as well as language and speech prosody such as pause and intonation. These wide-angled features actually incorporate a tapestry of sensory, motor and attentional skills. For children to find relevance and salience in activities, their motivational system, at neurotransmitter level, interweaves with the expression of all of these skills.

For many children with communication problems, the threads of other features are not taken into account, the communication seen as causative – a communication disorder is seen as the sole reason that they cannot sit still or concentrate. This may be the case, and intensive behavioural and language therapy methods, which address issues of attention, can make a huge difference. However, for certain children, intensive work on communication may fail to change the problem with concentration and/or perceptuo-motor impairments.

Children with language problems are often not recognised but if they are, they are most likely to receive limited language therapy. Very few children find that this continues into school. The therapy has tended to be in blocks and children are moved off the list to make room for others once some progress is seen. In general, if children perform within the broad average range on receptive and expressive language tests they are not a priority. Recognition of semantic-pragmatic disorders in vast numbers of the population has been a long time coming. The crucial need to improve basic attentional skills and help a child to shift focus from irrelevant sounds to language in the environment can be achieved by intensive support from well-qualified speech and language therapists.

However, even now an assessment by a local speech and language therapist may not address such issues, or a passing reference may be made without any input.

Recent research has indicated that there was no difference in terms of outcome between clinic-based standard speech and language therapy in a clinic setting and 'watchful waiting' (Glogowska et al. 2000). Given the increasing recognition of communication failure in many of our children, this is indeed a very worrying finding – until one looks closer at the nature of the input. It related to clinic based sessions limited in frequency, given the limitations of health authority resources. It may also not have addressed the wider communication difficulties or taken other threads into account. Nor was it intensive and the transfer of learning component was not considered.

Sensory and rhythmic motor action and planning

The use of visual clues and cues is known to be salient for all people, especially children. As we shift along the severity threads, we find that this becomes crucial to help children focus, associate, retain and consolidate learning about their world.

Some highly distracted children do not see relevance in symbols to start with and are more motivated if their attention can be drawn to objects that come to be associated in their minds with activities. In time, photographs of people they know in action help a child to develop strucutre and predict what is going to happen. Making up visual timetables of events that are going to happen, using visual prompts ranging from objects to photographs to symbols which represent action, undoubtedly helps children with developmental disorders and these methods have been used to very good effect in the work of Mesibov through the TEACCH programme in North Carolina (Schopler and Mesibov 1995).

The use of the TEACCH method was a huge step forward. Its innovative use of visual supports and sequential order to help autistic people has remained a very strong and efficacious intervention, even if the TEACCH programme is not fully implemented. This programme is regarded as cradle to grave, which reflects the opinion that we cannot shift a person out of autism.

Unfortunately, there has often been piecemeal use of visual methods, and I have seen many a chart or picture left attached to a report and stuck in the filing cabinet in schools, in some cases even strewn underfoot in the classroom. In schools for children with significant learning difficulties the workload for teachers can be impossible if they are expected to tend to the basic needs of profoundly handicapped children and at the same time successfully engage in detailed programmes designed to improve communication.

Stacked boxes and visual prompts neatly piled out of the reach of children pay lip-service to the methods, but scream out lack of commitment to it.

Parents have often told me that they have had just one or two laminated cards sent home over the period of years their child has spent in school. In severe cases these are likely to be for visiting the toilet and asking for a drink. This is light years away from what is required, and misses out intensity, repetition, training, monitoring, early intervention, crossing contexts and inclusion of parents to ensure that learning sticks.

In some cases the chart is on the wall but there is no systematic and consistent procedure which addresses any of the important features which facilitate learning. I have seen charts hanging off the wall with the occasional point towards it by overworked staff. This barely touches the sides.

Within the world of ADHD, there is little recognition of the need for such visual supports to aid early communication as the child gives the impression of being able to understand – but does not comply.

While some professionals have been in a position to undertake highly detailed work in, say, music integration therapy or auditory integration training, which has led to positive change in the clinic or music room setting, the transfer to wider areas of functioning and into other settings is often very disappointing. The breakthrough does not seem to happen.

Devices that in principle make a considerable difference to a child can soon fall by the wayside as the child either adapts to them or loses them. The support to intensify learning to change habits has not been put in place. To change entrenched behaviours requires a mix of methods that must include a motivator – for something new to be incorporated into settled habits there must be a reward.

While exercise and relaxation methods have been proven to be valuable, if not incorporated into a daily routine, they have little value. It is rather like food. We have to keep eating it or it loses its purpose.

Obvious motor problems in our population of children have led to the involvement of occupational therapists, as the problems mainly concern the putting into action of motoric skills. While the value of such therapy is undisputed, there has been very little available and poorly trained – if at all – assistants could find themselves with a list of activities to do in PE, not incorporated into an IEP and with no serious support to monitor and evaluate.

In the past there may have been a lack of recognition of the hidden sensory impairments including proprioception, vestibular and tactile processing as well as motor planning, sequencing and co-ordination.

It is very rare for a child to receive intensive support for such difficulties from occupational therapists. However, even when they do, and measures taken at baseline and after intervention, sometimes over years, show obvious improvements over time in clinic-based tests, certain features can remain unaltered, initially blamed on the motor difficulties. As motor difficulties subside, attentional and social problems can emerge. These are usually related to the interweave of attentional and wide-angled communication threads and the clinic-based nature of the activity.

Learning theories

Learning theory applies to all organisms. It expects learning to take place when individuals are motivated through their central nervous system and that this motivation can be enhanced through reward.

The principles of learning theory are well established and over the decades we have applied them to children with severe developmental disorders. Again, with mixed results. Again, not surprising in many cases as the efforts have been piecemeal, the training limited and commitment to the required effort not possible due to lack of training and resources.

Of fundamental importance is the drawing together of a functional analysis. This procedure attempts to analyse the detail within a child's world to determine how events might have been triggered and, in cases of severe language and communication problems, what the person intended by an action or behaviour. There can be difficulties with the latter when assumptions are made which are wide of the mark.

But close observation as part of a functional analysis can help to inform us about the way the child is learning as well as the traditional reasons for using these forms of analysis – to understand stress triggers and the meaning within a child's response. One young adolescent male with Asperger syndrome, the expected dyspraxia and a tic disorder used to become highly anxious when facing any challenge. When distressed his odd behaviours were rapidly demonstrated. He would become agitated, reverse his pronouns and echo the motor mannerisms of others. His learned social skills collapsed and he would often throw things. After improving his behaviour through intensive methods, on one day he sensed a difficult atmosphere when he walked into a room. He became rapidly agitated and smashed a plate. He then followed this by saying 'That wasn't me! It was my temper!'

Stress and anxiety can often be averted once we know the way a child reacts to events. However, we need to be as aware as possible of the triggers for the child. In some cases there appears to be no discernible trigger. It is likely that there will be neurochemical or electrical changes and charges that are not related to specific events but which can interfere with functioning. However, closer analysis can get us nearer to unseen triggers.

Within ABA learning theory, functional analysis involves tapestry type processes, which break down tasks into threads as simple or as complicated as you want them to be. So, careful evaluation of different responses in different contexts allows us to define the problem more clearly and better devise the solution.

Applying the reward principle in the ADHD world has tended to rely on various forms of behaviour modification techniques. While in general they work, it is the reasons why they have failed our severe children that hold the key to what to do next. The more severe the problem, the greater the need for absolute commitment to the method and precision in its application.

Knowing which rewards are salient – which comes down to truly knowing the child – and being flexible to allow for adaptation and/or over dependence are essential starting points. Knowing how to fade the rewarding over time – and whether to do so – is all part of the training that many who try these methods do not have. Principles of breaking things into small chunks, over-learning and backward chaining are all techniques that need to be precisely understood and applied.

Applying rewards too late – when the child cannot associate their action with the reward – can destroy a programme. Similarly, inconsistent use of rewards – sometimes rewarding the behaviour and other times failing to – will also confuse the child.

Learning theory has been used in applied research into autism, at the University of California, Los Angeles, initially by Lovaas (1987). The strict use of learning theory, that also brought into play aversion therapy, led to condemnation. Once the aversive components were removed, the research began to make an impact as there was an increase in autism and vast numbers of families became desperate to know what could be done. In their reading of the literature, most have told me that nothing compares with the research methodology and even if less than 50 per cent seemed to recover they set this against the less than 5 per cent in general studies of outcome in autism and compared the interventions.

Initially sceptical of this approach, given the early aversive interventions and my own knowledge of the entrenched nature of autism, I have been impressed by the improvement of some children. Indeed this programme, properly undertaken, can encourage compliance within a very short space of time. I have made a point of observing many children while in therapy and of assessing them all. I was also impressed by the way the programme covered crucially important issues pertaining to:

- Early intervention.
- Involvement of parents in training and programme.
- The use of imitation.
- Transfer of learning – recognised many years ago by Thorndike, and always seen as a significant problem in autism.
- Consistency.
- Salient reward at the point of performance.
- Techniques to maximise learning potential including backward chaining and modelling.
- Careful and precise baseline and ongoing monitoring and evaluation to fine-tune programme on an ongoing basis. With such a close and precise programme it is possible to check not only on

whether a target has been reached but also how a child responded to interventions and how that might have to be altered to achieve success. This includes undertaking a functional analysis that has been used within autism for many years, especially in very severe impairments.

- A well-developed system to allow a child to engage with other children as they developed skills, and shadows to attend with the child in nursery and school.

On arrival at the home of a little Kanner autistic child, whose early developmental video confirmed this diagnosis, two little children came toward me to say Hello, a little boy and his younger sister. I looked for the little boy I had come to assess, then his mother introduced me to him – he was the child next to me!

The family had become involved in an ABA programme and the child had shifted from drifting more and more into his own world into the social world. She recalled when she 'got her son back' and told me that she 'knew every drill' which had to be meticulously drawn up, put in place, repeated over and over, and measured. Each person who worked with her child had to be totally consistent in their approach and this had to extend across other tutors and the parents, requiring intensive training, dedication, financial commitment and video to ensure consistency. Rewarding and reinforcing are crucial elements of such behavioural shaping programmes, especially in the early stages. These can take the tangible form of a tiny bite to eat, through to social rewards, at the point of performance and at a high rate of frequency – maybe after a single appropriate social response.

By a painstaking process of planned manipulation of these fixed behavioural threads, the interactions and responses given and expected are made more and more complex so that the child copes with change and becomes more flexible in his dealings with the world and the people within it. First by achieving compliance so the child sits (our immobile infant?) he must then be able to *imitate* to move forward – so talking, pausing and stroking over and over and over with essential eye contacting is part of the basic process. 'Did it die when I wasn't looking?' asks tragic Kate. The magic for me swirls around the still beguiling mystery of how the threads result in the emergence of social consciousness, the tapestry of life. From this complex weave, in this case, emerged a social child – John.

John's mum had become an expert in the development of communication and the threads of engagement and I was very impressed. He could still be distractible but had shifted along the socially impaired severity thread, was biddable and could play with his sister. His pragmatic language problem was subtle and the most obvious sign that it existed was when I left the house and his Mum said, 'Say goodbye John'. As he waved to me he said: 'Goodbye John'.

Another little boy, Adam, who was also very classically Kanner, astonished and moved me when he rushed into the living room and straight to his mother, saying 'Mama'. It was just discernible and these dedicated and devoted parents told me of the painstaking and arduous road they had travelled to reach that joyous point – which they never expected to reach. Tragically, despite the incredible progress for a child with very severe autism, this family lost a tribunal and their son struggles without the intensive support he continues to need.

Dawson and Osterling (1997) analysed early intervention in autism that Jordan (1998) discussed in her survey. They analysed the common features in eight programmes that showed successful outcomes. They listed these as:

- family involvement
- highly supportive and intensive teaching environment and techniques to encourage generalisation
- routine and predictability
- a curriculum which includes selective attention to imitation of others and task demands
- social interactions
- ability to play with others and comprehension and use of language
- a functional approach to problem behaviours
- support in staged transition to school.

It was noted that normal peers were used as models and all but one of the programmes involved at least 20 hours per week of the intervention.

Knowing the child's basic tapestry through careful observation and assessment and knowledge of the child helps in this process. However, there is an issue in that some children, who one might predict would respond, do not do so.

From my perspective, certain forms of support and intervention need also to interweave. For instance, some children, despite compliance, which in itself was remarkable, could not easily sustain attention. One was clearly affected by an allergic system that made perseverative behaviours much worse. This boy was greatly helped by a casein- and gluten-free diet that reduced his tantrums and bowel problems but did not make a big difference to his distractibility. A child making no progress at all on expressive language was ultimately helped enormously by the use of the Picture Exchange Communication System (PECS: Bondy and Frost 1994). Another child was faced with lacklustre delivery from the tutor and very limited time on the programme, as parents could not afford it.

Some older children clearly needed social communication programmes to be sewn into their tapestry.

A nonverbal child with hyperactivity and increasing signs of autism was given Methylphenidate, which immediately improved his focus – unfortunately he also needed the intensive behavioural programme that would enable him to use that focus to learn. In this boy's case, the Methylphenidate seemed appropriate. In other cases it has led to a dramatic increase in repetitive behaviours and rituals and the overlap of autism and ADHD must be understood when prescribing, in my opinion.

Some families cannot engage in intensive home-based interventions for various reasons, including other children, limited finances, limited space and weariness from the child's escalating problems over the years. Many children with severe problems are now too old to benefit enough from school-only based programmes. For instance, tapestry children with no language and highly repetitive behaviours may become more controlling and manipulative within the family and increasingly aggressive when thwarted as they grow older. Limited high focused time within school may provide only an hour or so a week, which is woefully inadequate, the absence of focused reinforcing support in the times in between acting to destroy any benefits.

Most education authorities across the world do not provide home-based programmes linked with school for consistency across contexts. For autistic tapestry children, their communication level may be similar to that of an infant, whom we would not expect to cope within school based settings without intensive support and recognition. The best chance for such a child to weave that early engagement tapestry will be in the context in which babies find themselves – at home with the family. Unfortunately, if circumstances have moved on too far, the highly manipulative and controlling autistic child, instead of wearing a healthy tapestry suit of his own, could easily become painfully sewn into that of his first carers – usually his parents and most particularly his mother, by no fault of their own.

Behavioural learning theory used for severe ADHD

Within the world of ADHD, attempts to curb the hyperactive behaviours through the use of star charts met with very limited success with the severe groups. The children caused pandemonium in the home and the school setting. It was increasingly recognised that the more severe the problem, the more precise and intensive the methods and the greater the need for one-to-one support. Special schooling was the only setting where a child would find such a high staff to pupil ratio.

UCI–CDC Model (Swanson)

The University of California Irvine Child Development Center (UCI–CDC), a clinic and later an experimental school, based its methods on work by James Swanson and Marcel Kinsbourne from 1975 to 1980 (see, for example, Swanson and Kingsbourne 1978). Swanson along with Russell Barkley and others formed the Professional Group for Attention and Related Disorders (PGARD) in order to establish the importance of educational interventions and to create an educational definition.

The methods were developed by a tapestry of collaboration between clinicians and educationalists. They set up a school on the university campus 'to develop intensive school-based interventions combined with comprehensive clinical interventions' (Swanson 1992, p.9). They recognised the 'severity thread' requiring different levels of intensity of intervention which ranged from basic classroom modifications (Carlson and Lahey 1988) through increasingly intensive interventions.

The underlying principles of operant conditioning (Skinner 1987) and behaviour modification were used, as developed with the autistic children through ABA/Lovaas type therapies. Swanson referred to the theory of 'selection by consequences' (1992, p.132). The team developed three models related to severity of impairment:

- the parallel teaching model in which children with mild problems have their normal classroom altered to meet their needs

- the paraprofessional model which is intended to provide supplementary support in addition to classroom alterations for children with moderate impairment

- the multi-component (or multi-modal) model in which comprehensive educational and clinical interventions are provided to meet the considerable needs of children with severe impairments.

The use of operant models of behaviour modification requires careful measuring of baseline and ongoing behaviours, and specific techniques to shape behaviours including reward and a progression through clearly defined levels of treatment. It was recognised that it was difficult for children to maintain gains from reinforcement programmes over the long term, and the researchers sought to use specific operant conditioning techniques to enhance generalisation and maintenance. It was accepted that careful design and long-term treatment were necessary in order to see long-term effects from behaviour modification.

Level 1 involves continuous monitoring and direct feedback to the children through the use of social reinforcers and tokens. Success is defined as managing to earn 90 per cent of available tokens as rewards to trigger the neurotransmission system into action. For ADHD children, not regarded as autistic, this could take two or three weeks before a point is reached when the behaviour is maintained. Within the Lovaas treatments this is expected to take much longer given the extreme neurological deficits of the autistic group.

Once onto Level 2, the child engages in self-monitoring and self-evaluation with the intention of creating withdrawal from the need for constant monitoring and to foster generalisation, a problem with the ADHD and autistic groups in particular. This could take from four to ten weeks.

At Level 3, Swanson reports that intervention 'is based on responsibility/privilege contingencies (which reflect the uncertainties of natural consequences in the real world environment) instead of the standard token system' (1992, p.121).

Ultimately the researchers developed their programme based on a full year of intensive Level 1 and then Level 2 intervention, followed by the adapting of different programmes at transition over to the next placement for the child. The interventions were based on the knowledge that motivational problems were continuous through the day, therefore requiring *continuous* input.

The parallel teaching model

Teachers are trained to carry out a normal lesson plan and to provide redirection and reinforcement for the ADHD child after scanning the room. It was hoped that such techniques would become second nature. The teacher learns shaping and prompting techniques that are essential procedures. The need for a higher intensity and frequency of these methods with ADHD children, for instance reminders just before tasks begin and just before they are about to end, are facilitated by the trained classroom aide.

The paraprofessional model

In this model for moderately impaired children, there are three components:

- the teacher is provided with a facilitator, a paraprofessional who implements the token economy with frequent and consistent token reinforcements and activity reinforcers
- small group coaching and shaping of social skills and language using continuous reinforcement
- daily report cards, replacing the intensive point system over 12 weeks leading to a fading out of the facilitator.

The paraprofessional crosses small group to class group contexts to aid generalisation. The trained facilitator is provided for 15 hours per week – 3 hours per day for 5 days a week – for each classroom holding one or more ADHD students. These students attend in groups of four for twice-a-week 30–40 minute skill-training group lasting for 6–12 weeks.

The multi-component model

The third model, for severely impaired students, used a multimodal approach. It was recognised that these children have tangled tapestries, given co-morbidities such as dyslexia and emotional problems – which could have included some of our autistic spectrum tapestry kids:

- support is intensive, over six hours per day
- training groups run daily are operated by clinical and educational staff
- double blind assessments of pharmacological interventions
- parental involvement to cross contexts into the home setting occurred in groups and individual sessions.

The precision and labour required in these behavioural intervention programmes are very clear. It is also clear that without long-term commitment to the precise components, such a programme could easily fail. The research undertaken by Swanson (1989, 1990) and McEachin, Smith and Lovaas (1993) also reveals that the methods are reaching the correct parts of the brain.

Pharmacology *may* further improve the latter methods, as applied in the multi-modal programme, for some children.

The structured learning model

This psychoeducational approach (Goldstein *et al.* 1979) was used with ADHD adolescents needing to learn prosocial skills. The method includes the components of:

- modelling
- role playing
- feedback
- transfer of training.

Modelling relates to demonstration of the skill required, broken into small steps and demonstrated in various settings.

This is followed by role play in which the child rehearses the same skills in the same way, facilitated by the coach or assistant.

Feedback is evaluation, which will be augmented by rewards until the behaviour is shaped to be the same as the model.

Transfer of training recognises the problems with generalisation of skills and uses various methods to encourage transfer into real life settings. This last component is the most difficult, as children can perform well in situations with structure, guidance and appropriate language and instruction.

Group leaders must have good communication skills, be enthusiastic, flexible and sensitive with a knowledge of child development. More specifically, in relation to structured learning techniques, they must be able to orient the trainees and staff, present material in concrete, behavioural form, initiate and sustain roleplay and be sensitive in feedback. The more similar the context, the greater the chance of transfer of skills.

The principles of introducing friends and family to the sessions, and of homework assignments on the same skills, address issues which we have discussed in the context of other methods, whether dealing with communication, attention or specific social skills.

Using the adolescents to run groups was found to be very effective. It was found that the adolescents' own skills increased when they knew they were going to help teach others what they had learned. We used this with children in our 'Dwight's Party' studies, and found that the children adored to explain to the others how Dwight worked.

Finally, using this model of structured learning was found to 'increase the perspective-taking skill (i.e., seeing matters from other people's viewpoint) and also leads to consequent increases in co-operative behaviour' (Goldstein 1979, p.273).

Without a doubt, many interventions which improve a child's behaviour spring from a neuropsychological perspective and target the circuitry within the brain which is responsible for orienting, motivating, focusing, retaining, learning and shifting learning across contexts.

From this a behavioural programme is constructed; for example, highly intensive behavioural methods which improve the frontal lobe motivational system and incorporate knowledge of how learning develops from a neuropsychological perspective, i.e. UCLA interventions (Swanson 1992); Lovaas. However, a broad perspective informs us that many parents and teachers cannot undertake and sustain such programmes.

We are left with two thoughts. If we can provide the precise provision, we can move a number of children on, but not all. Other interventions through scientific advances (see Chapter 3) will help those children. Because many cannot move on, we must decide whether we should encourage those who can, and provide facilitators within the system to move as close to the ideal as possible.

Additional support: through closer attention to the unique child's needs

Dependent on the unique child, certain types of intervention may be implicated. These may come into place at the start of, during or after intensive early interventions, although some purists do not want confounding features that affect research outcomes. Parents, however, go with their child.

Musical integration therapy

There is evidence of this method working for some children, when it is appropriately applied. Intuitively, it should help the children and I would like to see it more widely available.

Auditory integration therapy

For some children, especially those with a history of ear, nose and throat problems, this method may help. There have been reports of improvement and families need to be able to access this therapy more easily as a standard medical intervention. It is intuitively appealing given balance and rhythm in association with the functioning of the inner ear. From my observations, a child needs first to be able to attend in order to value this intervention fully.

Holding therapy

This therapy attempts to override the tactile defensiveness that creates such interpersonal distance. Dependent on the child, this may prove helpful.

Options

Again there have been reports of good outcome in this intensive therapy which involves stepping inside the shoes of the child and imitating all that they do. Many aspects of the programme can be introduced and indeed I have observed them, in the day-to-day running of an ABA programme.

Use of medication

It is recognised that medications can allow a child's neurotransmission system to operate better, and in turn provide a window of opportunity to facilitate other forms of essential support. In the severe ADHD cases, they needed not just the medication, not just the behavioural interventions but *both* and *also* a great deal of one-to-one and precisely structured setting. Even then the learning did not transfer easily to other settings and the tasks were intensive to implement.

Many years ago it was found that highly hyperactive children could focus, often for the first time in their life, once they were given stimulant medications. For some children, however, this focusing was not enough. For others, the medication did not work or it improved focus but led to an increase in repetitive behaviours, which were unacceptable. From my perspective, these children are the ones with overlapping autistic and hyperactive traits.

Children with autism, Asperger syndrome and/or ADHD will be more amenable to developing social awareness and consolidating their learning if hyperactivity is reduced and focus improved through various methods which must be put in place and monitored.

The medication of choice for hyperactivity is Methylphenidate and there is overwhelming evidence for the efficacy of this dopamine focused drug. However, certain children do not respond and some react badly. If the treatment is properly monitored and finely tuned, such reactions may be modified.

For some, no amount of fine-tuning makes a difference – it just doesn't work for them.

In my experience, it is the child with co-morbidities – the tapestry child with obsessive features – who may be a poor responder and these children may form part of the 'anxious' (Goldstein 1996) or 'manic' (Biederman 1998) group who can react very badly. For the sake of balance, I have seen children with ADHD who are obsessive improve on Methylphenidate alone, but I have seen more of this group who do not.

However, many with complex disorders do respond and this provides an important window of opportunity to provide other forms of support. I was astounded when one tapestry child stopped her impulsivity and was able to stop and think for long enough to engage in reciprocal interactions and also reflect on her behaviour. She said: 'Why did I used to break windows?' Stopping the hyperactive and impulsive behaviour immediately allowed this child to communicate in a reciprocal manner, to consider the consequences of actions, pay attention to instructions and also reflect on past actions and their effect on others. She also won a prize at school for the first time.

Unfortunately, as her hyperactivity abated with medication and given her maturity, and as her mother had been blamed for her problems, the aim was to 'prove' that she was 'normal' by placing her in mainstream without support or recognition for the underlying semantic-pragmatic language problems which surfaced once the hyperactivity abated.

When there are very severe difficulties or a specific anxiety or tic disorder, other medications can be tried and have been successful for significant numbers of children whose lives were unbearable before.

Temple Grandin speaks of the change in her life since she began to take medications for anxieties which intruded so badly into her development.

One young man at college came to see me for an assessment with his mother. His history was very much one of Asperger syndrome and ADHD throughout his childhood. He became so desperately depressed and lonely at school that he attempted to take his own life. He had never been able to read other people, had never been a part of a group, did not know or care how to dress in order to fit, and eventually bullying and isolation nearly ended his life. With a combined plan which included the use of a selective serotonin re-uptake inhibitator (SSRI) this boy was able to mix with others and to dress appropriately; he even found that he could understand what others were trying to communicate. His mother was astounded. For many older adolescents who become depressed and anxious at that stage as part of their condition, the depression exacerbated as their lives crumble around them, such intervention trials can be imperative and this form of the medication is less controversial than stimulants.

Irlen lenses

Many children experience visual distortions which grossly affect their functioning. First noticed through problems with reading, there is a high incidence of this problem within the autistic, the ADHD and the head injured group. What is quite remarkable is how this non-invasive intervention can remove the distortions in an instant for many people.

Picture Exchange Communication System (PECS)

The visual methods, recognising that all people benefit from visual representations – hence the idea of the practical tapestry – met with success in all groups in that they helped provide a structure, an explanation and a guide to what was expected. The methods extended to helping a child to communicate through the ingenious use of cards, images pertaining to the child's life and needs and the invention of sticky-back Velcro! PECS uses visual augmentative methods as a means of communication for children and also involves the process of exchanging a card between the child and the adult to alert the adult to the child's needs. An overuse of this method before there has been a clear programme over some time to establish language could result in a child using the pictures instead of language. There is obviously a tension in terms of recognising how soon the cards are introduced.

Indeed this tension exists with all behavioural methods in which there is not expected to be any confounding interference of other methods. How long does this continue and would some children benefit form such methods from the outset? These questions are not yet answered.

Diet

The idea that what a child eats can cause hyperactivity either as part of ADHD or autism is variously accepted or refuted. In Sunderland, researchers Paul Shattock and Paul Whiteley have established certain types of metabolic functioning linked with bowel problems and autism that improve without having to metabolise casein and gluten (Shattock et al. 1990; Shattock and Lowdon 1991; Shattock and Savery 1997; Whiteley et al. 1999). Knowing the individual child enables fine-tuning to lead us to such possibilities, which are not applicable to all, but could make a considerable difference to some.

Speech and language therapy

This needs to address the subtle language problems and the paralinguistic features and also target attentional issues. The therapist needs to recognise the issues to do with transfer of learning and interweave his or her work with a language assistant in the classroom who can do the same. Ideally the therapist would work with the assistant in a one-to-one and also work for some time with the assistant in the classroom. Monitoring, evaluation and liaison with parents are crucial.

The therapist may feel that technology such as Speech Viewer is helpful. This enables a child to see on a screen the effect of his or her utterances. The child sits next to the therapist and each has a microphone. They work on numerous aspects of speech. For instance, a child may have a very high-pitched tone and will see perhaps a red balloon rise; the child has to lower the tone to make the balloon follow a path across the screen.

This technology incorporates important components: the salience of the computer, the one to one, visual and auditory interest, rewards and real tasks pertaining to multiple aspects of spoken language.

Occupational therapy (OT)

The important skills that can be taught by the occupational therapist need also to interweave with other staff in other settings to ensure transfer. Fundamental sensory-motor perceptual skills weave into early communication, attention and executive functioning.

The interweave

The interweave of essential processes at varying levels of explanation maps onto professional input and this also needs to interweave.

All those working with the child need to interweave their practice with one another. One problem at the root of all else does not describe our tapestry kids and will not lead to the rich tapestry of support and intervention they need.

First engagements

If a child cannot be engaged to learn basic skills, whether through disengagement or hyperactivity or aggression or all of these, we are in trouble. It is because certain methods seem to be able to achieve this state, which then provides a springboard for other skills to be learned, that I looked closer for myself. I found the following.

Positives

- Providing visual supports does enable children to feel a safe structure in their world, to improve their understanding of rules and the order of things around them, and offers some a means of communication.

- Methylphenidate does help some hyperactive children focus and sustain attention and while the medication is taken, they are in a much better position to learn the other skills which are impaired.

- Other medications can make a remarkable difference to behaviours such as tics, bed-wetting, sleep disorders etc.

- Casein- and gluten-free diets do help some allergic children with bowel problems, autism and often hyperactive behaviour.

- ABA interventions do work for some autistic children, which is to be expected given the robust base of behavioural learning theory – instrumental or operant conditioning. They were found to lead to remarkable states of recovery in 47 per cent of children undertaking Lovaas therapy.

- Speech and language therapy and occupational therapy can help to train a child in various crucial areas pertaining to wide-angled communication skills and motor planning etc.

Negatives

- Visual supports alone do not shift children dramatically along the spectrum, and are not intended to do so.

- Methylphenidate, for some children, can lead to overly receptive behaviours and an excessive hyperfocus in some areas for those who already hyperfocus.

- Side-effects of medications for some children can be unacceptable.

- Very strict diets can be difficult to put in place without very specific support and understanding from specialist medics.

- ABA interventions were found to fail to meet the aim of recovery in 53 per cent of children with autism (Lovaas 1987).

- Behavioural interventions hit problems with staff undertaking the work and learning did not transfer to other contexts in applied educational research (Swanson 1992).

Which principles or methods seem to help *all* children?

Early intervention

There is now a consensus of opinion that the earlier that one can intervene when children have developmental disorders, the greater the prognosis.

We discussed earlier how brain tapestries involve not only fixed sites relating to particular functions but also multiple pathways, which interweave between sites in a transactional manner. Chemical messages fired by electrical charges are passed along the pathways and these neurotransmission systems can be compromised, affecting function even if brain sites are perfectly intact. In turn, these warped processes can interfere with normal development of particular areas relating to emotions, perceptions and cognitions, and taking a wrong path can lead to the use of other parts of the brain, most likely during the early years when there are lots more neuronal connections in the brain and before patterns become entrenched. This early flexibility can be used to re-weave faulty webs of a number of children. The result may not lead to normal functioning, although it may in some, but it has the potential to create at least *some* positive change.

Our challenges include understanding how children learn and which mechanisms are failing to enable them to access social and educational opportunities.

The speed with which a child with neurodevelopmental disorders can deteriorate can be rapid, and certainly a lot more rapid than the speed of system support to help them. A little too late can be disastrous and is no longer acceptable. Therefore, early recognition within the family and then the system of the severity and extent of coexisting problems will help us to prioritise and tailor-make the support to the child.

Pre-verbal (touch–talk–gaze) paralinguistics weave with motor action

Recognising how these early processes interweave to form communicative images leads to a greater understanding of methods of intervention.

Learning theory

From my perspective, I was astonished to witness the efficacy of ABA compliance programmes for young (under the age of 5 years) children in a rapid space of time. When compared with the years and years of various efforts applied to a child becoming more aggressive, distant or hyperactive, this was very impressive. This was a crucial issue given the pivotal importance of gaining this compliance in order to begin the process of trying to engage the child to work on the processes to learn the skills!

Helping a child to attend, then to imitate and then to comply, comes absolutely first. When we look at the many failed attempts even to assess children with severe problems, it is these basic skills that are impaired. This then leads to no assessments and no involvement of therapists, who cannot even reach the child. If this programme proved anything for me, it was that these first skills can be rapidly learned in all children and if nothing else, this part of the programme is a breakthrough.

However, these skills can easily be lost and there is a fragile quality about the learning in the early stages. Many children clearly remained autistic, but they had moved forward and been able to learn and engage in activities with the family. These families were thrilled to have their child in communication with them, even though they recognised their obvious autism. For others, the child had broken through and did not present as autistic, but did continue to have ADHD and/or semantic-pragmatic type of language difficulties, and emerged more like a child with Asperger syndrome.

Augmentative visual support

There is no doubt that these methods, used appropriately, can truly help a child. The aims are different to the behavioural programmes but working together these methods should see greater success.

Simple general approach to giving instructions to younger children

All young children benefit from engaging in rhythmic games and attend better when eye contact is achieved, when some physical contact is made, such as a hug or a gentle touch on the arm or hand, and when language is clear. True to the principle of the thread or continuum from normal through to impaired, needs become magnified as we move further along the severity thread.

Therefore, incorporating the touch–talk–gaze principles, and our knowledge of poor understanding in children who can appear to have normal language and of their poor attentional skills, the following method should be used when instructions are given.

- Make sure you get eye contact.

- Touch child on arm or hand.

- Keep emotional tone low, otherwise the child just hears and feels all the emotions, especially if the language is complex.

- Limit the instruction to short attainable tasks – just one at a time, for example, 'Put the dolly away in the box now'. Some children need their name at the start of the task: 'Janie, put the dolly away in the box now.'

- Do not embellish the instruction with 'Can you…' and 'Would you mind…' and certainly not with 'If you don't then I'll…!!!' The child will miss most of what you say and so can't adhere to the instruction.

- Some children need visual cues, such as themselves putting the dolly in the box, maybe an actual photograph of them doing that. Others can learn by a symbol: this needs to be shown to them at the time of the instruction and while they are doing the task. This becomes associated with the activity.

- The task can be drawn onto a visual timetable and a matching card attached to it. The child takes the card when doing the task. The timetable shows the sequence and the structure in a typical day. The more severe the child's problem, the more important such structures are in the early stages.

- Others also need the action modelled for them.

- Others need the task breaking down into finer tasks.

- Others need visual clues: the task breaking down, the task modelling – starting with the last action and working backwards, the child copying and if necessary hand over hand guidance.

- None of this must be done in a threatening way. If you feel angry cool off first. All the tension will totally prevent the child from understanding.

- Constant repetition of this action will lead to success.

- All children need actions to be reinforced so they can learn. The more severe the problem, the more intensive and finite the tasks and the rewarding. Older children with less severe problems still need a reward and this can take the form of tangible rewards such as money or tokens leading to money and outings etc. Social rewards such as a smile can be enough after a while for some children.

In summary:

Gain eye contact, hold arms gently, and give one short instruction which is achievable. Model behaviours. Don't verbally elaborate and keep emotional tone down.

What can go wrong even though you achieve compliance in the young child with development disorders?

If a child can sit at table-top tasks and engage, however minimally, this is a major step forward. However, the next challenge is that the child does not often shift learning easily from one context to another. The more we move along the *shift* thread, the more rigid and severe is this problem. In the worst case scenario we can have a highly frustrated child with no language, no ability to comply in order to learn and years spent mainly being kept under control within education. I have assessed children in their teens who have not moved forward since they were 4 years old and who can't sit at a table for more than five minutes. But I have seen, to my complete and utter surprise, children at the age of 4 with very similar tapestries, achieving compliance within a week. At least then they can begin the learning process.

Improving problems with shift could be expected to improve this problem, and it has also been shown to change through intensive and focused methods involving people working with the child in one context interweaving into the other and vice versa. For instance, the teacher can become involved with language therapy and with the family in the home, and the therapists and the family can become more involved in the school. This way, the child begins to make associations between people and contexts to improve learning. Within ABA therapy, there are quite intensive and specific methods that involve different skills being mastered and maintained within different contexts and with different people, all of which is charted, monitored and evaluated.

Very young pre-school children with severe presentations of autism, ADHD and other associated developmental disorders such as Tourette syndrome, oppositional defiance disorder, or early onset conduct disorder must be provided with early intensive support which needs to tackle all recognised problems through an appropriate treatment tapestry before the child's problems become entrenched – and this can happen long before a child is 5 years of age, in extreme cases.

Perry, Cohen and DeCarlo (1995) argue in favour of very early intensive support such as the ABA methods for extreme cases of autism and refer to the potential for entrenchment of quirky brain patterning without intrusive support.

However, we can learn a great deal about the development of autism and ADHD from what is emerging at case study level using these types of methods.

Weaving a tapestry of methods and treatments, which are increasingly better focused through careful evaluation and research, on precisely the failing learning mechanisms, can not only improve the child's pivotal problem but also in some cases shift them into a different intellectual category.

This is very important as many children with these disorders which interfere with intellectual development are denied specific and intensive support, instead dismissed as 'children with severe learning difficulties', their pivotal problems blamed, oddly, on the learning difficulties rather than the underlying processes leading to it, which we can target! Obviously, as time passes without reaching into the minds of such children to grab the faulty weave, they may never begin to associate, consolidate and recall *in order to learn* – so this early designation becomes a reality, a squatting albatross, firmly settled on our children's shoulders forever.

In almost all the families whose children I have assessed, the parents wanted desperately to understand and to make positive change, and were prepared to climb very steep and often very emotionally and physically exhausting learning slopes to do so.

Under which circumstances, with which children, do seemingly robust methods fail?

This brings us to crucial issues. There is a consensus of opinion that even though a child may be seen to be learning in a strict clinic or laboratory setting, this can easily fall away:

1. if certain principles are not understood

2. if certain children have particular tapestries requiring alterations.

Lovaas (1987) recognised that children who were auditory learners were more likely to develop language, which in turn vastly improved their chances of success on his programme. Indeed, it is well recognised that children who develop language in the autistic population by the age of 7 years have a much better prognosis than those who do not.

Although Lovaas recognised that 53 per cent of the children in his research did not recover he remained convinced for some years that there should be no intrusions of other methods if the programme was to be successful, also requiring consistency across parents and tutors, intensity of methods, at least 40 hours a week over two to three years. I have personally seen some remarkable changes when these principles have been adhered to. However, I have also seen children who, despite compliance, remain very difficult to shift. In cases where the programme is being properly implemented, for some children, this seems related to the interwoven effects of allergic reactions and extreme distractibility. In others it related to revealed motor impairments once compliance was achieved and wider communication problems not directly addressed through social communication programmes or methods such as PECS.

In a recent paper written by Glen Sallows (200?, in reply to a critique by Rita Jordan (1998), it is now acknowledged that some children do require those additional forms of support as they move through the programme.

Swanson's recognition of the problems with context and the difficulties of engaging the family are addressed by the work of Lovaas through flexible methods applied in different contexts and the maintenance of learning consolidated in those various contexts. Additionally, involving the family addresses pivotal interpersonal issues. From Chapter 5, focusing on infants and parents, it should not be a surprise that children need to be brought back to the first communicating environment as a springboard before they can be expected to relate to peers and operate in a 'school' environment.

It seems entirely appropriate for models of good practice to allow for flexibility in school systems and to shift the learning environment to the home, or something which can be made to feel like home, and involve parents, when these fundamentals are being taught.

I have seen many children who cannot engage at all with people except in one-to-one settings with an adult, as the young infant does. Expectations that these children at the severe end of our reciprocity thread should be able to learn from others in a group peer setting are not realistic. However, once engagement can be achieved, built on and expanded, then the influence of normally developing peers becomes crucial as part of the tapestry of intervention.

The unique child tapestry informs us how our interventions should be applied.

When we look at these severe cases and the methods which are needed to make them work for many children – not considering the fine-brush needs of this population – there are some pointers as to why many of the intuitively correct interventions (speech and language therapy and occupational therapy) have not always led to the changes expected:

- they have not been intensive
- they have not crossed contexts
- they have not applied learning theory
- they have not been woven into the day-to-day communicative setting within which the child lives and learns for most of the time – home and school
- they have not considered co-morbidities including entrenched hyperactivity requiring a medication trial
- they have not considered allergies and dietary intervention.

When I look at how even these methods fail, in both ADHD and autism, despite achieving initial compliance, it is because there is:

- a lack of consistency of methods across contexts
- a lack of novelty to inspire flagging neurotransmission systems
- delivery which is too slow and boring
- adults giving up on behavioural methods
- failure to understand the unique child tapestry.

It may also be important to interweave occupational therapy (OT) and speech and language therapy (SaLT) with visual, auditory and behavioural methods.

Components

Whatever methods are used, the following are important components.

Delivery

The delivery of the activities needs to alternate pausing with fun, fast paced and repetitive action. In my opinion, touch–talk–gaze processes need to be interwoven. This means that the interpersonal functions need to be seen as basic. Normal and natural delivery will incorporate these behaviours of ensuring a child is looking and you look at the child – leaping on every flashed and fleeting glance to reward it. Gentle hand, shoulder and arms touching at the same time as well as positive facial expressions and brief comments ensure that this interweave is used as standard.

Pauses

As part of the essential process, pauses are crucial for assimilation of learning and children can be engaged in alternative activities and also in play of their own choice. These pauses allow children to take alternative perspectives, to let their minds process information on other tasks and then be better able to understand and retain that information. Children also need time alone, to reflect and relax.

Balance

There is a balance to be struck between providing the essential intrusion to weave them into the real world, and not overstimulating a quiet child. This particularly applies to a medically vulnerable, very premature infant. With touch–talk–gaze processes, a child's needs are easier to read.

Context

This relates to the various settings and various people that the child experiences. The learning tapestry must include the practise of skills in a variety of contexts, repeated as part of an over-learning activity. So, an essential activity will be repeated with different people and in different places. To assist this process, there must be a physical transfer of people between and overlapping the different settings. There can also be a transfer of photographs to enable the child to connect one place or another, for children with severe problems and for very young children.

Description
The description of the child and his or her skills and problems must be clear, not derogatory, phrased in concrete description so that concrete methods can be put into place to help.

Monitoring and evaluation
Close monitoring helps in many ways: these include being more able to know a child's strengths and weaknesses, to fine-tune programmes as the child progresses and to enable parents and professionals to see even the tiniest change which encourages. Without such close monitoring, it can be very difficult to see any real changes for some time. This could lead to people becoming disheartened and not implementing programmes properly, which in turn will definitely lead to no change.

Summary
- Programme in the home with parents – the first communicating environment. If this is impossible, a local nursery incorporating methods below and involving parents.
- The compliance training from ABA programmes, which astonished me when I first saw the results in children who, in the past, would have simply become increasingly difficult, distant and unmanageable. Making rapid change which enables an autistic or hyperactive child to sit and face a person during the pre-school years provides a window of opportunity to put other methods in place.
- Organise learning environment according to child's tapestry.
- Visual methods e.g. from TEACCH.
- Intensive multi-modal methods.
- Limited verbal instruction.
- Non-confrontational.
- Positive application.

- Communication games.
- Rich encouragement and focused description of a child's appropriate action in all situations in the home.
- Modelling of appropriate behaviour, language and gesture.
- Sensory and motor planning exercises and games.
- Music and rhythm games and activities.
- Fast delivery at times.
- Pauses and time for quiet reflection.
- Across contexts.
- Over-learning.
- Mini targets.
- Frequent rewards for reinforcement.
- Staff training in appropriate methods.
- Consideration of possible reasons for failure when fine-tuning.

Simple general approach to giving instructions to school aged children

Returning to the tapestry of each child, the methods discussed in respect of younger children can be applied to older children, but do not need to be so extensive. They do, however, need to be intensive.

Many of the expected interventions have partially failed in the past because of factors which include long periods of time on a waiting list to receive piecemeal support every few weeks and outside the situation in which the child lives, plays and studies, hampering transfer of skills. In my opinion, it also relates to a lack of recognition of the interweave of needs and a tradition of assuming the most obvious problem causes all learning difficulties.

Social communication programmes

Unique problems such as sensitivities and the myriad of difficulties which make up expressive and receptive social confusion can be addressed using social communication packages, visual supports and the parent + professional + facilitator (coach) model.

However, the need for careful planning, based on individual assessment and the essential interweave of intervention pertaining to attention or motor and communication should, in my opinion, apply as standard, methods and forms of delivery varying dependent on the age, gender and ability level of the child and the unique weave of co-morbidities.

Learning from the severe cases and the researchers working with them, skills of any kind will not shift for these children unless the principles of applying what they need occur in varied contexts. I am also of the opinion that we need to move to a position in which the use of the well-trained facilitator or coach model is standard practice in social work and school systems and their positive involvement needs to be applied daily, watered down as ongoing monitoring and evaluations determine the child's needs – not what the resources allow.

Years ago when I was first describing my 'transactional mediational problems', there was nothing on the market which could be easily obtained, especially for parents. This has vastly improved. Now there are programmes which offer to include parents, provide training and offer purchasable packages to support the children. One of these relates to the work of Carol Gray (1994, 1995). I was drawn to her many methods as they attempt to engage the child in fun activities which improve their communications; she also refers to the use of colour given the emotional impact. Details of the programme of Comic Strip Conversations are given in Appendix 2.

Social skills training

Many of these older methods are very helpful and include essential components of reward, breaking tasks down, visual supports, role play etc. Programmes such as Skill Streaming and I Can Problem Solve are easily available (see Appendix 2).

ABA

Although ABA methods have been used mainly on the most severely affected autistic children, very early to maximise the chance of success, Eikeseth (1999) has used such methods with reported success in older groups and in principle, as with Swanson with the ADHD children at UCI, these methods should be effective. Schools should introduce the trained coaches who can interweave their knowledge through in-service training, ongoing external professional development and hands-on applied work in the school system.

School milieu

The learning environment of the first school (up to 7 or 8 years of age) is nurturing, structured in a way which allows for greater flexibility and in which a child is not faced with multiple changes of class and teacher or expectations to work in the abstract with very little support, especially visual, and through oversight and prompting by a friendly teacher. The very large classes, however, are not helpful.

Within such settings all the valuable visual support systems, the rewarding and ABA should be possible. Social communication and skills training should not be difficult to put in place.

If children have embarked on an ABA programme which has proved to be successful, leading to opportunities to attend mainstream and weave into the normal environment, things can soon fall apart if they are simply expected just to fit in without the facilitator or 'shadow', as Lovaas refers to such support. Nor can the LEA, school or family expect that the support person will be able to maintain the success unless they are properly trained and engaged in monitoring and evaluation in the appropriate manner. All the good work could fall away.

Furthermore, through a recognition of a child's particular tapestry, his or her responses in varied contexts will be better understood and this will lead to a better fine-tuning of the programme – providing someone is engaged to do this work. There have been expectations that children who have been on ABA programmes will be able to manage without any support, but this is unfair to the child. They are experiencing a condition in the severest form, which just a few years ago we could not intrude upon at all, the only option being special school. While this remains the only option for some, others are taking their place in mainstream without the desperate angst experienced by any of their predecessors who suffered terribly in mainstream. If this is at all possible, for however few, we have a duty to support the child. This cannot be done blindly, and the unique needs of the individual determine which placement or programme would meet their needs. This should not be an exercise in testing out the robustness of ABA by giving the child nothing and watching him or her fail.

Mainstream or nothing must also not be the rallying call. Many children have been destroyed by lack of recognition, insensitivity, lack of resources, lies about improvement, parent blame and so on. If a system cannot incorporate the respectful models of practice advocated in this book – and parents must discover this on visits to school and talks with other families – then alternative schooling is the only option.

I would envisage that alternative models of education incorporating the above will find a place in our system without stigmatising the child.

In my opinion, no child with a history of autism or severe ADHD should move through any school system without very specific support. Thanks to the years of insight and respect for children with autism emanating from researchers such as Lorna Wing and the tapestries of new methods including ABA, visual support systems and programmes, social communication packages, and focused communication work in one-to-one and mapped onto various communicative contexts through trained tutors, some will be able to access mainstream education and the costs to the public purse will be minimal by comparison with what might have been. The benefit to individuals who can use their brain to learn and to engage with others is incalculable.

Once into the 8 years and older sector of schooling, the demands for independent working increase and the prompts, support and nurturing decrease. The language of instruction becomes more complex and abstract with few visual supports or multisensory methods in place to reduce confusion. The child with severe early problems will continue to need a tapestry of support which will increasingly focus on more subtle semantic-pragmatic problems and fine motor difficulties, problems of interpretation in social contexts which need to be discussed and perhaps avoided if reactions are extreme. Difficulties with work production need to incorporate new technologies including word recognition software for those who are articulate but have praxis problems. Information technology can be used as a means to produce work through a word processor or as a way of helping children gain some control over their learning by using appropriate software which helps with impairments.

It is during these years when earlier efforts need consolidating, and the children need to work on areas of difficulty before they move up to secondary school. This is a very difficult time when children with these problems are hugely vulnerable. Terrible fears and anxieties can overwhelm them if their problems have not been recognised and expecting them to cope with no support, even though they have made such great strides, is unrealistic.

Transitions need to be very carefully handled and staged through interwoven crossed contextual action. Throughout at least the whole of the last term before a child moves on, there need to be carefully organised visits to the next school and visits from the secondary school to the primary. Ideally, facilitators will be able to move up with their child in certain cases and there needs to be the flexibility built into the system to do this. If a child is expected to cope with massive change on all fronts in a very large school with large classes, this could lead to considerable problems. A plan is essential in all situations. A plan of action for transitions with our tapestry kids is imperative.

Once into the secondary sector, the challenges are much greater because the days are fragmented into many lessons in many classes with many teachers and many teaching styles. The main focus is on subject learning, and teachers are more likely to say that they are there only to teach. This misses a crucial point. They are actually there to *assist children to learn* and gain access to education and the wider social world. This has to be facilitated in the most efficacious manner. As we have established, in severe cases children will not be in the mainstream of education, but many are and it is their fundamental developmental disorder which prevents them from accessing the opportunities laid before them.

However, it is also recognised that teachers cannot be expected to be all singing, all dancing and able to meet the commitment to the precision of learning theory approaches and methods, as well as teaching – nor should they be expected to do so.

Instead, the system must ensure that teachers are helped to facilitate the learning of their students through appropriate training and through provision of resources such as the therapists and the facilitators – to enable teachers to play the role they are dedicated to fulfil.

Communication sessions which focus on various aspects of basic communication should be incorporated into the curriculum and enjoyed by students. Increasingly packages that address the various aspects of communication are being developed for various ages and levels of ability. Understanding our fundamental responsibilities to each other in society cannot be left to chance. Furthermore, through facilitating attentional, motor and communication skills, learning is more efficacious. It is these strands which make it happen.

The ongoing interweave of OT and SaLT into school systems is also crucially important, even at secondary level, and professional models of intervention incorporating the crucial interweave that maps onto the underlying essential processes will need to evolve gradually in normal school systems.

Despite the increasing optimism about the way we can make changes for our children, some children's tapestries are too tangled, they have too many co-morbidities, support never provided or coming too late, and the specialist school is very important for such children. If this is necessary, there should not be despair but rich interwoven models must also operate in those schools.

Indeed the training for staff in such schools is crucially important and needs to move away from the 'slow learner' idea which leaves many children screaming inside or off on another planet. It may take some children a long time to process information – hence the 'slow' idea – but for many, they actually need quite fast, intensive and repetitive methods to trigger sluggish neurotransmission systems and help the children find salience in what they are learning, retain, consolidate and sustain that learning. I have observed many a slow learner rapidly working out ways to avoid the dread dullness of the excessively slow wheels of teaching methods provided for them.

The interweave of neurodevelopmental processes including those we refer to currently as frontal lobe functioning – regulating, planning, focusing, shifting, sticking, sustaining, motivating – sewn into communication and motor skills disorders is indisputable and requires the psychological understanding of theories of behavioural intervention which facilitate these processes. Psychologists, speech and language therapists and occupational therapists need to weave their own focused one-to-one work with children in with appropriate training and monitoring of facilitators who will work intensively in one-to-one sessions, and develop focused methods of generalisation. In turn, this will increase the potential for success in those one-to-one therapies for those who need it. As we move back along the severity thread it is obvious that some children will now need the facilitator support, but they must have facilitators who have the training and the abilities for ongoing monitoring.

I also know many teachers who would rather leave the profession than continue with limited training, limited support and limited resources. We can be quite sure that the teaching profession will not be able to incorporate these methods into the system without commitment at LEA and government level to the interweave of working practice between professionals and the training of facilitators. Brain-storming sessions need to start the reweaving process with some urgency.

Summary

Older children currently in the school system will not have benefited from early intensive interventions. There are methods which can also apply to them and an increasing number of resources and important training courses are available.

Some of the difficulties in the past need to be recognised to pave the way forward:

- Perceiving a single problem as causing all else – therefore a single focus on one type of treatment. Professional input needs to be interwoven to map onto essential interwoven development threads to reweave impairments.

- Failing to understand the complex interweave of co-morbid conditions. Knowing the interweave helps with accessing interventions which work for various groups. Some forms of input will obviously pertain only to the single defining strand, but those that are shared provide rich weaves for positive change.

- The difficulties with the transfer of learning can be reduced by recognising the interweave of contexts – people, settings, conditions in the learning environment etc.

- Very limited resources in health and educational systems are not conducive to the need for real commitment to change and new ideas.

- None, limited or inappropriate training for professionals and parents make the starting tasks impossible.

In turn this will result in piecemeal support relating to one thread which also fails in terms of:

- intensity
- frequency
- duration.

Crucial intervention threads must take into account:

- The contexts within which learning takes place including within the family – parents also need training and supporting.

- How a child can be helped to orient to the learning environment before the bells goes and class/therapy ends.

- The factors which stimulate a child's motivation to learn.

- How any learning can be generalised from one setting to another.

- Training of staff and parents to help them weave the communication tapestry across home and school contexts.

- Ongoing monitoring and evaluation of progress through precise behavioural descriptions set within clear records.

In the past and continuing:

- Many children never have their needs recognised.
- Many do have their needs recognised but do not receive appropriate interwoven support.

In the older child the following benefit all:

- Learning environment organised according to child's tapestry.
- Visual supports to augment language-based lessons.
- Visual supports to provide information, rules, instructions, daily timetables.
- Limited verbal instruction.
- Rewards for reinforcement – perhaps a token system or the use of response cost. In the latter a child starts the day with a certain amount of tokens and must work to keep them.
- Positive application.
- Structured programmes.
- Evaluation and monitoring involving the child.
- Incorporation of social communication programmes and games.
- Facilitator or coach support who thoroughly knows the child and who can help to guide the child through the day with prompts, advice, gentle reminders and focused problem-solving discussion in relation to their specific needs. These could include sensitivity to sounds and fears associated with them; particular social awareness failings; repetitive behaviours and language etc. Once the child is *engaging* he or she can be helped to reduce anxieties and rigid behaviours. The facilitator coach needs to understand learning theory so that they do not inadvertently reinforce behaviour that they are trying to reduce.
- Facilitator or coach who can help children plan and structure their work or colour codebooks etc.
- Facilitator or coach who can chart change and liaise with parents, other teaching staff and therapists.
- Parents' involvement with the programme.

Suggestions for action

First

- Fully understand the child's tapestry including the salient factors which *prevent* learning taking place.
- Fully understand the child's tapestry including the salient factors which *enable* learning to take place.

Second

- Recognise underlying mechanisms such as warped motivational processes linked with poor focus and attention to what is relevant, poor orienting skills, poor regulation (the rhythm).
- Recognise limited ability to *sustain* and *retain* processed information and inability to *shift* learning from one context to another. These underlying processes and others act in concert with the development of nonverbal skills, then language, motor co-ordination and motor planning, and form the essential communicating interweave of the tapestry.

Third

- Establish how these essential processes can be rewoven by putting in place methods which incorporate our knowledge of essential processes and our knowledge of success in the most severe cases. If this can be achieved in severe cases, the same principles can be watered down as we move along the severity threads.

The successful interweave

From increasing awareness of how children learn within autism or language impairments and ADHD research it is clear that combinations of the most efficacious methods are likely to be needed, especially for complex tapestry cases.

Learning theory

Closely monitored behavioural programmes do show evidence of success across contexts and in different domains of functioning, to an extent that we would never have believed possible, and this must not be forgotten.

I hope to see a greater availability of such programmes and training to undertake them woven through school systems but, first and most important, available for parents.

However, researchers emphasise the effort and commitment involved to achieve success in the programmes and both recognise a group who, while definitely benefiting from such interventions in ways which provide a window of opportunity, require additional support for their long-term needs.

Various forms of support could be interwoven depending on the unique child tapestry, and the following is just a sample.

Communication and motor training packages

Intensive communication programmes; intensive monitored motor planning activities; sensory integration; visual methods of communication such as PECS; social communication packages such as Social Stories and Comic Strip Conversations are increasingly available for parents and professionals and include training in some cases.

Visual methods

These involve a commitment to precise implementation of procedures incorporating visual timetables, cards, photographs, etc. The older child can help with the timetables and graphs.

Reward systems

These depend on the setting, the severity, age and ability level of the child, and also what motivates him. The methods can range from token systems in school to ABA methods at home.

Interweave of psychologist, language therapist and OT

Involvement of speech and language therapists alongside psychologists and occupational therapists should interweave in programmes put into place in the home and school. The areas of motor planning, proprioception and kinaesthetics woven with visual perception and pre-verbal communication skills, gestures, expressions etc. is a good start and incorporates the essential instinctive processes which are impaired.

The direct delivery of therapeutic interventions with the speech and language therapist and occupational therapist is implicated at the severe end of communication and motor skills threads, while the delivery for less severe problems can be put into place by facilitators working one-to-one with the child. However, the programme, initial introduction and ongoing evaluation of progress must always be put into place by the professional therapists.

Irlen lenses

Children with autism need sensitivities reduced by other methods if improving communication does not change these problems. I have now seen numerous children who suffered from perpetual sensitivities that were immediately relieved when they used an overlay or Irlen lenses. Donna Williams reports the remarkable difference when she wears the lenses.

Improving communication and attention to what is relevant to reduce sensitivities

I have seen some cases in which ritualising behaviour and sensitivity to sound in particular were reduced after children improved their communication skills and learned what was salient in the environment – i.e. language – and focused on this instead of other sounds, or learned to ignore those sounds. Two children with Asperger syndrome, one aged 10, the other 15, had a crippling fear of sudden sounds including thunder, fire bells etc. In neuropsychological assessment they jumped every time an auditory bleep went off, and were too distressed to continue. However, when the bleeps were accompanied by short stories which they also had to listen to, they did not jump and were able to function much better. This verbal distraction took their minds off the bleeps.

Expert speech and language therapists focus on work to help children improve their selectivity of environmental sights and sounds; improve their recognition and category of sound; improve the abstraction of saliency and meaning from auditory stimuli; and learn active neglect of sounds in the learning environment and passive neglect of background noise (Cathy MacLennan, speech and language therapist, personal communication).

Eastern methods to calm

Other temporary methods can be put into place to help with sensitivities, fears and anxieties. These include relaxation using aromatherapy and sensory integration and Eastern methods of meditation. For some, intense exercise alters neurotransmission processing and this shifts problems. As with massage for back problems, the difficulties will return and so if there is improvement for the individual child, the methods must be part of the ongoing programme.

Forms of words

Using language to mediate is the sine qua non of human existence and impairments in these areas for the children interferes with the perception of all kinds of normal environmental events. This can lead to great anxieties, obsessive and catastrophic thinking. Discussion of obsessions can help the older child with language, but there will need to be visual support and repetition. The language and even the single words used can alter how the child overcomes or manages such anxieties but without any doubt, the use of language and discussion can help reduce anxiety, augmented in some cases by the use of methods such as aromatherapy, with help to calm the nervous system.

I worked with one young boy with Asperger syndrome who was obsessional about light bulbs. He thought he had some magic power as they kept 'blowing'. When he went to bed he could not sleep for the fear that influences out of his control would lead to disaster. The sleep deprivation and lying awake worrying in turn affected him during the day.

Staff were able to reduce this child's fears through lavender baths calming him at bedtime and through clear explanation about the light bulbs. Through a simple survey he was able to work out that the bulbs blew when he was not there – so it was not him doing it; that they were cheap so more likely to blow. Drawing up tables and doing his own survey helped him, but he needed the structure and guidance of a coach or facilitator who could remind and reassure regularly and repeat the exercise if necessary.

This child and others were also helped by the well-known stop and think procedures which were drawn out to look like a traffic light.

Newer medications

In extreme cases of anxiety, medication can be very appropriate and can release a person from mind-numbing fears. There are obvious concerns about the effects of certain medications on developing nervous systems but for some children, the damage to their system could be much greater if fundamental neurotransmission problems cannot be changed by intensive methods in the severely affected child.

The regulating mechanism of the newer medications may be as important to such children as medications for asthma and diabetes. Specialists must be involved to fine-tune any interventions and to monitor closely any increase in obsessions that can be triggered by certain medications.

Diets

Terrible tantrums and bowel problems as part of the new variant autism can be considerably relieved by casein- and gluten-free diets. Tests on urine samples at Sunderland University's Allergy Induced Autism Department (in north-east England) can establish whether the individual child would be a good candidate.

Computers

Our younger generation are naturals on computers. For many with developmental problems using a computer each day with planned material can be highly salient and motivating. In the late eighties, when a very talented special education computer programmer, an occupational therapist and I recognised the problems with very basic processes which preceded reading development, we got together and designed a computer program for 5–7 year olds which we called 'Dwight's Party'. At that stage, there was simply nothing available and computer graphics were poor. The programmer used the now departed Amiga as its graphics were so strong and appealing. That program also excited the children because coloured images came out from a black non-distracting screen. At that point in time no programmes had such backgrounds. They liked the engaging character 'Dwight', who would put his thumb up or down and say 'That's right' or a 'not right' buzzer would go off. Thanks to the enthusiasm and encouragement of two forward-thinking headmistresses, we were able to introduce Dwight to children in two West Sussex infant schools in southern England with a variety of tasks including sequencing and face matching; this helped all but two of a pilot group of children to improve sequencing skills on standardised tests. One of these children was so autistic and so distracted that the images on the screen were not salient to him and he either looked at reflections on the glass screen or at the lights above him. The other child could not do any better than she did on the baseline assessment!

Our lack of funds ensured that we could not afford to develop more programmes even though we were told it had enormous potential given the need for salient programs that would work for young children. We sent detailed letters to all and sundry and also sold a few copies, but that was as far as it went. Nevertheless, our experience proved to us the value of such interventions and we are very happy to see that there is now an enormous choice of software material available to help children with a variety of skills.

These programs can also be integrated into group, home and classroom work and one family used a program to wean their Asperger son from his knife fascination. The program showed articles such as knives being gathered up and put away. This was augmented by repetitive modelling within the home and rewards for appropriate action. As they held their son's shoulders or arms gently and ensured he was looking at them, specific and limited 'stop' instructions delivered using low emotion also accompanied these events in the early stages. His extreme hyperactivity, bowel and motor problems also meant that he needed medication for the hyperactivity, which worked for that thread, a casein- and gluten-free diet and sensory integration. Thus, behavioural interventions, touch–talk–gaze methods for engagement, diet and therapies formed the intervention tapestry for this child. Given the severity of this little boy's problems, ongoing evaluations are necessary to fine-tune the various forms of professional support. This child was also enrolled on a class-based communication programme but applied his rigidity to the off-the-shelf scenarios he learned. Specific, tailor-made programmes have been necessary.

The trained facilitator

Without a coach or facilitator, fully trained and supported, who charts and monitors, prompts and provides support, liaises with teaching staff, professionals and parents – none of this can work.

Summary of key ideas

Key threads

Interwoven communication and 'executive' impairments replace 'behaviour' as the main focus.

Severity and hue of tapestry determines how tried and tested interventions are put in place.

Unique child demands unique methods

Facilitators or coaches for each child or family are crucial.

In severe cases, support needs to be intensive and early (pre-school) to maximise chances of improvement and before the tapestry becomes tangled with further secondary problems.

Older, tangled tapestry kids previously unrecognised will pose great challenges and these children are the ones who are most likely to need alternative schooling.

The 'golden children' who remain after appropriate interventions will require a 24-hour curriculum that crosses environmental and communicative contexts, if the autistic or communication thread is severe.

Impossible tasks

In some cases normal families are simply not able to undertake intensive programmes within their home, even with a trained facilitator, and the child runs riot on return from the school which has been able to control and hold him or her during the day. In the past and currently, the only option in these cases has been for respite care by services which know nothing about autism and severe ADHD as the child becomes increasingly more demanding and challenging. While parent involvement is highly desirable, and many argue against residential schools, for some children with severe problems, this is the only possible option.

The severity tapestry allows you to determine how intensive, how structured, how limited a time period, how detailed the nature of consistency, how many rewards, how much reinforcement etc. are necessary for the individual child.

Functional analyses allow you to fine tune each thread of behaviour as you analyse how behaviours are shaped.

Monitoring and evaluating

Monitoring of progress, involving careful charting and daily discussion of exactly how a child responded in a given situation, is a crucial component and must occur on an ongoing basis to fine-tune the programme.

Real world setting

The interventions need to occur within the real world of that child – the home for the pre-schooler and a combination as he or she improves and moves into the school system or in the care or school settings in residential school.

Crossing contexts

Crossing contexts to maximise reinforcement of learning requires a mixing of home or care and school staff, therapists and parents.

Behavioural interventions

Interventions which have proven efficacy in both autism and ADHD must be put into place, the extent determined by the slide-rule of severity.

Small chunks of required learning must be presented in numerous ways and by various people in different situations, then repeated to ensure mastery and constantly evaluated for fine-tuning.

Repetition of small step learning is imperative.

Model behaviour

Salient rewards are essential – at the right time and consistently applied.

Visual support systems should be carefully applied.

Trials of medications may be necessary.

Diet modification may be necessary in medically vulnerable or allergic children.

Breakthrough

The child reaches the stage when he or she can tolerate other children and to attempt to reach the point when more useful communication skills can emerge from the tapestry of support, repetitive interventions must occur within the communicating environment by trained facilitators. In some cases additional language work will be needed in the one-to-one and in some cases this will also need to be augmented with an interweave of language or motor and attentional support, social communication and motor activity packages, diets, lenses and new technologies. However, any gain from piecemeal sessions of support can be rapidly lost in a matter of minutes, which calls out for intensity of methods. Without close evaluation and monitoring to fine-tune programmes, we are working blind.

Last threads

We are developing the knowledge to recognise which methods work for different groups and which methods work *across* groups. Dependent on the severity of a particular problem, our efforts must be increasingly magnified to expose the fundamental glitches, the work then more intensive, repetitive and extensive. Like our babies in Chapter 5, repeat it, pause, look, hold, touch, sing, laugh, joke over and over and over again in different contexts and with varying reinforcements.

Inevitably, given the tapestry nature of people, rock solid proof of 'success' has not been easily found in the academic literature within which the traditional population evaluations of numerous interventions have not been able to assess properly tapestry effects on tapestry people – are we surprised?

What we do find, however, is evidence of processes that are generally helpful and need to be woven into our interventions and very specific evidence of success in particular programmes which is often anecdotal. We all understand that this area of work is not an exact science, as much as we might like to think it is. Our insights are as valuable as evidence from a cold study in which we *know* all the threads or variables in the tapestries will not be matched. All it takes is to not ask the right questions.

The danger is that we can leap from our insight with success in one person and imagine that we will find the same in another, or leap from success in a highly controlled clinical situation into real life and expect the same.

As long as we realise that development is a tapestry of art and science, we can apply our best bet – what is the *probability* that this will help this particular child? – from the increasing amount of information available to us, our knowledge of our child through the tapestries we have built, set within our own personal life context.

In other words, does this seem to be an approach that will work for this particular child and will the child, family, professionals and school be able to manage? Can they do this?

Weaving this chapter's tapestry is as crucially important as the previous tapestries. Families should not find that they are meeting considerable professional resistance despite honest and respectful attempts to resolve differences. New ways forward should not have to involve armed battle with education and health systems. Certain professionals should cease to conspire with each other to hide evidence of a child's problems, denying them their human rights.

Fortunately, most parents have benefited from an educational system also enjoyed by the professionals to whom they turn. This is not meant to imply that parents are experts in medical and psychological fields – although some will be – but that parents are intelligent people who are experts in relation to their own children. It is enormously frustrating for an intelligent parent to be disregarded by a professional who has spent little or no time with their child. Parents are now empowering themselves with knowledge and in some cases taking this to the professionals. The information and the work undertaken by the parents will excite those with integrity. Parents and professionals need to collaborate as discoverers.

Parents are not professionals to their own children. They cannot leave work at the end of the day and put it behind them. They cannot leave the job if it is too demanding. They cannot hand over to someone else. From my experience, when methods fail at home it is for such reasons. Furthermore, children who feel isolated at school or who are failing will return home feeling depressed and frustrated. This will be worse if they have felt constrained during the day.

Many tapestry kids who have shown typical profiles at pre-school are *not* always seen as a problem initially in school. This is particularly the case if the child is under the age of 7 and still in awe of teachers. If children are in a school with small classes with a highly structured day and attentive empathic teachers and assistants, they will be provided with what they need to contain their difficulties. Often the problems emerge first in the less structured playground activities. As time passes, and demands increase, expectations growing and the language of instruction increasingly abstract with less and less support, many of this group of children will begin to demonstrate the difficulties which parents saw at pre-school.

The intensive methods described above need to be considered within the school system, but it is imperative that facilitators are trained and that the procedures are understood and implemented intensively as appropriate.

The same types of programmes, designed for the home and for very young children with autistic spectrum disorders, cannot be imposed on families. It must be their decision as to whether they can undertake the effort, cost and commitment involved and if they do, the local authority should work with them.

The system should aim for the following:

- improved knowledge within the health service about polygenetic effects on various body systems relating to autistic spectrum and the interwoven ADHD spectrum of disorders, and the vulnerability of many children within this group to knock-on effects as problems accumulate
- rigorous assessments – baseline and then ongoing
- methods of multi-modal working including the use of ABA

- educational authorities' commitment to the provision of trained facilitators within schools to develop tapestries and undertake interventions according to efficacious models

- individual tapestries which would include not only the IEP but also the health and social plans which make up the whole and unique person tapestry

- various measures put into place as appropriate.

Other texts deal in detail with specific interventions for different groups and Appendix 2 gives some details.

I have been enormously impressed by parents' integrity and their desire to understand problems which their child may experience, and I understand the frustration when their considerable knowledge meets increasingly higher stone walls within the system. Our future aims must be:

- to understand how problems can develop from conception onwards by weaving a positive tapestry of the most intuitive and valuable knowledge of the child; sharing meanings within and between professionals is an essential prerequisite to an understanding of the processes involved in sharing meaning in infant development

- to reduce complex problems as early as possible before tangled interweaving effects compound existing difficulties, by creating a support tapestry in order to reweave the original

- to improve social communication, academic, vocational and creative success through appropriate and positive treatment plans and ongoing evaluation

- ultimately to improve social competence and creativity within successful families, communities and the wider society

- to protect the golden children through specialised schooling, caring and creative trained staff who can lead them forward into an adulthood which lessens confusion and fear and provides then with a purpose in their isolation.

Legal issues

Vast numbers of parents of older children within the school system in various countries find that their children's difficulties are complex enough to warrant support at a level which the school is unable to provide from its own resources.

Appendix 2 lists websites and addresses of groups which can advise about legal rights.

If the school is unable to access the appropriate support from health and education authorities, and given that children have various rights to support to meet their needs, it falls to their parents, as their advocates, to find them this support.

Accessing this support requires considerable effort on the part of parents who can find themselves in a minefield. Arguments usually swivel on the nature and extent of the child's needs to start with, and on their response to broad-band provision. Chapter 6 dealt with some of the problems which can arise when parents, trying to help their child, face local authorities trying to spread limited resources out to help many.

At the extremes, and in the minority, there will be parents who exaggerate a child's problems and make unreasonable demands and complaints, and inevitably there will be LEAs which prevent any recognition of a child's needs by various underhand means. Unfortunately, professionals working in many authorities in both health and education have found themselves compromised with implied threats of job loss unless they shift their position. Many professionals have straddled the roles of administrator and impartial professional and the roles became blurred. Some professionals simply working as professionals, obviously with a mind toward resource implications but not responsible for them, are more able to provide honest reports.

One psychologist was actually sacked for naming where a child should go to school. Most now are discouraged from making diagnoses and this confuses parents. 'Why was I never told?' they will ask, when it is obvious their child was experiencing a particular problem for many years. Cynically, many defend themselves by taking the moral high ground and dismissing the use of labels for children. However, failing to recognise clusters of problems can lead to a lack of recognition of the child's real difficulties and needs. Preventing recognition of problems stymies social systems.

The use of the tapestry enables us to address some of the arguments inherent in fixed categorisation – thereby feeding into the 'don't label them' argument widens the perspective and allows for growth of understanding rather than restriction.

From this base of comprehensive tapestry-type assessments, many of the problems within the system can be highlighted as well as providing a true picture of the child. As even teaching hospitals have been targeted by certain authorities (in the UK) to change their diagnoses, it will continue to require totally independent professionals to assess properly and guide in such cases.

Given the problems of poor recognition and limited provision and the social outcomes of rising crime and rising mental health problems, we cannot continue to bury our heads under the sand of local authority money and power issues.

Many parents of children with various special needs have campaigned over decades to improve the lot for their child. As a result, large parent driven support groups have been developed – for instance, CHADD for the ADHD children in the USA and the NAS for autistic children in the UK. Other support groups pertaining to these and other conditions in both countries are mentioned in Appendix 2.

Legal initiatives have evolved resulting in protection of children's rights to have their needs met. Constant political change leads to revisions and families need to be advised about the legal situation for their child. The large support groups for different conditions can usually guide a parent who may need to approach groups which provide legal support, and in some cases lawyers are necessary. Battles about children's rights and needs may then need to shift to tribunals and courts but may bring the changes to the law which in turn guide and drive how systems support children.

IPSEA was founded by John Wright in the late 1980s, in response to concerns across the UK pertaining to children and the struggle to recognise and provide support for their special needs. This group helps families understand what they need to do if they are unhappy with their child's progress and provision of support set out in the legal document which is called a Statement of needs, following a formal assessment.

For many years LEAs could find ways of dodging their responsibilities and if they could not avoid a child's needs being recognised they could limit the support by writing statements which were not clear. This changed in 1996 when the authorities were obliged to quantify and specify provision, but as I write the July 2000 draft of a new Code of Practice has left out the guidance pertaining to quantifying and specifying special educational provision.

Action on Entitlement (AoE), representing 16 parent groups and voluntary organisations concerned with children with special educational needs, wrote to the government stating:

> [T]he proposals would seriously undermine the long-standing legal entitlement of some of the most vulnerable children to educational provision. If needs are not matched by specific provision detailed in the Statement,

the Multi-Professional Assessment (The Formal Assessment) becomes a hollow exercise. If Statements are vaguely written, parents will be unable to judge whether the extra help for their child will be sufficient or appropriate or whether a particular school is fulfilling the statement. The Statement will therefore be unenforceable.

The Special Educational Consortium (SEC) representing 247 organisations wrote:

> There is concern that these proposals erode the very structures that can give parents the confidence that their child's needs can be met in mainstream school. The Consortium has consulted with a number of groups of parents in different parts of the country. Some talk positively about the progress of their child in a mainstream school, but many had sought a special school place because the struggle to secure support for their child in mainstream had become too great, or because they had seen what other parents had experienced and this made them feel unequal to the task. It would appear that there are many parents of children in special schools who are, in effect, refugees from mainstream and would have chosen a mainstream school had they been able to secure the necessary support.

Every group sent in its own concerns referring to many matters including the risk of misinterpretation, the reduction of support, the fact that the Code of Practice was put in place in the first place because local authorities were evading their responsibilities in law.

In reaction to the concerns, changes were announced in December 2000. However, these are still not satisfactory, stating that provision should be 'quantified as necessary' and leaving the interpretation of 'as necessary' wide open to abuse. These struggles show how politically difficult it can be for parents to attain a true understanding of their child's tapestry of problems and match these with an appropriate tapestry of interventions.

In the UK the Special Educational Tribunal exists independently to adjudicate on issues between parents and LEAs. They have powers that enable them to order a local authority to put certain support in place or name an alternative school for the child.

However, before such a happy state is reached, the parents will find they have been through numerous hoops in the school system and will have spent years trying to understand what is wrong with their child. Ideally, rules of thumb and then thorough assessments will lead educationalists and health professionals to determine which children need support. As this is also determined by resources, criteria have to be set down. These criteria are usually quite strict and less than 2 per cent of the population will be considered eligible for a formal assessment which may, or may not, lead onto a Statement in which a child's needs are set out. There is current controversy over whether new legislation will remove the clause that states that provision has to be quantified and specified. If this was to happen, vague and woolly statements could easily become the order of the day again.

As schools have been given their own resources, taken away from the LEA, it is understandable that LEAs insist on making sure that school systems have put everything in place they possibly could before a child is considered to need more resources – from the LEA – or alternative schooling. This will include therapies; IEPs which detail programmes of intervention and outcomes of such programmes. Unfortunately, there is not a culture of providing facilitator or coach models into schools. Instead, classroom assistants are employed and most have very little training in the methods discussed above. Additionally, school systems are not encouraged to put children forward for formal assessments and the parents may find themselves in the outrageous situation of having a school admit their child's difficulties but when forced to attend tribunal, to say something quite different. In many cases the school will not admit it from the outset but with the new laws that enable parents access to their files, they often find that the truth behind the comments is quite different. In one case known to me a head teacher begged for extra help for a child, in lengthy letters to the powers that be. To the parents he reported absolutely no problems at all and queried the mental health of the mother. On accessing the files the truth came to light. This behind-the-scenes honesty and front-of-house lying does nothing for desperate parents. The LEA is unlikely to budge, especially as it knows the head teacher will not reveal his duplicity to the parents and so the secret information will remain so – right though to tribunal.

It is in cases such as these that independent specialist assessors are helpful. They can independently view the papers, assess the child and determine the nature of the support required. They can also report openly on any duplicity.

IPSEA (UK) can support families with opinions and advice about their exact case, help with forms and paperwork, advise on the workings of the tribunal and education law in general and attend as a representative if necessary. The representative exists separately from the expert witness, but families can actually attend tribunals on their own and organise their appeal by themselves.

In the USA, legislation has been put in place following parental drives to recognise the most vulnerable children. Website details are provided in Appendix 2.

Tapestry blanket to wrap around your child

To weave this rainbow blanket you need the following strands of silk:

SHIMMERING GOLD:	positive, non-blaming support and training for parents and children who take priority in our society – they represent the future
SYMPHONY SILVER:	touch–talk–gaze – woven sensory skills
FLUORESCENT YELLOW:	attention and engagement
INDIGO BLUE:	taking turns and listening
PINK:	regular pauses threaded throughout
BREEZE BLUE:	imitation – expression, gesture, motor action and language
PURPLE:	rich, respectful, novel experiences
AQUAMARINE:	calm, cool, non-confrontational responses when tempers flare
SUNRISE RED:	times for fun, fast, joyful delivery
SEA GREEN:	balanced, wave-like interactions
MELLOW YELLOW:	recognise child's need for quiet times alone
TERRACOTTA:	down-to-earth, straightforward descriptions of skills and problems
SUNSET ORANGE:	consistent, salient rewards for all successes and positive behaviour
SOLID SILVER:	functional analyses weaving basic 'unique child tapestry'
PACIFIC BLUE:	clear, simple, precise instruction – one at a time
BRIGHT WHITE:	keeping simple clear records of progress, for ongoing fine-tuning
BURNISHED BLACK:	protecting the human rights of your child through legal action if necessary

This weaving process is repeated over and over again – the emerging image will be better control of your own destiny – parent and child – and maybe even a happy, successful, sociable child!

Diagnostic criteria

Table 1

Childhood autism (Closest to Kanner's type): ICD-10

For childhood autism (F84.0), impaired or abnormal development must be present *before* 3 years, manifesting the *full triad* of impairments:

1. in reciprocal social interaction

2. in communication

3. in restricted stereotyped, repetitive behaviour.

Table 2

Diagnostic criteria for attention deficit and hyperactivity disorder: DSM-IV

Either (1) or (2):

(1) Six (or more) of the following symptoms of inattention have persisted for at least six months to a degree that is maladaptive and inconsistent with developmental level.

INATTENTION

1. often fails to give close attention to details or makes careless mistakes in schoolwork or other activities

2. often has difficulty sustaining attention in tasks or play activities

3. often does not seem to listen when spoken to directly

4. often does not follow through on instructions and fails to finish schoolwork, chores or duties in the workplace (not due to oppositional behaviour or failure to understand instructions)

5. often has difficulty organising tasks and activities

6. often avoids, dislikes or is reluctant to engage in tasks that require sustained mental effort (such as schoolwork or homework)

7. often loses things necessary for tasks or activities (e.g. toys, school assignments, pencils, books or tools)

8. is often easily distracted by extraneous stimuli

9. is often forgetful in daily activities

(2) Six (or more) of the following symptoms of hyperactivity or impulsivity have persisted for at least six months for a degree that is maladaptive and inconsistent with developmental level.

HYPERACTIVITY

1. often fidgets with hands or feet or squirms in seat

2. often leaves seat in classroom or in other situations in which remaining seated is expected

3. often runs about or climbs excessively in situations in which it is inappropriate (in adolescents or adults, may be limited to subjective feelings of restlessness)

4. often has difficulty playing or engaging in leisure activities quietly

5. is often 'on the go' or often acts as if 'driven by a motor'

6. often talks excessively

IMPULSIVITY

1. often blurts out answers before questions have been completed

2. often has difficulty awaiting turn

3. often interrupts or intrudes on others (e.g. butts into conversations or games)

Some hyperactive-impulsive or inattentive symptoms that caused impairment were present before age 7 years.

Some impairment from the symptoms is present in two or more settings (e.g. at school or work and at home).

There must be clear evidence of clinically significant impairment in social, academic, or occupational functioning.

The symptoms do not occur exclusively during the course of a pervasive development disorder, schizophrenia, or other psychotic disorder and are not better accounted for by another mental disorder (e.g. mood disorder, anxiety disorder, dissociative disorder or a personality disorder).

Table 3

Diagnostic criteria for hyperkinetic disorder: ICD-10

A. Demonstrates abnormality of attention and activity at home, for the age and developmental level of the child, as evidenced by at least *three* of the following attention problems:

   (a) short duration to spontaneous activity

   (b) often leaving play activities unfinished

   (c) over-frequent changes between activities

   (d) undue lack of persistence at tasks set by adults

   (e) unduly high distractibility during study.

And by at least two of the following activity problems:

   (f) continuous motor restlessness

   (g) markedly excessive fidgeting or wriggling during spontaneous activities

   (h) markedly excessive activity in situations requiring relative stillness

   (i) difficulty in remaining seated when required.

B. Demonstrates abnormality of attention and activity at school or nursery, for the age and developmental level of the child, as evidenced by at least two of the following attention problems:

   (a) undue lack of persistence at tasks

   (b) unduly high distractibility, i.e. often orienting towards extrinsic stimuli

(c) over-frequent changes between activities when choice is allowed

(d) excessively short duration of play activities.

And at least *two* of the following activity problems:

(e) continuous and excessive motor restlessness in school

(f) markedly excessive fidgeting and wriggling in structured situations

(g) excessive levels of off-task activity

(h) unduly often out of seat when required to be sitting.

C. Directly observed abnormalities of attention or activity. This must be excessive for the child's age and developmental level. The evidence may be any of the following:

(a) direct observation of the criteria in A or B above

(b) observation of abnormal levels of motor activity, or off-task behaviour, or lack of persistence in activities, in a setting outside home or school

(c) significant impairment of performance on psychometric test of attention.

D. Does not meet criteria for pervasive developmental disorder, mania, depressive or anxiety disorder.

E. Onset before the age of 6 years.

F. Duration of at least 6 months.

G. IQ above 50.

Table 4

Diagnostic criteria for 299.00 autistic disorder: DSM-IV

A. A total of six (or more) items from (1), (2) and (3), with at least two from (1) and one each from (2) and (3):

(1) Qualitative impairment in social interaction, as manifested by at least *two* of the following:

(a) marked impairment in the use of multiple non-verbal behaviours such as eye-to-eye gaze, facial expressions, body postures, and gestures to regulate social interaction

(b) failure to develop peer relationships appropriate to developmental level

(c) a lack of spontaneous seeking to share enjoyment interests, or achievements with other people (e.g., by lack of showing, bringing or pointing out objects of interest)

(d) lack of social or emotional reciprocity.

(2) Qualitative impairment in communication as manifested by at least *one* of the following:

(a) delay in, or total lack of, the development of spoken language (not accompanied by an attempt to compensate through alternative modes of communication such as gesture or mime)

(b) in individuals with adequate speech, marked impairment in the ability to initiate or sustain a conversation with others

(c) stereotyped and repetitive use of language or idiosyncratic language

(d) lack of varied, spontaneous make-believe play or social imitative play appropriate to developmental level.

(3) Restricted repetitive and stereotyped patterns of behaviour, interests, and activities, as manifested by at least *one* of the following:

(a) stereotyped and restricted pattern of interest that is abnormal either in intensity or focus

(b) apparently inflexible adherence to specific, non-functional routines or rituals

(c) stereotyped and repetitive motor mannerisms (e.g. hand or finger flapping or twisting, or complex whole-body movements)

(d) persistent preoccupation with parts of objects.

B. Delays or abnormal functioning in at least one of the following areas, with onset prior to age 3 years: (1) social interaction, (2) language as used in social communication, or (3) symbolic or imaginative play.

C. The disturbance is not better accounted for by Rett's disorder or childhood disintegrative disorder.

Table 5

Diagnostic criteria for Asperger syndrome (Gillberg and Gillberg 1989)
SOCIAL IMPAIRMENT (EXTREME EGOCENTRICITY)
At least *two* of the following:

    (a) inability to interact with peers

    (b) lack of desire to interact with peers

    (c) lack of appreciation of social cues

    (d) socially and emotionally inappropriate behaviour.

NARROW INTEREST
At least *one* of the following:

    (a) exclusion of other activities

    (b) repetitive adherence

    (c) more rote than meaning.

REPETITIVE ROUTINES
At least *one* of the following:

    (a) on self, in aspects of life

    (b) on others.

SPEECH AND LANGUAGE PECULIARITIES
At least *three* of the following:

    (a) delayed development

    (b) superficially perfect expressive language

    (c) formal pedantic language

    (d) odd prosody, peculiar voice characteristics

    (e) impairment of comprehension including misinterpretations

(f) of literal/implied meanings.

Non-verbal communication problems

At least *one* of the following:

(a) limited use of gestures

(b) clumsy/gauge body language

(c) limited facial expression

(d) inappropriate expression

(e) peculiar stiff gaze.

Motor clumsiness

Poor performance on neurodevelopmental examination.

Table 6

Diagnostic criteria for Asperger syndrome (Szatmari, Bremner and Nagy 1989)

SOLITARY

At least *two* of the following:

(a) no close friends

(b) avoids others

(c) no interest in making friends

(d) a loner.

IMPAIRED SOCIAL INTERACTION

At least *one* of the following:

(a) approaches others only to have own needs met

(b) a clumsy social approach

(c) one-sided responses to peers

(d) difficulty sensing feelings of others

(e) detached from feelings of others.

IMPAIRED NON-VERBAL COMMUNICATION

At least *one* of the following:

(a) limited facial expression

    (b) unable to read emotion from facial expression of child

    (c) unable to give messages with the eyes

    (d) does not look at others

    (e) does not use hands to express oneself

    (f) gestures are large and clumsy

    (g) comes too close to others.

ODD SPEECH

At least *two* of the following:

    (a) abnormalities in inflection

    (b) talks too much

    (c) talks too little

    (d) lack of cohesion to conversation

    (e) idiosyncratic use of words

    (f) repetitive patterns of speech.

Does not meet DSM-111–R criteria for autistic disorder.

Table 7
Diagnostic criteria for Asperger disorder: DSM-1V

A. Qualitative impairment in social interaction, as manifested by at least *two* of the following:

    1. marked impairment in the use of multiple non-verbal behaviours such as eye-to-eye gaze, facial expression, body postures and gestures to regulate social interaction

    2. failure to develop peer relationships appropriate to developmental level

    3. a lack of spontaneous seeking to share enjoyment, interests, or achievements with other people (e.g. by a lack of showing, bringing or pointing out objects of interest to other people)

    4. lack of social or emotional reciprocity.

B. Restricted repetitive and stereotyped patterns of behaviour, interests and activities, as manifested by at least one of the following:

1. encompassing preoccupation with one or more stereotyped and restricted patterns of interest that is abnormal either in intensity or focus

2. apparently inflexible adherence to specific, non-functional routines or rituals

3. stereotyped and repetitive motor mannerisms (e.g. hand or finger flapping or twisting, or complex whole-body movements)

4. persistent preoccupation with parts or objects.

C. The disturbance causes clinically significant impairment in social, occupational, or other important areas of functioning.

D. There is no clinically significant general delay in language (e.g. single words used by age 2 years, communicative phrases used by age 3 years).

E. There is no clinically significant delay in cognitive development or in the development of age-appropriate self-help skills, adaptive behaviour (other than in social interaction), and curiosity about the environment in childhood.

F. Criteria are not met for another specific pervasive developmental disorder or schizophrenia.

Table 8

Diagnostic criteria of Asperger syndrome: ICD-10

A. There is no clinically significant general delay in spoken or receptive language or cognitive development. Diagnosis requires that single words should have developed by 2 years of age or earlier and that communicative phrases to be used by 3 years of age or earlier. Self-help skills, adaptive behaviour, and curiosity about the environment during the first three years should be at a level consistent with normal intellectual development. However, motor milestones may be somewhat delayed and motor clumsiness is usual (although not a necessary diagnostic feature). Isolated special skills, often related to abnormal preoccupations are common, but are not required for diagnosis.

B. Qualitative abnormalities in reciprocal social interaction are mani-fested in at least *two* of the following areas:

    (a) failure adequately to use eye-to-eye gaze, facial expression, body posture, and gesture to regulate social interaction

    (b) failure to develop (in a manner appropriate to mental age, and despite opportunities) peer relationships that involve a mutual sharing of interests, activities and emotions

    (c) lack of social-emotional reciprocity as shown by an impairment or deviant response to other people's emotions: or lack of modulation of behaviour according to social context: or a weak integration of social, emotional and communicative behaviours

    (d) lack of spontaneous seeking to share enjoyment, interests, or achievements with other people (e.g. a lack of showing, bringing, or pointing out to other people objects of interest to the individual).

C. The individual exhibits an unusually intense, circumscribed interest or restricted, repetitive and stereotyped patterns of behaviour, interests, and activities manifest in at least one of the following areas.

    (a) an encompassing preoccupation with stereotyped and restricted patterns of interest that are abnormal in content or focus: or one or more interests that are abnormal in their intensity and circumscribed nature though not in the content or focus

    (b) apparently compulsive adherence to specific, non-functional routines or rituals

    (c) stereotyped and repetitive motor mannerisms that involve either hand/finger flapping or twisting, or complex whole body movements

    (d) preoccupations with part-objects or non-functional elements of play materials (such as their colour, the feel of their surface, or the noise/vibration that they generate).

However it would be less usual for these to include either motor mannerisms or preoccupations with part-objects or non-functional elements of play materials.

D. The disorder is not attributable to the other varieties of pervasive developmental disorder: simple schizophrenia, schizo-typal disorder, obsessive compulsive disorder, anankastic personality disorder, reactive and disinhibited attachment disorders of childhood.

Table 9

Triad of impairments in autism (Wing 1981)

Triad of impairments in:

1. social communication

2. social interaction

3. imagination.

Appendix 2

Resources

This list is separated into categories covering support groups, websites, and some practical resources. It provides information for various countries, but obviously cannot cover all available information.

SUPPORT GROUPS
ADHD

UK

There is limited awareness of ADHD in the UK, and still much cynicism, but each area's Health and Education Department should be able to direct you to local services/universities or hospitals with a developing expertise in this area.

ADDISS (ADD Information Services)
ADHD National Registered Charity run by Andrea Bilbow.

The support group provides information and training and runs conferences. They sell books, videos and resources on ADHD and related disorders, and produce a mail order catalogue.

The ADDISS Resource Centre
10 Station Road, Mill Hill, London, NW7 2JU
Email: info@addiss.co.uk
Website: www.addiss.co.uk

USA
CHADD – Children and Adults with Attention Deficit Disorder

A highly influential group set up by parents in 1987 to provide support and information given the serious lack of understanding about ADHD in the USA at that time, both professionally and in the lay public. This organisation runs a highly informative yearly conference at various venues in the USA, publishes literature, and has influenced policy making for the child and adult with ADHD. From just one support group in Florida there are now many 'Chapters' of voluntary workers across the United States. Floods of information in relation to ADHD, treatment, assessment, education, advocacy and support are provided by this inspiring group.

8181 Professional Place
Suite 201, Landover, MD 20785
Tel: (001) 800 233 4050 or Tel: (001) 301 306 7070. Fax: (001) 301 306 7090
Website: www.chadd.org

NETHERLANDS

ADHD Stichting (Duch ADHD Foundation)
Dion Kobussen (Chairman)
Eendrachtsweg 21, NL 3012 lb, Rotterdam
Tel: (00) 31 616 818 576
Email: kobussen@adhd.nl Website: www.adhd.nl

AUTISM
UK
NAS (National Autistic Society)

A very large charity, originally set up by parents, which runs education and adult centres, publishes many books and other materials on autism and Asperger syndrome, trains and supports local authorities to develop services, organises conferences and training programmes, and offers specialist diagnostic assessment services. There are NAS area groups all over the UK and Ireland.

Head Office
393 City Road, London, EC1V 1NG
Tel: (0044) (0) 20 7833 2299. Fax: (0044) (0) 20 7833 9666
Email: nas@nas.org.uk Website: www.nas.org.uk

National Helpline: 020 7903 3597

NAS (Wales)
Tel: 01792 815915. Fax: 01792 815911

NAS (Scotland)
Tel: 0141 221 8090. Fax: 0141 221 8118

USA

In addition to well-recognised centres in hospitals and university departments across the United States, the dramatic real increase in the incidence of autism since the late 1980s has resulted in powerfully expressed parent concerns. In turn, and quite appropriately, this has resulted in the rapid growth of early interventions; support groups; legal challenges in terms of educational rights; the right to explore the cause of autism in each child; and the right to be informed/determine the best forms of intervention for each unique tapestry child.

Autism Society of Los Angeles
www.autismsocietyla.org

Aspergers and ADD
www.users.primushost/~dmoisan

OASIS – Autism
www.udel.edu/bkirby/asperger.html

ASPEN of America – Autism
www.asperger.org

Families for Early Autism Treatment – FEAT
www.feat.org

An active group with their own newsletter.

Autism Research Institute, San Diego
www.autism.com/ari

Oops Wrong Planet Syndrome – Asperger syndrome
www.isn.net/-jypsy

A website full of information by jypsy.

CANADA
Geneva Centre for Autism
www.autism.net

Lovely website homepage. Various links and lots of information.

AUSTRALIA

Autism Victoria co-ordinates activities of all other groups.
Website for behavioural interventions is: www.home.vicnet.net.au

Autism Association of South Australia
www.span.com.au

NEW ZEALAND

AutismNZ

Provides information and support, sells video and audio tapes, books etc.

www.autismnz.org.nz

There are branches in about 14 areas including the main cities of Auckland and Wellington, and also in towns such as Hawkes Bay, Tauranga and Manawatu.

The Auckland branch can be contacted on:

Tel: (0064) (09) 276 1396. Fax: (0064) (09) 276 8790
Email: autism_auck@xtra.co.nz

DEVELOPMENTAL CO-ORDINATION DISORDER (Dyspraxia)
UK

When interwoven with attentional problems this condition meets DAMP criteria. The combination commonly co-exists with evidence of poor social awareness, in some cases reaching criteria for Asperger syndrome.

Dyspraxia Foundation, 8 West Alley, Hitchin, Herts, SG5 1EG
Helpline: (0044) (0) 1462 454 986. Fax: (0044) (0) 1462 455 052

DYSTONIA
UK
The Dystonia Society
46/47 Britton Street, London, EC1M 5UJ
Tel: (0044) (0) 207 490 5671

They can provide details of various types of dystonia including torticollis, eye blinking, tics and writer's cramp. Although this condition is recognised by extreme muscular distortions and gross involuntary spasms due to inherited and acquired (secondary) factors which emerge from brain changes, researchers also recognise motility problems – such as swallowing and dysphagia and the link to gastroesophageal reflux and neuromuscular disorders – all of which may be diagnosed differentially.

Website: www.dystonia-foundation.org

HEAD AND BRAIN INJURIES

UK

Headway – Brain Injury Association
4 King Edward Court,, King Edward Street,, Nottingham, NG1 1EW
Tel: (0044) (0)115 924 0800. Fax: (0044) (0)115 958 4446
Email: enquiries@headway.org.uk Website: www.headway.org.uk

US

The Brain Injury Association
105 North Alfred Street, Alexandria, VA 22314
Tel: (001) 703 236 6000. Fax: (001) 703 236 6001
Family Helpline: (001) 80 444 6443

This website provides a rich seam of information and links to pages from which you can download detailed advice – for instance on how to cope with a child who has a brain/head injury in hospital, at home, at school etc. It provides forms and advice about how to talk to the doctors, questions to ask, how to inform the school and ongoing monitoring of progress and needs.

Website: www.biausa.org

There is also a professional link to PROLINK.

Lash and Associates Publishing/Training
708 Young Forest Drive, Wake Forest, NC 27587-9040
Tel/Fax: (001) (0) 919 562 0015
Email: lapublishing@earthlink.net

This organisation can be found through the biausa site but also through its own address:

www.lapublishing.com/attention_memory_training_tools.htm

This site is also rich in information about how to help a child with a head or brain injury in terms of skills relating to attention and memory. Training can be provided to help professionals with rehabilitation work. One of the training tools is 'Pay Attention!' Attention Training for Children Ages 4–10. There are Tip cards, links to other resources, free catalogues etc.

Suite 101

Award-winning website in the category of Disabilities Advisory. Up-to-date information on various disorders.

www.Suite101.com

AUSTRALIA

Headway Victoria: Acquired Brain Injury Association Inc.

2nd Floor, 212 King Street, Melbourne 3000

Tel: 03 9642 2411. Fax: 03 9642 2522

Freecall: 1800 817 964

Email: hmvceo@vicnet.net.au

Headwest (Head Injured Society of WA Inc.)

645 Canning Highway, Alfred Cove, WA 6154

Tel: 09 330 6370. Fax: 09 317 2264

NEW ZEALAND

Brain Injury Association of New Zealand

PO Box 74, 323 Market Road, Auckland

Tel: 0064 (0) 9623 1540. Fax: 0064 (0) 9623 1813

Email: bionz@xtra.co.uk Website: www.brain-injury-nz-org

HYDROCEPHALUS AND SPINA BIFIDA

UK

Website: www.asbah.demon.co.uk

New international website launched at the XIIth International Conference.

Website: www.ifglobal.org

USA

Institute for Neurology explores innovations in treating hydrocephalus in children.

Website: www.nyneurosurgery.org/child/hydrocephalus

Website linking to many sites for information, treatment etc.

www.healthlinkusa.com

Hydrophalus.html

CANADA
Spina Bifida and Hydrocephalus Association of Canada
Website: www.sbhac.ca

IRLEN SYNDROME

The Irlen Website, www.irlen.com, is packed with information about this perceptual disorder and every single Irlen practitioner across the world can be found on this site – specifically at www.irlen.com/centers.htm

Originally recognised as helpful for dyslexic children, these lenses have been found to relieve perceptual distortions in a number of disorders, for both children and adults, including autism, ADHD, stroke, seizures, head and brain injuries, and migraine.

Main office where all the action takes place – run by the highly professional team headed by Helen Irlen:

Irlen Institute, 5380 Village Road, Long Beach, California 90808, USA
Tel: (001) 562 496 2550. Fax: (001) 562 429 8699
Email: irlenInstitute@Irlen.com

Examples of some contacts around the world for readers without computers are listed below:

UK
Don Riley, 17 Ashford Drive, Kingswood, Maidstone, Kent, ME17 3PA
Tel/Fax: (0044) (0) 1622 842764
Email: DonRiley@compuserve.com
North-west England
Joan Hillary, Beacon Lodge, Macclesfield Road, Over Alderley, Macclesfield, Cheshire, SK10 4UB
Tel: (0044) (0) 1625 583841. Fax: (0044) (0) 1625 584441
Email: 106123.1264@compuserve.com

EGYPT
Pauline Smith, The Middle School, Cairo American College, PO Box 39, Maadi, Cairo 11431

ISRAEL
Shulamit Elad, 16 San Martin, Jerusalem 93343
Tel: 9722 6792773

UKRAINE

Olga Bogdashina, PO Box 47, Gorlovka 26 338026
Tel: 01484 681471

There is a desperate need for more knowledge and support in her country, especially for children with autism.

AUSTRALIA

New South Wales

Dr Gregory L. Robinson, Special Education Centre, University of Newcastle, University Drive, Callaghan, NSW 2308
Tel: (0) 2 4946 8576. Fax: (0) 2 4921 6939
Email: scglwr@cc.newcastle.edu.au

Queensland

Peter Freney, PO Box 733, Buderim, QLD 4556
Tel: (0) 7 5445 2458. Fax: (0) 7 5476 9556
Email: pjfreney@babe.net.au

Victoria

Gloria Thomas, PO Box 463, Brentford Square, Victoria 3131
Tel: (0) 3 9877 6388. Fax: (0) 3 9877 0389. Mobile: 0419 874566
Email: gloria@dyslexia.aust.c

NEW ZEALAND

John Anstice, 10 Clyde Road, Ilam 8004, Christchurch
Tel: (0) 33 43 3909. Fax: (0) 33 43 2723
Email: JAnstice@compuserve.com

David T.Wardell, PO Box 38893, Howick, Auckland
Tel: (0) 9 534 1619. Fax: (0) 9 534 1640
Email: kmec@voyager.co.nz

MYALGIC ENCEPHALITIS (ME)
UK

National charity dedicated to support young people with ME, their families and professionals:

Tymes Trust
Chelmsford, Essex

Tel/Fax: (0044) (0) 1245 263482
In partnership with www.youngactiononline.com
Email: jane@youngactiononline.com

Sheffield
Local site with lots of help and links.
www.sheffieldMEgroup.co.uk

NEUROLOGICAL DISORDERS INCLUDING STROKES
NIH/National Institute of Neurological Disorders and Stroke (NINDS)
9000 Rockville Pike, Bethesda, MD20892
Tel: (001) (301) 496-5751 or (001) (800) 352-9424
Website: www.minds.nih.gov/

NONVERBAL LEARNING DISABILITIES
USA
Nonverbal Learning Disabilities
www.nldontheweb.org/tanguay_3.htm

SPEECH AND LANGUAGE DELAYS AND DISORDERS
UK
AFASIC
69–85 Old Streeet, London, EC1V 9HX
Tel: (0044) (0) 20 7841 8900
www.afasic.uk

AFASIC Hampshire
Paul Burrows
Tel: (0044) (0) 23 92719644
E-mail: paulburrows@afasichampshire.org

TOURETTE SYNDROME
UK
Tourette Syndrome Association
1st Floor Offices, Old Bank Chambers, London Road, Crowborough, East Sussex, TN6 2TT
Tel: (0044) (0) 1892 669151. Fax: (0044) (0) 1892 663649
Website: www.glaxocentre.merseyside.org/tsa.html

USA

Tourette Syndrome Association
40–42 Bell Boulevard, Bayside, NY 11361–2820
Tel: (718) 224-2999 or (800) 237-0717
E-mail: tourette@ix.netcom.com Website: http://tsa.mgh.harvard.edu/

Tourettes Syndrome of Arizona
Chapter 3400, East Speedway Boulevard, Suite 118–194, Tucson, Arizona 85716
Tel/Fax: (001) 520 622 3068
Website: www.ycom/logical/tourette

ASSESSMENTS
UK
AUTISM

There are a number of centres for assessment of autism by teams within the UK. These assessments are purchased through local health and education authorities and waiting lists can be long. Some local teams have become trained, and have set up their own assessment clinics.

INDEPENDENT ASSESSMENTS

There will be a number of people undertaking independent assessments. Support groups and lawyers will be able to direct families.

The author, Lisa Blakemore-Brown, undertakes independent psychological assessments of any child from any area and any country. She is fully trained through the NAS to diagnose autistic spectrum disorders. The author has also recognised ADHD presentations since the mid eighties. Assessments include pre-assessment preparation of information through questionnaires sent to families, discussions of history including exploring attentional and executive difficulties experienced by the child, as well as direct testing of attentional skills, psychometric and attainment testing. Pre- and post-assessment consultations, advice, full report and Tribunal/Court attendance if necessary.

Lisa Blakemore-Brown
Tel: (0044) (0) 1243 262227. Fax: (0044) (0) 1243 264900
Email: ltapestry@aol.com

PROFESSIONAL TRAINING AND INFORMATION

Apart from the usual routes for Continuing Professional Development, the following may be helpful in addition to the websites.

ADHD

USA

ADHD REPORT

Professor Russell Barkley from University of Massachusetts Medical Center, Worcester, MA edits this informative monthly newsletter for professionals with articles, Research News and Case Study Section. Subscriptions available from:

Guilford Publications, 72 Spring Street, New York, NY 10012
Inside US and Canada: Toll-Free: 800 365 7006
Outside US and Canada: (001) 212 431 9800 Ext: 3
Fax: (001) 212 966 6708
Email for samples: samples@guilford.com Website: www.guilford.com

CHADD

Yearly conference held in October/November at a different US city each year. Hugely informative event with many strands. Lectures are available for professionals in various fields and parents, and there are some events for adolescents with ADHD. Exhibition hall and lots to buy including testing equipment, books etc.
Website: www.chadd.org

UK

ADDISS

Runs a yearly conference in London in the spring. Respected speakers from various countries.

British Psychological Society

Has published guidance for psychologists on ADHD.

BPS, St Andrews House, 48 Princess Road East, Leicester, LE1 7DR
Tel: (0044) (0) 116 254 9568. Fax: (0044) (0) 116 247 0787
Email: mail@bps.org.uk Website: www.bps.org.uk

AUTISM
UK

National Autistic Society (details as above)

Provides training and conferences for professionals.

Distance Learning Degree Course
School of Education, University of Birmingham

Rita Jordan heads this important Distance Learning Course. Two options are available – one for those working with children with autism and Asperger syndrome, and the second for those working with adults.

Tel: (0044) (0) 121 414 4866. Fax: (0044) (0) 121 414 4865
Email: G.E.Jones6bham.ac.uk or R.R.Jordan6bham.ac.uk
Website: www.edu.bham.ac.uk

COACHING

Virtual (so applicable worldwide)

ADD Coach Training

Optimal Functioning Institute
Website: www.addcoach.com Email: support@addcoach.com

Francena Hancock is a virtual coach for this.

US based coaching group which provides many forms of support from individual coaching needs to training to become a Coach.

This type of support should be woven through Education and Social Services systems as a matter of course. The coach/facilitator should provide the strucutre and guidance which triggers salience provided it is intensive and focused enough.

UK

ADDISS can redirect you to coaches – www.addiss

Dianne Zaccheo (Bostonian based in London)
Tel: (0044) (0) 20 7603 0368. Fax: (0044) (0) 20 7603 5359
Email: Dzaccheo@aol.com

UNIQUE EXAMPLES OF FOCUSED EDUCATIONAL PROVISION

ADHD

USA

CHADD will be able to direct parents to details of provision for ADHD across the US

University of California Irvine (UCI)

The Child Development Centre School, established by James M. Swanson in 1982, is a specialised school program for children aged 5 to 11 years with ADHD which uses behavioural principles.

Director: Ron Kotkin
Tel: (001) 949 824 2343
www.communications.uci.edu/

UK

The London-based day school Centre Academy was set up with the ADHD/ dyslexic child in mind. Individualised programmes and a structured curriculum are provided to build on positive and successful experiences.

92 St John's Hill, Battersea, London, SW11 1SH
Tel: (0044) (0) 20 7738 2344. Fax: (0044) (0) 20 7738 9862
Email: ukadmin@centreacademy.com Website: www.centreacademy.com

ADHD AND AUTISTIC SPECTRUM

Dyslexia Teaching Centre (DTC)

Liverpool

Run by Director Michele Pemberton, this unique Assessment and Teaching Centre has evolved from its initial main focus on dyslexia, given a growing awareness and knowledge by the Director of the 'tapestry' nature of learning difficulties for many children she saw. The Centre provides specialist teacher assessments, referrals to psychologist Lisa Blakemore-Brown and to speech and language therapists, and other assessments as appropriate. Standard DTC assessments include Conners' Continuous Performance tests for computerised measures of attention and screens for Asperger syndrome and DAMP. Multi-sensory after-school/weekend/summer small group and 1:1 ABA interventions.

The Centre Director encourages ongoing professional development of her staff. They attend the CHADD conference each year. Collaboration with CARD has also lead to an ABA intervention base being set up in 2001. Local health and education authorities are now keen to be involved with the Centre to help the children of Liverpool.

Tel: 0151 280 0317. Fax: 0151 280 0299
Website: www.Dyslexiateachingcentre.co.uk

AUTISM

UK

The NAS can provide considerable detail on schools and colleges throughout the country. The website of a Surrey based NAS group, www.mugsy.com, also holds a vast amount of information on schools and many other issues of importance to parents of children with autism. Their website also picks up on any articles in the UK or the USA which refer to autism.

Ashleigh Further Education College (Day and Residential)

Currently the only one of its kind in the UK for further education students with Asperger syndrome. The College takes students from the age of 16 years. It provides an extended curriculum to teach social, emotional and life skills in the community.

ESPA (European Services for People with Autism)
9 The Cedars, Ashbrooke, Sunderland, Tyne and Wear, SR2 7TW
Contact Mike Smith (Admissions Manager)
Consultant Psychologist for the group: Lynne Moxon
Tel: (0044) (0) 191 213 0833. Fax: (0044) (0) 191 213 2614

NAS support scheme for university students in the UK with autism and Asperger syndrome
Prospects, part of the National Autistic Society
Tel: 020 7704 7450
E-mail: prospects@nas.org.uk
Information within www.users.dircon.co.uk

INTERVENTION PROGRAMMES

ABA (Applied Behavioural Analysis)

USA

LIFE (Lovaas Institute for Early Intervention)

Lovaas was the first person to apply the principles of behavioural analysis to the education of autistic children. His early aversive methods do not form any part of the modern day ABA therapies.

Based at the University of California, Los Angeles (UCLA).

Website: www.lovaas.com

CARD (Centre for Autism and Related Disorders)

University of Florida

The ABA principles of the Lovaas method are threaded through these research based interventions, but there is flexibility which allows for the recognition of the individual and the additional introduction of other methodologies sewn into the ABA fabric if impasses are reached.

www.card.ufl.edu

WEAP (Wisconsin Early Autism Project)

This group is directly affiliated with Dr Ivor Lovaas at UCLA. The training, interventions, monitoring and evaluation procedures are grounded in his research. Methods are highly detailed and intensive leading to often startling outcomes for some children who were 'slipping away' into autism. Not all children who are provided with this therapy are able to attend mainstream school, which is the Gold Standard aim of the intervention. Intensive and creative methods must be maintained to ensure reinforcement occurs as there can be a rapid falling away of skills, especially if a child's course finishes too soon.

www.wiaautism.com

UK

PEACH (Parents for the Early Intervention of Autism in Children with Autism)

Carrie Haslett heads this group, providing support and help to callers interested in early intervention programmes. It is also involved with training, provision of ABA programmes, fundraising, and produces a newsletter, SPEACH.

Tel: (0044) (0) 208 891 0121 Ext: 2348. Fax: (0044) (0) 208 891 8209
Email: peach@brunel.ac.uk

CARD (Centre for Autism And Related Disorders)
Orpington, Kent
Tel: (0044) (0) 1689 837373. Fax: (0044) (0) 1689 896656

Charlotte Atkins heads this centre and has worked unremittingly to develop an ABA service in various parts of the country, in individual homes and also in schools.

London Early Autism Project (LEAP)
699 Fulham Road, London, SW6 5UJ

The principles and methods are the same as for WEAP, above.

Tel: (0044) 0207 736 6688. Fax: (0044) 0207 736 8242
Email: Judith.Taylor@londonearlyautism.com

OPTIONS
SON-RISE PROJECT

This project helps families to design and implement home-based programmes which develop emotional connections between parents and autistic children through using intensive imitative methods to break into their world.

www.son-rise.org

TEACCH
University of North Carolina at Chapel Hill

This intervention was developed by Eric Schopler in 1972. It was designed to ease the anxieties of autistic individuals in communities through highly structured, visual sequential methods. Recognition of the unique individual is central to the philosophy as well as respect for the 'culture of autism'. Existing skills and interests are built on. Many workers include some aspects of TEACCH into their own methodology even if the entire programme is not used. Training provided.

www.unc.edu/depts/teacch

USA and UK PECS

Pyramid Educational Consultants produce interventions using cards to improve communication skills in young children. Training provided. The very clear visual stimulus attracts and maintains attention, and many formerly non-communicative children and adults now find a voice through PECS.

www.pecs.com

Social Stories and Comic Strip Conversations

Carol Gray developed these programmes to help children learn about their world and their place in it, through creative methods which intrigue the child.

The Gray Center, PO Box 67, Jenison, MI 49429
Tel: (001) 616 667 2396
www.thegraycenter.org

Hanen Programme

This programme helps parents whose children have language development problems. Strong emphasis on early intervention and the crucial nuts and bolts of reciprocity.

Hanen Centre, Suite 403–1075 Bay Street, Toronto, Ontario, M5S 2B1
Tel: 001 416 921 1073. Fax: 001 416 921 1225
Website: www.hanen.org

AIT (Auditory Integration Training)

Integrating the Senses for Successful Learning

Communication Therapies Ltd, Rosemarie Mason – Administrator, 58 Brisbane Road, Ilford, Essex IG1 4SL
Tel/Fax: (0044) (0) 208 554–6522
Email: 100533.145@compuserve.com or COTHLD@AOL.com

The Tomatis Method

A listening therapy for ADHD and autism.

www.tomatis.com

Teach me language: A language manual for children with autism, Asperger's syndrome and related developmental disorders

For parents and therapists to teach language to visual learniers who can communicate minimally and can work on table top activities. Freeman, S.K., Dake, L. and Tamir, I. Available from www.amazon.com

PRODUCTS TO AID LEARNING

WatchMinder

Device to train and remind children and adults with attention deficits as part of self-monitoring procedures. Order from:

PO Box 19565–226, Irvine, CA 92623-9565
Tel: 800 961 0023.. Fax 949 854 1843
www.watchminder.com

Interactive Metronome

Exercise device to improve cognitive timing. Recognises the importance of rhythm and balance in relation to planning, sequencing and executing activity.

Interactive Metronome, 2500 Weston Road, Suite 403, Weston, Florida 33331
Tel: (001) 954 385 4660 28. Fax: (001) 954 385 4674
www.interactivemetronome.com

Irlen Lenses and Overlays

Recognition that colour can improve distorted perceptions. Thorough assessments determine which colour is appropriate for each individual.

www.irlen.com

Telephone numbers listed above.

Organisation providing a variety of products - send for catalogue
Winslow Press
Education and Special Needs, Goyt Side Road, Chesterfield, Derbyshire S40 2PH
Tel: 0845 921 1777. Fax: 01246 551195
Email: sales@winslow-cat.com

Noise reducing device
Noisebuster, Educational Solutions, PO Box 2204, Broken Arrow, Oklahoma 74012
Tel: (001) (918) 451–9485

DoToLearn

Very helpful, practical website. Recognises need for small incremental steps and detailed visual aids. Online support provides considerable step-by-step guidance in all areas, for example, living skills; reducing injurious behaviour; interacting;

understanding and managing time; feelings; school and homework etc. This is done through picture cards, story strips, graphs, tables and schedules which are copyrighted to the company but can be downloaded for a child to colour in and adult to complete – children who can complete such graphs also enjoy seeing their progress. There are also advice and tips on how to use these aids practically.

You can download many pictures, schedules etc. for your own use.

www.do2learn.com

Different Roads to Learning

Online catalogue with many toys, tools and books. Including: PECS, audio and video tapes, discrete trial teaching, manipulative toys etc.

Tel: Toll free (001) 800 853 1057
(001) 212 604 9637
www.difflearn.com

DIETARY INTERVENTIONS TO REDUCE/REMOVE HYPERACTIVITY AND DISTRACTIBILITY
Autism Research Unit

Research into gluten- and casein-free diets, examination of biomedical factors associated with autism, urinary analysis etc. Urine samples can be sent for analysis.

Paul Shattock and Paul Whiteley, School of Sciences (Health), University of Sunderland, Sunderland, SR2 7EE
Tel: (0044) (0) 191 510 8922. Fax: (0044) (0) 191 510 8922

ANDI (Autism Network for Dietary Interventions)

First page of this website refers to recognition that an immune system dysfunction is found in many cases of autism which affects how the body breaks down proteins and how it deals with bacteria and yeasts.

Parent researchers developed the website, produce newsletters and so on and there are translations of information into Spanish, French and German.

There are many links, hard to find books, audiotapes, diets etc.

Website: www.autismndi.com

Books:

A User Guide to the GF/CF Diet for Autism, Asperger Syndrome and AD/HD, by Luke Jackson

Diet Intervention and Autism: Implementing the Gluten and Casein Free Diet for Autistic Children and Adults - A Practical Guide for Parents, by Marilyn Le Breton

Special Diets for Special Kids: Understanding and Implementing Special Diets to Aid in the Treatment of Autism and Related Developmental Disorders, by Lisa Lewis

All published by Jessica Kingsley Publishers.

www.jkp.com

LEGAL ADVICE FOR FAMILIES

Please note that neither the author or the publisher of this book can be held responsible for the quality of advice received as a result of contacting the following organisations. As with the rest of this Resources section, the details here are provided for information only, with no warranty as to their suitability for a reader's particular situation.

Educational Rights

UK

Action on Entitlement

AoE, 17 Cumberland Road, Kew TW9 3HJ
Tel: 0208 948 1746
Email www.aoe.org.uk

IPSEA (Independent Panel for Education Advice)
John Wright, Woodbridge, Suffolk
Tel/Fax: (0044) (0) 1394 380518

Provides support for parents of children with special educational needs.

USA

Legal Representatives
www.wrightslaw.com
www.reedmartin.com
www.ideapractice.org

Parent attorneys
www.copaa.net

Vaccination disputes

USA

Law firm handling claims against manufacturers on the basis that autism has been caused by mercury and in particular Thimerosal in vaccine.

Waters and Kraus, LLP, 400 Oceangate, Suite 800, Long Beach, CA
(001) 562 436–8833

UK

Law firm handling claims that vaccines caused autism.

Alexander Harris
South: (0044) 0207 430 5555
North: (0044) 0161 925 5555

MISCELLANEOUS

MAMA (Mothers Against Munchausen by Proxy Allegations)

www.msbp.com

US website devoted to raising awareness of tragic outcomes when mothers are falsely accused of causing their children's real developmental problems through msbp (Munchausen Syndrome by Proxy).

Site developed by tragic mother Julie Patrick whose son died because she was accused of causing his problems which in turn led to medical investigations not being undertaken.

CHAOS THEORY

…and finally…to see how small changes/interventions can make big differences to tapestries – check out the Chaos Theory Sites

To learn more about Chaos:

James Gleick's homepage:

www.around.com

To view and 'manipulate' the Mandlebrot Set and other fractal images:

www.neutrino.physics.ucsb.edu/people/piro/mandlebrot

References

Achenbach, T.M. (1986) *Child Behaviour Checklist – Direct Observation Form.* Burlington, VT: University Associates in Psychiatry.

Achenbach, T.M. and Edelbrock, C. (1988) *Manual for the Child Behaviour Checklist and Revised Behaviour Profile.* Burlington, VT: University Associates in Psychiatry.

Aitken, K.J. and Trevarthen, C. (1997) 'Self–other organisation in human psychological development.' *Development and Psychopathology 9,* 651–675.

American Psychiatric Association (APA) (1994) *Diagnostic and Statistical Manual of Mental Disorders,* 4th ed (DSM-IV). Washington, DC: APA.

Asperger, H. (1944) 'Die Autistischen Psychopathen im Kindersalter.' *Archiv. fur Psychiatrie und Nervenkrankheiten 117,* 76–136.

Attwood, T. (1997) *Asperger's Syndrome: A Guide for Parents and Professionals.* London: Jessica Kingsley Publishers.

Bachevelier, J. (1990) 'Ontogenic development of habit and memory formation in primates.' In A. Diamond (ed) *Development and Neural Bases of Higher Cognitive Functions.* New York: New York Academy of Science.

Bailey, A., Phillips, W. and Rutter, M. (1996) 'Autism: Towards an integration of clinical, genetic, neuro-psychological, and neurobiological perspectives.' *Journal of Child Psychology and Psychiatry 37,* 89–126.

Barbolini, G., Caffo, E., Robinson, G. and Wright, A. (1998) 'Light sensitivity and some pervasive developmental disorders: Autistic disorder, Asperger disorder.' Paper presented at the Modena International Conference on Autism and Pervasive Developmental Disorders. University of Modena, March.

Barkley, R., (1997) *ADHD and the Nature of Self-Control.* New York: Guilford Press.

Barkley, R. (1995) *Taking charge of ADHD: The complete, authoritative guide for parents.* New York: Guilford Press.

Barkley, R. (1990) *Attention deficit hyperactivity disorder: A handbook for diagnosis and treatment.* New York: Guilford Press.

Barkley, R. (1989) 'Linkages between attention and executive functions.' In G.R. Lyon and N.A. Krasnegor (eds) *Attention, Memory and Executive Function.* Baltimore, MD: Paul H. Brookes.

Barkley, R. (1981) *Hyperactive Children: A handbook for diagnosis and treatment.* New York: Guilford Press.

Baron-Cohen, S., Cox, A., Baird, G., Swettenham, J., Nightingale, N., Morgan, K., Drew, A. and Charman, T. (1996) 'Psychological markers in the detection of autism in infancy in a large population.' *British Journal of Pyschiatry.*

Baron-Cohen, S., Leslie, A.M. and Frith, U. (1985) 'Does the autistic child have a "theory of mind"?' *Cognition 21,* 37–46.

Baron-Cohen, S., Mortimore, C., Moriarty, J., Izaguirre, J. and Robertson, M. (1999) 'The prevalence of Gilles de la Tourette Syndrome in children and adolescents with autism.' *Journal of Child Psychology and Psychiatry 40,* 2, 213–218.

Biederman, J. (1988) 'Children and adults with Attention Deficit Disorder.' Paper given at CHADD Conference, New York, November.

Biederman, J., Faraone, S., Milberger, S., Guite, J., Hick, E., Chen, L., Hennin, D., Marrs, A., Oullette, C., Moore, P., Spencer, T., Norman, D., Wilens, T., Kraus, I. and Perin, J. (1996) 'A prospective 4-year follow-up study of attention deficit hyperactivity and related disorders.' *Archives of General Psychiatry 148,* 564–577.

Biederman, J., Faraone, S.V., Spencer, T., Norman, D., Lapey, K.A., Mick, Lehman, B.K. and Doyle, A. (1993) 'Patterns of psychiatric comorbidity, cognition, and psychosocial functioning in adults with Attention Deficit Disorder.' *American Journal of Psychiatry 150,* 12, 1792–1798.

Biederman, J., Newcorn, J. and Sprich, S. (1991) 'Comorbidity of diagnosis in Attention Deficit Disorder.' In G. Weiss (ed) *Attention Deficit Hyperactivity Disorder.* Philadelphia, PA: W.B. Saunders.

Bishop, D.V.M. (1989) 'Autism, Asperger's Syndrome and Semantic Pragmatic Disorder: Where are the boundaries?' *British Journal of Disorders of Communication 24,* 107–121.

Blakemore-Brown, L.C. (1998a) 'Braking the mode.' Paper presented at Northampton General Hospital.

Blakemore-Brown, L.C. (1998b) 'False illness in children – or simply false accusations?' In D. Winn (ed) *The Therapist 5,* 2, 24–29.

Blakemore-Brown, L.C.'(1998c) Paper presented at the Promoting Parenting Skills Conference, Birmingham UK, September.

Blakemore-Brown, L.C. (1998d) 'Weaving the tapestry of Asperger Syndrome.' Paper presented at the tenth Annual CHADD Conference, New York.

Bondy, A.S. and Frost, L.A. (1994) 'The Delaware autistic program.' In S.L. Harris and J.S. Handleman (eds) *Pre-school Education Programs for Children with Autism.* Austin, TX: Pro-Ed.

Bowler, D.M., and Worley, K. (1994) 'Susceptibility to social influence in adults with Asperger syndrome: a research note.' *Journal of Child Psychology and Psychiatry 35,* 4, 689–97.

British Psychological Society (BPS) (1996) *Attention Deficit Hyperactivity Disorder (ADHD): A Psychological Response to an Evolving Concept.* Leicester: BPS.

Brown, T.E. (1994) 'Many faces of ADD: Comorbidity.' *Attention! 1,* 2, 29–36.

Carlson, C.L. and Lahey, B.B. (1988) 'Behaviour classroom interventions with children exhibiting conduct disorders or attention deficit disorders with hyperactivity.' In J.C. Witt, S.M. Elliott and F.M. Gresham (eds) *The Handbook of Behaviour Therapy in Education.* New York: Plenum Press.

Cassily, J.F. (1999) 'Rhythmic control and the developing brain.' *Advance Magazine for Occupational Therapy Practitioners and for Speech-Language Pathologists and Audiologists.*

Charman, T. (1996) 'Psychological markers in the detection of autism in infancy in a large population.' *British Journal of Psychiatry 168,* 158–163.

Clarke-Stewart, K.A. (1973) 'Interactions between mothers and their young children.' *Monographs of the Society of Research in Child Development 38, 513,* 35–43.

Clarke-Stewart, K.A. and Hevey, C.M. (1981) 'Longitudinal relations in repeated observations of mother-child interaction from 1–2 and a half years.' *Developmental Psychology 17,* 127-145.

Comings, D.E. (1996) *The Gene Bomb. Do Technologically advanced societies accelerate the selection of genes for addictive and disruptive behaviours?* Duarte, CA: Hope Press.

Comings, D.E. (1996) *Search for the Tourette Syndrome and human behaviour genes.* Duarte, CA: Hope Press.

Comings, D.E. and Comings, B.G. (1993) 'Comorbid behavioural disorders.' In R. Kurlan (ed) *Tourette Syndrome and Related Disorders.* New York: Marcel-Deeker, 111–147.

Comings, D.E. and Comings, B.G. (1988) 'Tourette's Syndrome and Attention Deficit Disorder.' In D.J. Cohen, R.D. Bruun and J.F. Leckman (eds) *Tourette's Syndrome and Tic Disorders: Clinical Understanding and Treatment.* New York: Wiley.

Conners, C.K. (1986) 'How is a teacher rating scale used in the diagnosis of Attention Deficit Disorder?' *Journal of Children in Contemporary Society 19,* 33–52.

Davis Gammon, G. and Brown, T. (1993) 'Fluoxetine and Methylphenidate in combination for treatment of Attention Deficit Disorder and Comorbid Depressive Disorder.' *Journal of Child and Adolescent Psychopharmacology 3,* 1–10.

Dawkins, R. (1998) *Unweaving the Rainbow: Science, Delusion and the Appetite for Wonder.* London: Allen Lane.

Dawson and Osterling (1997) 'Early intervention in autism.' In M. Guralnick (ed) *The effectiveness of early intervention.* Baltimore, MD: Paul H. Brookes.

Denckla, M.B. (1995) 'A theory and model of executive function from a neuropsychological perspective.' In G. Reid-Lyon and N. Krasnegor (eds) *Attention, Memory and Executive Function.* Baltimore, MD: Paul H. Brookes.

Dewart, H. and Summers, S. (1988) *The pragmatics profile of early communication skills.* Windsor: NFER-Nelson.

Dowker, A., Hermelin, B. and Pring, L. (1998) 'A Savant Poet.' Paper presented at British Association Annual Meeting, Cardiff, 9 September.

Ehlers, S. and Gillberg, C. (1993) 'The epidemiology of Asperger Syndrome: A total population study.' *Journal of Child Psychology and Psychiatry 34,* 1327–1350.

Ehlers, S., Nyden, A., Gillberg, C., Sandberg, A., Dahlgren, S., Hjelmquist, E. and Oden, A. (1997) 'Asperger Syndrome, autism and attention disorders: A comparative study of the cognitive profiles of 120 children.' *Journal of Child Psychology and Psychiatry 38*, 207–217.

Eikeseth, S. (1999) 'Intensive school based behavioural treatment for four to seven year old children with autism: A one-year follow-up.' Paper presented at the PEACH *Putting Research into Practice* Conference, 18 June.

Farrington, D.P. (1994) 'Early developmental prevention of juvenile delinquency.' *Criminal Behaviour and Mental Health 4*, 209–27.

Farrington, D.P. and West, D.J. (1990) 'The Cambridge Study in delinquent development: A prospective longitudinal survey of 411 males.' In H-J. Kerner and G. Kaiser (eds) *Criminality: Personality, Behaviour and Life History*. New York: Springer-Verlag.

Fogel, A. and Hannan, T.E. (1985) 'Manual actions of nine-to-fifteen-week-old human infants during face to face interactions with their mothers.' *Child Development 56*, 1271–9.

Fogel, A., Toda, S. and Kawai, M. (1988) 'Mother-infant face to face in Japan and the U.S.: A laboratory comparison using 3-month-old infants.' *Developmental Psychology 24*, 398–408.

Frith, U. (1991) *Autism and Asperger Syndrome*. Cambridge: Cambridge University Press.

Frith, U. (1989) *Autism: Explaining the Enigma*. Oxford: Basil Blackwell.

Frith, U. and Happé, F. (1994) 'Autism: Beyond Theory of Mind.' *Cognition 50*, 115–132.

Galaburda, A.M., Menard, M.T. and Rosen, G.D. (1994) 'Evidence for aberrant auditory anatomy in developmental dyslexia.' *Proceedings of the National Academy of Science USA 91*, 8010–13.

Gerring, J.P *et al.* (1998) 'Premorbid prevalence of ADHD and developmental of secondary ADHD after closed head injury.' *Journal of the American Academy of Child and Adolescent Psychiatry 37*, 6, 647–54.

Gillberg, C. (1991) 'The Emanual Miller Memorial Lecture. Autism and autistic-like conditions: Subclasses among disorders of empathy.' *Journal of Child Psychology and Psychiatry 33*, 813–842.

Gillberg, C. (1992) 'Autism and autistic-like conditions: Subclasses among disorders of empathy.' *Journal of Child Psychology and Psychiatry 33*, 813–42.

Gillberg, C. and Gillberg, I.C. (1989) 'Asperger Syndrome: Some epidemiological considerations: A research note.' *Journal of Child Psychology and Pyschiatry 30*, 631–638.

Gillberg, C. and Hellgren, L. (1996) 'Outcome of attention disorders.' In S. Sandberg (ed) *Hyperactivity Disorders*. Cambridge: Cambridge University Press.

Gleick, J. (1987) *CHAOS: Making a New Science*. New York: Penguin.

Glogowska, M., Roulstone. S., Enderby, P. and Peters. T.J. (2000) 'Randomised controlled trial of community based speech and language therapy in preschool children.' *British Medical Journal 321*, 923.

Goldstein, S. (1996) Paper given at CHADD Conference, Chicago, October.

Goldstein, A.P., Sprafkin, R.P. and Gershaw, N.J. (1979) *Skill streaming the adolescent: A structured learning approach to teaching pro-social behaviour.* Champaign, IL: Research Press.

Gray, C. (1994) *Comic Strip Conversations.* Arlington, TX: Future Horizons.

Gray, C. (1995) 'Teaching children with autism to read social situations.' In K.A. Quill (ed) *Teaching Children with Autism Strategies to Enhance Communication and Socialisation.* London: International Thomson.

Grossman, K.E. (1988) 'Longitudinal and systemic approaches in the study of biological high and low risk groups.' In M. Rutter (ed) *The Power of Longitudinal Data: Studies of Risk and Protective Factors for Psychological Disorders.* Cambridge: Cambridge University Press.

Headway (1999) *The Way Ahead,* monthly newsletter, June.

Hepper, P. (1995) 'The behaviour of the foetus as an indicator of neural functioning.' In J-P. Lecanuet, W. Fifer, N. Krasnegor and W. Smotherman (eds) *Foetal Development: A Psychobiological Perspective.* Hillsdale, NJ: Erlbaum.

Hobson, R.P. (1993) *Autism and the Development of Mind.* Hove: Lawrence Erlbaum.

Hobson, R.P. (1989) 'On sharing experiences.' *Development and Psychopathology 1,* 197–203.

Howlin, P. (2000) 'Assessment instruments for Asperger Syndrome.' *Child Psychology and Psychiatry Review 53,* 120–129.

Howlin, P. (1998a) *Children with Autism and Asperger Syndrome. A Guide for Practitioners and Carers.* Chichester: Wiley.

Howlin, P. (1998b) 'Psychological and educational treatment for autism.' *Journal of Child Psychology and Psychiatry 9,* 3, 307–322.

Hubel, D.H., Henson, C.D., Rupert, A. and Galambos, R. (1959) '"Attention" units in the auditory cortex.' *Science 129,* 1279–80.

Irlen, H. (1983) 'Successful treatment of learning disabilities.' Paper presented at the 91st Annual Convention of the American Psychological Association, Anaheim, California.

Irlen, H. (1991) *Reading by the colors.* New York: Avery Publishing Group Inc.

Jordan, R., Jones, G. and Murray, D. (1998) *Educational interventions for children with autism: A literature review of recent and current research.* London: DFEE Publications.

Kadesjo, B. and Gillberg, I.C. (1999) 'Developmental coordination disorder in Swedish 7-year-old children.' *Journal of the American Academy of Child and Adolescent Psychiartry 38,* 820–8.

Kanner, L. (1943) 'Autistic disturbances of the affective contact.' *Nervous Child 2,* 217–50.

Klin, A., Volkmar, F.R., Sparrow, S.S., Cichetti. D.V. and Rourke, B.P. (1995) 'Validity and neuropsychological characterisation of Asperger Syndrome: Convergence with nonverbal learning disabilities syndrome.' *Journal of Child Psychology and Psychiatry 36,* 1127–40.

Kuhn, P.K. and Meltzoff, A.N. (1988) 'Speech as an intermodal object of perception.' In A. Yonas (ed) *Perceptual Development in Infancy*. Minnesota Symposia on Child Psychology, Volume 20. Hillside, NJ: Erlbaum.

Ladd, G. (1981) 'Effectiveness of a social learning method for enhancing children's social interaction and peer acceptance.' *Child Development 52*, 171–8.

Lane, D. (1992) 'Music Therapy: A gift beyond measure.' *Oncology Nursing Forum 19*, 6.

Leekham, S., Libby, S., Wing, L., Gould, J. and Gillberg, C. (2000) 'Comparison of ICD-10 and Gillberg's criteria for Asperger Syndrome.' *Autism 4*, 1, 11–28.

Lord, C., Rutter, M., Goode, S., Heemsbergen, Jordan, H., Mawhood, L. and Schopler, E. (1989) 'Autism diagnostic observation schedule: a standardised observation of communicative and social behaviour.' *Journal of Autism and Developmental Disorders 19*, 185–212.

Lorna, V. (1999) 'Easy listening'. *Sunday Times Style Magazine*, 31 January, 34–5.

Lovaas, O.I. (1987) 'Behavioural treatment and normal educational and intellectual functioning in young autistic children.' *Journal of Consulting and Clinical Psychology 55*, 3–9.

Lovaas, O.I. and Leaf, R.L. (1981) *Five videotapes for teaching developmentally disabled children.* Austin, TX: Pro-Ed.

McEachin, J.J., Smith, T., and Lovaas, O.I. (1993) 'Long-term outcome for children with autism who received early intensive behavioural treatment.' *American Journal of Mental Retardation 97*, 359–372

McGinnis, E., Goldstein, R.P., Sprafkin, R.P. and Gershaw, N.J. (1984) *Skill Streaming the elementary school child: A guide for teaching pro-social skills.* Illinois: Research Press.

Marcotte, A.C. and Stern, C. (1997) 'Qualitative analysis of graphomotor output in children with attentional disorders.' *Child Neuropsychology 3*, 147–53.

Messahel, S., Pheasant, A.E., Pall, H., Ahmed-Choudhury, J., Sungum-Paliwal, R.S. and Vost, P. (1998) 'Urinary levels of neptorin and biopterin in autism.' *Neuroscience 241*, 1, 17–20.

Molfese, D.L., (1999) 'Predicting dyslexia at 8 years of age using neonatal brain responses.' *Brain Language 72*, 3, 238–45.

Newson, J. (1979) 'The growth of shared understandings between infant and caregiver.' In M. Bullowa (ed) *Before Speech: The Beginnings of Human Communication.* Cambridge: Cambridge University Press.

Niemann, G.W. (1996) 'The neurodevelopment of Autism: Recent advances.' *Advances in the Assessment and Management of Autism*, ACPP Occasional Papers 13. London: Association for Child Psychology and Psychiatry.

Ornitz, E.M. and Ritvo, E.R. (1968) 'Perceptual inconstancy in early infantile autism: The syndrome of early infant autism and its variants including certain cases of childhood schizophrenia.' *Archives of General Psychiatry 18*, 76–98.

Ozofsky, J.D. and Danzger, B. (1974) 'Relationships between neonatal characteristics and mother–infant interaction.' *Developmental Psychology 10*, 124–30.

Ozonoff, S., Strayer, D.L., McMahon, W.M. and Filloux, F. (1998) 'Inhibitory defects in Tourette Syndrome: A function of co-morbidity and symptom severity.' *Journal of Child Psychology and Psychiatry 39*, 8, 1109–18.

Panksepp, J. (1979) 'A neurochemical theory of autism.' *Trends in Neuroscience 2*, 174–7.

Papousek, M. and Papousek, H. (1981) 'Musical elements in infants' vocalisation: Their significance for communication, cognition and creativity.' In L.P. Lipsitt (ed) *Advances in Infancy Research*, vol. 1. Norwood, NJ: Ablex.

Pennington, B.F. and Bennetto, L. (1993) 'Main effects or transactions in the neuropsychology of conduct disorder? Commentary on "the neuropsychology of conduct disorder".' *Development and Psychopathology 5*, 153–64.

Pennington, B.F. and Ozonoff, S. (1996) 'Executive functions and developmental psychopathology.' *Journal of Child Psychology and Psychiatry 37*, 51–87.

Perry, R., Cohen, I. and DeCarlo, R. (1995) 'Case study: Deterioration, autism, and recovery in two siblings.' *Journal of the American Academy of Child and Adolescent Psychiatry 34*, 232–7.

Pope, A.W., McHale, S.M. and Craighead, W.E. (1988) *Self esteem enhancement with children and adolescents*. Maryland: Allyn and Bacon.

Prior, M., Eisenmajer, S., Leekham, L., Wing, L., Gould, J., Ong, B. and Dowe, D. (1998) 'Are there subgroups within the autistic spectrum? A cluster analysis of a group of children with autistic spectrum disorders.' *Journal of Child Psychology and Psychiatry 39*, 6, 893–902.

Rambihar, V.S. (2000a) *A New Chaos Based Medicine beyond 2000*, Vol. 2. Toronto: Vashna.

Rambihar, V.S. (2000b) 'A Chaos Theory for Health Care.' *The Medical Post 36*, 16.

Reddy, V. (1991) 'Playing with others' expectations; teasing and mucking about in the first year.' In A. Whiten (ed) *Natural Theories of Mind: Evolution, Development and and Simulation of Everyday Mindreading*. Oxford: Blackwell.

Reddy, V., Havy, D., Murray, L. and Trevarthen, C. (1997) 'Communication in infancy: Mutual regulation of affect and attention.' In G. Bremner, A. Slater and G. Butterworth (eds) *Infant Development: Recent Advances*. Hillside, NJ: Erlbaum.

Reddy, V. and Simone, L. (1995) 'Acting on attention: Towards an understanding of knowing in infancy.' Paper given at Annual Conference of the Developmental Section of the British Psychological Society, Strathclyde.

Reichelt, K.L., Hamberger, A. Saelid, G., Edminson, P.D., Braestrup, C.B., Lingjaerde, O., Ledaal, P. and Orbeck, M. (1981) 'Biologically active peptide containing fractions in schizophrenia and childhood autism.' *Advances in Biochemistry and Psychopharmacology 28*, 627–43.

Reichelt, K.L., Hole, K., Hamberger, A. *et al.* (1993) 'Biolgically active peptide-containing fractions in schizophrenia and childhood autism.' *Advances in Biochemistry and Pharmacology 28*, 627–43.

Reichelt, K.L., Lindback, T. and Scott, H. (1994) 'Increased levels of antibodies to food proteins in Down syndrome.' *Acta Paediatrica Jpn 36*, 5, 489–92.

Robinson, G.L. (1998) 'The effects of Irlen coloured filters on eye treatments.' Paper presented to the Fifth International Conference on Perceptual and Learning Development. Cambridge University, July.

Robinson, G.L. and Miles, J. (1987) 'The use of coloured overlays to improve visual processing: A preliminary survey.' *The Exceptional Child, 34*, 65–70.

Rutter, M. (1996) 'Developmental psychopathology: Concepts and prospects.' In M.F. Lenzenweger and J.J. Hangaard (eds) *Frontiers of developmental psychopathology*. New York: Oxford University Press.

Rutter, M. and Bartak, L. (1973) 'Special educational treatment of autistic children: A comparative study. II. Follow-up findings and implicaions for services.' *Journal of Child Psychology and Psychiatry 14*, 241–2.

Rutter, M., Taylor, E. and Hersov, L. (1994) *Child and Adolescent Psychiatry: Modern Approaches*. 3rd edn. London: Blackwell Scientific.

Rylander, G. (1939) 'Personality changes after operations of the frontal lobes.' *Acta Psychologica et Neurologica Scandinavia*, Supplement 2.

Sallows, G. *Educational interventions for children with autism in the UK: Comment on the Jordan et al. June 1998 final report to the DfEE.*

Schopler, E. and Mesibov, G. (1995) 'Structured teaching in the TEACCH approach.' In E. Schopler and G. Mesibov (eds) *Learning and cognition in autism*. New York: Plenum Press.

Scifo, R., Cioni, M., Nicolosi, A., Batticane, N., Tirolo, C., Testa, N., Quattropani, M.C., Mo, M.C., Gallo, F. and Marchetti, B. (1996) 'Opioid-immune interactions in autism: Behavioural and immunological assessment during a double-blind treatment with naltrexone.' *Annals 1st Super Sanita 32*, 3, 351–9.

Shallice, T. (1988) *From Neuropsychology to Mental Structure*. Cambridge: Cambridge University Press.

Shallice, T. (1982) 'Specific impairments of planning.' *Philosophical Transactions of the Royal Society of London 298*, 199–209.

Shattock, P., Kennedy, A., Rowell and Berney, T.P. (1990) 'The role of neuropeptides in autism and their partnership with classical neurotransmitters.' *Brain Dysfunction 3*, 328–45.

Shattock, P. and Lowdon, G. (1996) 'Urinary profiles of people with autism: Possible implications and relevance to other research.' In *Proceedings of Conference on Therapeutic Intervention in Autism: Perspectives for Research and Practice*. Autism Research Unit.

Shattock, P. and Lowdon, G. (1991) 'Proteins, peptides and autism. Part 2: Implications for the education and care of people with autism.' *Brain Dysfunction 4*, 323–34.

Shattock, P. and Savery, D. (1997) 'Evaluation of urinary profiles obtained from people with autism and associated disorders. Part 1: Classification of subgroups.' In proceedings of conference *Living and learning with autism: Perspectives from the individual, the family and the professional*. Sunderland University: Autism Research Unit, 199–208.

Skinner, B.F. [1948] (1987) *Upon Further Reflection*. Englewood Cliffs, NJ: Prentice Hall.

Sonuga-Barke, E.J.S., Williams, E., Hall, M. and Saxton, T. (1996) 'Hyperactivity and Delay Aversion 111: The effect on cognitive style of imposing delay after errors.' *Journal of Child Psychology and Psychiatry 37*.

Spencer, T. (1995) 'The nature and treatment of combined ADHD and Tic Disorders.' Paper presented at the CHADD Seventh Annual Conference, Washington, DC.

Spencer, T., Biedmann, J., Harding, M., O'Donnell, D., Wilens, T., Faraone, S., Coofey, B. and Geller, D. (1998) 'Disentangling the overlap between Tourette's Disorder and ADHD.' *Journal of Child Psychology and Psychiatry 39*, 7, 1037–44.

Stern, D.N. (1985) *The Interpersonal World of the Infant: A View From Psychoanalysis and Developmental Psychology*. New York: Basic Books.

Stern, D.N. (1977) *The First Relationship: Infant and Mother*. Cambridge; MA: Harvard University Press.

Still, G. (1902) 'Some abnormal psychical conditions in children.' *Lancet* 1008–12, 1077–82, 1163–68.

Swanson, J.M. (1992) *School based assessments and interventions for ADD students*. Irvine, CA: K.C. Publishing.

Swanson, J.M. (1989) 'Paired-associate learning in the assessment of ADDH children.' In L. Bloomingdale and J. Swanson (eds) *Attention Deficit Disorder IV*. New York: Pergamon.

Swanson, J.M. (1988) 'Discussion: Attention Deficit Disorder.' In J.F. Kavanagh and T.J. Truss (eds) *Learning Disabilities: Proceedings of the National Conference*. Parkton, MD, York Press, 532–46.

Swanson, J.M. and Kinsbourne, M. (1978) 'Should you use stimulants to treat the hyperactive child?' *Modern Medicine 46*, 71-80

Swanson, J.M., Sargeant, J.A., Taylor, E., Sonuga-Barke, E.J.S., Jenson, P.S. and Cantwell, D.P. (1998) 'Attention-deficit hyperactivity disorder and hyperkinetic disorder.' *Lancet 351*, 429–33.

Swanson, J.M., Simpson, S., Agler, D., Rotkin, R., Pfiffner, L., Bender, M., Rosenau, C., Mayfield, K., Ferrari, L., Holcome, L., Prince, D., Mordkin, M., Elliott, J., Hivra, S., Shea, C., Bonporte, S., Youpa, D., Phillips, L., Nash, L., McBurnett, K., Lerner, M., Robinson, T., Levin, M., Baren, M. and Cantwell, D. (1990) UCI–OCDE *school based treatment program for children with ADHD/ODD*. Irvine, CA: K.C. Publishing.

Sykes, D.M., Hoy, E.A., Bill, J.M., McClure, B.G., Halliday, H.L. and Reid, M.M. (1997) 'Behavioural adjustment in school of very low birthweight children.' *Journal of Child Psychology and Psychiatry 38*, 3, 315–25.

Szatmari, P., Bremner, R. and Nagy, J. (1989) 'Asperger's Syndrome: A review of clinical features.' *Canadian Journal of Psychiatry 34*, 554-60.

Tantam, D., Holmes, D. and Cordess, C. (1993) 'Non-verbal expression in autism of Asperger's type.' *Journal of Autism and Developmental Disorders 23*, 111–113.

Taylor, E. (1986) 'Childhood hyperactivity.' *British Journal of Psychiatry 149*, 562–573.

Taylor, E. and Hemsley, R. (1995) 'Treating hyperkinetic disorders in children.' *British Medical Journal 310*, 1617–18.

Taylor, E., Schachar, R., Thorley, G. and Weiselberg, M. (1986) 'Conduct disorder and hyperactivity.' *British Journal of Psychiatry 149*, 760–7.

Trevarthen, C. (1998) *Children with Autism.* London: Jessica Kingsley Publishers.

Trevarthen, C. (1993) 'The function of emotions in early infant communication and development.' In J. Nadel and L.Camaioni (eds) *New Perspectives in Early Communication Development.* London Routledge, 48–81.

Trevarthen, C. (1979) 'Communication and co-operation in early infancy. A description of primary intersubjectivity.' In H. Bullowa (ed) *Before Speech: The Beginnings of Human Communication.* London: Cambridge University Press.

Trevarthen, C. (1977) 'Descriptive analyses of infant communicative behaviour.' In H.R. Schaffer (ed) *Studies in Mother-Infant Interaction.* London: Academic Press.

Wakefield, A.J., Murch, S.H., Anthony, A., Linnell, J., Casson, D.M., Malik, M., Berelowitz, M., Dhillon, A.P., Thomson, M.A., Harvey, P., Valentine, A., Davies, S.E. and Walker-Smith, J.A. (1998) '1 leal-lymphoid-nodular hyperplasia, non-specific colitis, and pervasive developmental disorder in children.' *Lancet 351*, 637–41.

Weber, E. (1846) 'Der Tastsinn und das Gemeingefühl.' In Wagner (ed) *Handwirterbuch der Physiologie 3*, 481–588.

Wechsler, D. (1991) *Wechsler Intelligence Scales for Children*, 3rd Edn. San Antonio, TX: Psychological Corporation.

Whiteley, P., Rodgers, J., Savery, D. and Shattock, P. (1999) 'A gluten-free diet as an intervention for autism and associated spectrum disorders: preliminary findings.' *Autism 3*, 1, 45–65.

WHO (1989) *The International Classification of Disease, Tenth Revision.* Geneva: World Health Organisation.

Williams, D. (1998) *Somebody Somewhere.* London: Jessica Kingsley Publishers.

Wine, T. and Bayer-Sager, C. (1965) 'A Groovy Kind of Love.' London: EMI.

Wing, L. (1996) *The Autistic Spectrum. A Guide for Parents and Professionals.* London: Constable.

Wing, L. (1981) 'Asperger Syndrome: A clinical account.' *Journal of Psychological Medicine 11*, 115–29.

Wing, L. (1969) 'The handicaps of autistic children: A comparative study.' *Journal of Child Psychology and Psychiatry 10*, 1–40.

Wing, L. and Gould, J. (1979) 'Severe impairments of social interaction and associated abnormalities in children: Epidemiology and classification.' *Journal of Autism and Childhood Schizophrenia 9*, 11–29.

Subject Index

Name index